# Sustainable Materialism

A growing number of environmental groups focus on more sustainable practices in everyday life, from the development of new food systems, to community solar, to more sustainable fashion. No longer willing to take part in unsustainable practices and institutions, and not satisfied with either purely individualistic and consumer responses or standard political processes and movement tactics, many activists and groups are increasingly focusing on restructuring everyday practices of the circulation of the basic needs of everyday life. This work labels such action sustainable materialism, and examines the political and social motivations of activists and movement groups involved in this growing and expanding practice. The central argument is that these movements are motivated by four key factors: frustration with the lack of accomplishments on broader environmental policies, a desire for environmental and social justice, an active and material resistance to the power of traditional industries, and a form of sustainability that is attentive to the flow of materials through bodies, communities, economies, and environments. In addition to these motivations, these movements demonstrate such material action as political action, in contrast to existing critiques of new materialism as apolitical or post-political. Overall, sustainable materialism is explored as a set of movements with unique qualities, based in collective rather than individual action, a dedication to local and prefigurative politics, and a demand that sustainability be practiced in everyday life – starting with the materials and flows that provide food, power, clothing, and other basic needs.

**David Schlosberg** is Director of the Sydney Environment Institute and Professor of Environmental Politics at the University of Sydney. His main theoretical interests are in environmental and climate justice, ecological and multispecies justice, climate adaptation and resilience, and environmental movements and the practices of everyday life– what he terms sustainable materialism. Professor Schlosberg's more applied work includes public perceptions and experiences of climate resilience and adaptation, the social impacts of climate change, and innovative local food policy. His previous authored, co-authored, or co-edited books with Oxford include Defining Environmental Justice, The Climate-Challenged Society, and The Oxford Handbook of Environmental Political Theory. Professor Schlosberg has been a visiting scholar at the London School of Economics, Australian National University, Princeton University, University of Washington, and UC Santa Cruz, among others.

**Luke Craven** is a Visiting Fellow, School of Business, UNSW Canberra. His research focuses on developing new tools to understand and address complex policy challenges. He works with a range of public sector organisations to adapt and apply systems frameworks to support policy design, implementation, and evaluation. He is known for developing the System Effects methodology, which is widely used to analyse complex causal relationships in participatory and qualitative data. He is also involved in a number of collaborative projects to support community-led systems change, both in Australia and internationally. Dr Craven holds a PhD and BA (Hons 1, Medal) in Political Science at the University of Sydney.

# Sustainable Materialism

*Environmental Movements and*
*the Politics of Everyday Life*

DAVID SCHLOSBERG AND LUKE CRAVEN

OXFORD
UNIVERSITY PRESS

# OXFORD
## UNIVERSITY PRESS

Great Clarendon Street, Oxford, OX2 6DP,
United Kingdom

Oxford University Press is a department of the University of Oxford.
It furthers the University's objective of excellence in research, scholarship,
and education by publishing worldwide. Oxford is a registered trade mark of
Oxford University Press in the UK and in certain other countries

First published 2019
First published in paperback 2022

Published in the United States of America by Oxford University Press
198 Madison Avenue, New York, NY 10016, United States of America

British Library Cataloguing in Publication Data
Data available

Library of Congress Cataloging in Publication Data
Data available

ISBN 978-0-19-884150-0 (Hbk.)
ISBN 978-0-19-286704-9 (Pbk.)

*This book is dedicated to all of the activists working to create more sustainable, just, and inclusive material systems.*

# Acknowledgements

These things take time. And help. From initial idea to completed book, we've been discussing, interviewing, engaging, presenting, writing, and getting feedback on this project for about seven years. And we have a lot of people and organizations to thank for help along the way.

The framework for this research was first articulated in print in 2011 by co-author Schlosberg in a commentary for the Carnegie Council on Ethics in International Affairs online forum on 'What are the Limits and Benefits of the Sustainability Approach?' The focus was then on two explanations or frameworks, using in part a Foucauldian understanding of power, but more broadly it was where Schlosberg began thinking about the politics and practice of new materialism, and first used it to explain the political motivations and material practices of a number of newly growing environmental movements. This initial set of ideas was extensively expanded in an incredibly fruitful and rewarding collaboration with Rom Coles, which eventually led to a co-authored piece, 'The New Environmentalism of Everyday Life: Sustainability, Material Flows, and Movements', published in *Contemporary Political Theory* (online in 2015, and in print in 2016). This piece added a third explanatory framework, a frustration with conventional political processes. As an initial overview of the idea of sustainable materialism, updated parts of this piece appear throughout the book, perhaps most extensively in our introduction, but also in Chapter 4, on power. Our first major debt of gratitude, then, must go to Rom, who has been a constant source of inspiration, feedback, and support over the course of this project.

In the time between the original idea and that initial publication, the Australian Research Council provided support in the form of a Discovery Project grant to co-author Schlosberg. Officially, this was DP140103863, on 'The New Environmentalism of Everyday Life: Sustainability, Material Flows, and the Evolution of Environmental Movements'. Funding, which began in 2014, supported the extensive interview fieldwork and the research assistantship that brought Luke Craven on board. (Needless to say, the discussion here is our own, and the views expressed here do not necessarily reflect those of the Australian Research Council.) We are heartfully thankful for a funding body that continues to support a broad range of research in the public interest.

In the academic realm, there were three major events that helped us to articulate various parts of this project, and included some major engagement and collaborative reflection with colleagues across numerous disciplines. The first was held at the University of Sydney, November 2012, as a Sydney Environment Institute event and companion symposium on 'What is Sustainable Materialism? An Environmentalism of Everyday Life'. There, thanks go especially to participants Fiona Allen, Bobby Banerjee, Jodi Frawley, Andrea Gaynor, Tess Lea, John Meyer, Jeff Neilson, Elspeth Probyn, Tom Roper, Zoe Sofoulis, and Eric Enno Tamm.

The second influential and reflective event was on 'The Greening of Everyday Life: Reimagining Environmentalism in Post-Industrial Societies', organized by John Meyer and hosted by the Rachel Carson Centre at the University of Munich in June 2014. Here, thanks go to Fiona Allen, Andrew Case, Jonathan Clapperton, Rom Coles, Teena Gabrielson, Yogi Hendlin, Jens Kersten, Karen Litfin, Michael Lorr, Cecily Maller, Brad Mapes-Martins, Shannon Orr, Thomas Princen, Sarah Randle, Jennifer Robinson, Chelsea Schelly, Nicole Seymour, and Piers Stephens. The feedback at this engaging workshop was both substantive and encouraging, and we thank all of the participants and organizers. That event culminated in an important collection on *The Greening of Everyday Life*, edited by John Meyer and Jens Kersten and published by Oxford University Press in 2016, which includes the Schlosberg and Coles co-authored piece.

The third major event where we received invaluable feedback was a workshop on 'Environmental Social Movements and the New Politics of Consumption', at the European Consortium for Political Research Joint Sessions of Workshops, in Pisa, April 2016. Here, we are particularly indebted to discussions that included Massimiliano Andretta, Viviana Asara, Elizabeth Bennett, Mario Diani, Brian Doherty, Sophie Dubuisson-Quellier, Francesca Forno, Graeme Hayes, Eleftheria Lekakis, Herman Lelieveldt, Angelos Loukakis, Sherilyn Macgregor, Michelle Micheletti, Chris Rootes, Mundo Yang, and Luke Yates. This workshop led to a special issue of the journal *Environmental Politics* on the New Politics of Consumption, to which we contributed two articles: David Schlosberg, 'From Postmaterialism to Sustainable Materialism', which contributes to Chapter 2, and Luke Craven, 'The Neoliberal Ties that Bind? Prefigurativism and the New Politics of Consumption', which contributes to Chapters 6 and 7.

Along the way, co-author Schlosberg gave numerous invited talks as the project developed. This included two presentations at the University of California Santa Cruz, including the Jessica Roy Memorial Lecture in 2016; the Energy

Resources Group at UC Berkeley in 2013; the Global Environmental Justice Research Group at the University of East Anglia and the Environmental Research Group and the Institute for Social Change at the University of Tasmania in 2015; Swarthmore College, the Green City Lecture Series at Lehigh University, and the Department of Political Science at the University of Oregon in 2016; Centre for the Study of International Relations at Science Po Paris, Environmental Studies Seminar Series at the University of Colorado, the School of Geography and Sustainable Communities at the University of Wollongong, and the Department of Sociology and Human Geography at the University of Oslo in 2017; and at Yale-NUS Singapore and the Sustainable Consumption Institute at the University of Manchester in 2018.

In these various venues, a sincere thank you again for insightful questions, suggestions, critiques, and more go to Noel Castree, Brendan Coolsaet, Ben Crow, Giovanna Di Chiro, Gareth Edwards, Iokine Rodriguez Fernandez, Stephen Gardiner, Herman Gray, Ben Hale, Jill Harrison, Burke Hendrix, Breena Holland, Sherilyn Macgregor, Michael Maniates, Dick Norgaard, Karen O'Brien, Devon Pena, Michelle Phillipov, Andy Szasz, Steve Vanderheiden, and more who we would identify had we taken better notes. Many thanks also to the Departments of Sociology and Environmental Studies at the University of California at Santa Cruz, and the Program on Values in Society and the Department of Philosophy at the University of Washington, which hosted Schlosberg as a visiting researcher in 2016.

Conference presentations of various chapters include the Australian Political Studies Association in Hobart in 2012, the British Political Studies Association in 2015, the Agriculture Food and Human Values Society in 2015, the Australasian Agri-food Research Network in 2015, the Australian Political Studies Association in 2015, the American Political Science Association in San Francisco in 2015, the European Consortium for Political Research General Conference in Oslo in 2017, the Society for the Advancement of Socio-Economics in 2017, and the American Association of Geographers in New Orleans in 2018. Most importantly, and most rewardingly, various parts of this project were presented in the section on environmental political theory of the Western Political Science Association in Portland 2012, San Diego 2016, Vancouver 2017, and San Francisco 2018. At the WPSA, colleagues in environmental political theory have been invaluable sounding boards, critics, and supporters. In particular, thanks to John Meyer, Teena Gabrielson, Andrew Biro, Joe Bowersox, Peter Cannavo, Steven Cauchon, Giovanna Di Chiro, Lisa Disch, Farah Godrej, Breena Holland, Matt Lepori, Sean Parson, Justin Williams, Rafi Youatt, and many more.

We also want to give a particular thanks to the journal *Contemporary Political Theory*, its editor Sam Chambers, and the initial reviewers of the first theoretical piece from this project, authored by Schlosberg and Coles. We are quite proud that the piece was named the best article in CPT in 2016, especially given the consistently creative, innovative, and important work being published there. Not so much thanks to the two previous journals that rejected the piece—one simply desk-rejected by an editor for not being grounded enough in the discipline of political science. Discipline indeed, but these hurdles need to acknowledged.

We also owe an immense and substantive debt to the attendees of a manuscript review seminar we held in Sydney after a long week of environmental justice conferencing in November 2017. Sherilyn Macgregor and Gordon Walker offered comments and critiques on chapters, and a substantive, critical, and incredibly helpful discussion included Julian Agyeman, Devita Davison, Lisa Heinze, Leslie Lindo, Alana Mann, Miranda Sharp, Elyse Stanes, and Margaret Steadman. We hope we have done all of their comments, critiques, and suggestions justice.

Thanks also to the anonymous reviewers for Oxford University Press, who really helped us fine-tune some key chapters. And, as always, a deep appreciation to our editor at Oxford, Dominic Byatt, who has supported (and published) Schlosberg's work for what is now twenty years.

At the University of Sydney, we are privileged to have the incredible and supportive atmosphere of the Sydney Environment Institute, a multidisciplinary initiative focused primarily on the environmental social sciences and humanities. Nothing there gets done without the immense energy, incomparable abilities, and sheer unending will of our Deputy Director, Michelle St Anne. The SEI seminar series on *Food@Sydney*, curated by Michelle and our incredibly generous and knowledgeable colleague and collaborator in all things food, Alana Mann, was also a key avenue for both learning more about food movements and engaging others around our work. Staff at SEI, including Eloise Fetterplace and Anastasia Mortimer, have consistently supported this project and all of the various travel, events, symposia, visitors, grant management, communications, social media, and blogging that has gone along with it. A particular and additional thank you to Anastasia for her thorough edit of the manuscript and her combined determination and magic with Endnote and the references. Other academic colleagues at Sydney have been helpful and/or inspiring on this project in particular; they include Robyn Alders, Ruth Barcan, Charlotte Epstein, Tess Lea, Rosemary Lyster, Iain McCalman, Astrida Neimanis, Susan Park, Bill Pritchard, and Elspeth Probyn.

A special thanks to Lisa Heinz, both for her inspiring work on sustainable fashion and her assistance reaching some of our key interviewees.

So much of academia, including political theory, remains an individual endeavour—and one almost exclusively focused on the academic applying expertise in a singular direction, to theorize the world. This work stands in direct opposition to that one-way approach, as it has emerged from an ongoing conversation *with* and *by* a community of activists and practitioners that has richly welcomed us along this journey as interlocutors, collaborators, and, ultimately, friends. We were particularly fortunate to have the chance to meet Devita Davison, Kath Delmeny, Jamie Facciola, Peter Kenyon, Leslie Lindo, Sandy Murray, Smita Narula, Sharelle Pollack, Carmen Rojas, and many more who taught us more than we ever expected, and whose voices resonate throughout the argument within. This book is for them.

Finally, and forgive us while we slip into the first person, there are those we need to thank individually.

David: Of all of the above names, I want to particularly thank my long-time colleagues and friends Rom Coles, Teena Gabrielson, John Meyer, and Sherilyn Macgregor. All have been particularly supportive—or supportively critical—at the necessary times, and I find myself repeatedly coming back to their contributions to my own thinking about various aspects of sustainable materialism. They each make the field of environmental political theory rich, vibrant, engaging, and rewarding. Of course, much thanks must go to Luke Craven, who started as a research assistant and quickly became a co-creator and co-author; it has been a pleasure to watch someone grow from student, to scholar, to colleague and collaborator. But my deepest appreciation goes to my wife and partner Sheila Clancy. This is usually where the author notes all of the emotional and caring support that he or she gets at home, and I have most certainly experienced and valued that for over thirty years now. But Sheila has offered much more to this project. As a sustainable materialist long before me, and as a textile designer, seamstress, and producer of 'sustainable intimates', it was her insistence that I look beyond food movements and into sustainable fashion as something worthy of academic study that initially pushed me down this track. Ever ahead of the trend, her foresight was spot on, invaluable, and incredibly rewarding. I must also thank my daughters, Mira and Valerie, who also see and use sustainability as a form of power; Mira's insistence as a teen that darning socks was an act of resistance was one of the initial things that got me thinking about the very material nature of contemporary movements.

Luke: I am of course, most grateful to David Schlosberg, a colleague, mentor, and friend, who indelibly changed the course of my life by inviting me to be part of this project—a decision I made, unbelievably for those that know me well, on a whim. David has been the perfect collaborator. Strategic, attentive, intellectually generous, he endlessly pressed upon me the merits of listening deeply and of believing in what does not seem immediately possible. I also owe the deepest of thanks to my closest family and friends, whose wisdom and constancy have kept me afloat these past five years: Dan who reminds me that common sense is not seeing things as they are, but as they ought to be; Sam who always makes time when I need it most, and Clare whose kindness and presence have helped this book emerge in the quiet moments. Finally, I am forever grateful to my loving parents, Jeni and Kerry, who from my earliest moment have helped me find the words, and given me the tools to use them. This book is immeasurably better for that moment, and each one since.

# Contents

# List of Tables

# List of Boxes

# PART I

# INTRODUCING SUSTAINABLE MATERIALISM

# 1

# An Introduction to Sustainable Materialism

This is a book about possibilities—possibilities in everyday practice. It is about the construction of different practices, institutions, systems for meeting some of our basic material needs—food, energy, and clothing—in more just and sustainable ways. And it is about the motivations, in particular the political motivations, for activists and practitioners working in these areas, building alternatives.

Humanity faces a broad range of ills, from ecological devastation to racist authoritarian nationalism; we live in a world of constant ignorance, hate, manipulation, greed, and damage. We hear of these realities and their obvious injuries every day, as well as the reactions against them—the tweets and replies, demonstrations and counter-demonstrations, bullshit claims and corrective narratives. Yet much of this argumentation remains in the realm of discourse, and the academic realm tends to follow. There is, for example, in reaction to the growth of right-wing figures and parties, a host of new academic tomes on authoritarianism and populism and the political actors that define, embrace, and use them. There is also a growing focus on localist politics and the potential of radical municipalism and urbanism. As important as these discourses may be, in both the public realm and the academy, our focus in this work is purposely different. Here, we examine real and growing innovations in alternative forms of practice and material flows. The focus is on the stuff of everyday life, on the basic material needs of our lives, and on the development of alternative systems and counterflows of both power and goods through the lives of individuals, communities, and environments. This is what we are calling sustainable materialism.

If Foucault taught us anything, it is that power is embedded and embodied in the practices of everyday life. For example, as much as we can lay the responsibility for climate change at the foot of the fossil fuel industry and the denial machine and politicians they funded, for most of us climate change is also linked to the simple act of turning on a light or getting in a car, given the way that energy is still generated with carbon-emitting fossil fuels. Similarly, we can talk about, and clearly lay out, the incredible power of industrialized and globalized agriculture, but in our everyday lives, the destruction of rivers, deltas, and reefs caused by contemporary agricultural practice is linked to the simple act of eating food grown and raised in industrialized food systems, where runoff from fields does damage downstream. We can be aware of, understand, and broadcast the very real human and environmental toll of fast fashion and waste, while the very clothes we put on our bodies everyday leave behind a trail of harms, from pesticides sprayed on cotton fields to the deaths of sweatshop workers. A focus on the material flows of these necessities of everyday life starkly illuminates the impacts of corrupt politics, abuses of power, a range of injustices, and the ecological unsustainability of the satisfaction of material needs in highly industrialized societies. And it illustrates one way to step out from the power behind it, and create new systems.

Our goal here is to simply illuminate and start to explore the existence and reasoning behind the development of *alternative* systems and flows for the provision of such material needs—the expansion of what we are calling sustainable materialism. Given the growing development of social movements around these very practices of everyday life, it is becoming increasingly possible to eat, to power, and to clothe ourselves and our communities outside of traditional industrialized practices. The focus here is specifically on the *why* of such movements—in particular the political, social, and ecological motivations of the activists creating these new and material systems and flows. It is about the politics of the shift in everyday material practice.

Ultimately, our argument is that there is a way to theorize, understand, and link a wide variety of these new movements and practices around the idea of sustainable materialism. Activists and groups are themselves responding to, and tying together, concerns about, and resistance to, the disconnect and capture of the political process, the everyday reality of social and environmental injustice, the dominant and encompassing circulations of power, and the alienation and resultant destruction of the non-human realm. These movements represent a new politics of sustainable materialism, an environmentalism of everyday life and practice.

## The Cases

We examine a number of new social movements in three industrialized countries—the US, the UK, and Australia. These movements represent the growth of material practice, in ways that illustrate innovative collective responses to, and critiques of, a range of problems with the production, supply, and circulation of everyday material needs. From fast-growing parts of the local food and food justice movements, to community responses to a post-carbon necessity and a climate-challenged world, to an embrace of a new vision of more sustainable fashion production and circulation, a range of movements offer new modes of practice, organization, resistance, and prefigurative models of democratic living, all immersed in re-formed relations with each other and the natural world.

We readily acknowledge that our cases are limited; our focus is a set of movements in industrialized nations—and primarily English-speaking contexts at that. While we address activism and developments in these three countries, our goal is *not* a comparative study, examining differences. Rather, we focus on the similarities and crosscurrents, the overlapping motivations and articulations of activists in different countries and different sectors—primarily in food, energy, and fashion. Our intent is not to universalize from what we explore, nor to discount the wide variety of movements and organizations we do not. The goal is to theorize the connective tissue that seems to hold very different kinds of movements together to form a pluralistic picture of a unique form of environmental action. We aim simply to develop a theoretical approach for understanding a range of these unique movements, to draw political and strategic links between seemingly disparate groups and foci, and to provide a framework for examining additional movements and contexts.

Clearly, there are multiple potential critiques of theoretical positions of the movements, groups, and activists we examine. There are also numerous examples of these movements that have arisen in other countries, both north and south, and reflections on such movements, in particular in the south, inform our approach (for example, Guha and Martinez-Alier, 1997; Shiva, 2008; Esteva and Prakash, 2013). In this sense, the cases for this initial study are limited—and there is potential to expand the scope of the idea, practice, and evaluation of sustainable materialism to other countries and material sectors.

The premise here is that a variety of movements can be viewed through the sustainable materialist frame we discuss. Recent food movements serve as one example—the growth of farmers markets, community supported agriculture, food policy councils, and more. These are rapidly growing new food institutions that, on the one hand, resist junk food in schools, food insecurity, food deserts in urban areas, unsustainable agriculture, and, on the other hand, work to construct food systems which are good for farmers, the health of consumers, the food insecure, and the environment (Winne, 2011; Agyeman, 2013; Alkon and Guthman, 2017). We wanted to get at the difference between the *consumers* of organic food, for example, and those that were focused on the development of distinct food *systems* and the relationships between producers and consumers. There has been an immense growth of these integrated food systems, and quite a bit of innovative research on them, but our focus is on the collective motivations of the breadth of actors creating these alternative and attentive food systems.

These groups have often developed out of previous social justice and environmental concerns and struggles. It is not uncommon to see areas with histories of radical politics or environmental justice organizing turn to the reconstructive focus of food. Detroit, for example, has one of the most promising alternative urban agriculture food justice movements in the US. While some early environmental justice advocates eschewed the whole idea of food self-sufficiency (as it reminded them of a sharecropping past), concerns with food access, economic development, health, community revitalization, cultural preservation, and connection to land and environment have helped anchor and drive these new movement organizations—and the development of empowered food systems. Similar concerns with social justice and community functioning and development are manifest in food justice movements in many cities, from London to Melbourne.

The point is not simply that food movements are growing, but that they are being articulated as alternative structures of community organization and material flows—simultaneously, if in different ways, in many communities across the globe (Shiva, 2007, 2008; Petrini, 2010; Esteva and Prakash, 2013; Sbicca, 2018). Whether it is based in response to hunger, food insecurity, and/or food deserts in inner cities, or a more direct response to the carbon outputs of industrialized agriculture, or the loss of traditional foods and practices, these movements share many of the same goals—challenging power and creating new collective institutions and food systems that embody sustainable material relationships between human communities and the natural world that supplies our needs. Combined, these movements represent the development of a new model of circulation around agriculture and food.

Likewise, energy movements—from the increasing number of community energy initiatives in the UK (Walker et al., 2010; Bomberg and McEwan, 2012), to the growing network of transition towns and initiatives across Europe (Barry, 2012), to a growing focus on 'just transition' or 'nature-based transformation'— are expanding the way that energy is produced and distributed, and how communities will design themselves for a post-carbon future. We focus in particular on the rapid development of community energy—again, not just individual homeowners buying solar panels, but those involved in collective ownership, neighbourhood and cooperative solar, and small-scale grids, in addition to participants in just transition and green city groups.

Because wind and solar are widely dispersed they have often been taken to be particularly amenable to—and even richly suggestive of—highly decentralized production and distribution, in ways that could release contemporary economies from the powerful circulations of fossil fuels. As such, alternative energy practices illustrate sustainable materialist possibilities akin to those emerging in agriculture. Shared energy generation is an aspect of this shift, but much of the early literature was focused on the business potential of collaborative consumption (Botsman and Rogers, 2010), rather than movement motivation and meaning. In contrast, the growing number of community energy cooperatives suggests that movements themselves are intentionally linking new flows of energy, finance, technology, and political communities to resist and create alternatives to the mega-circulations of the carbon industry (Abramsky, 2010; Walker et al., 2010). Such movements demand study that is complex, systematic, and multiscalar (Creamer et al., 2018).

Another aspect of the new sustainable materialist focus has come together around alternatives to fast fashion. Rather than focus solely on protesting sweatshops and working conditions and the increasing disposability of fashion, more alternatives are proliferating around sustainable fashion. Here our focus is primarily on new producers of more sustainable clothing that is attentive to the full supply chain. Over the lifetime of this project, starting in 2011, all of these areas have exploded in popularity, but none more so than sustainable fashion. We have seen critiques of fast fashion, labour practices in the industry, and sustainability come together in both the proliferation of new designers and companies, as well as in the industry as a whole— including traditional producers and high-end fashion houses. Training in the practice has grown in very traditional fashion institutions, such as Parsons School of Design, with textbooks and guides (Gwilt, 2014), and the academic study, mainly focused on design and practice, has grown as well (Gordon and Hill, 2015; Heinze, 2017). And yet, again, while there is growing literature on sustainable fashion, there is very little attention to the motivations and meaning of such a shift in attentiveness to fair, just, and sustainable supply chains in terms of social movements, collective action, and new material politics.

Throughout the text, we will highlight a few of the organizations in each of these material areas, with boxes in each chapter, to give a bit more depth to some of the particular cases.

In all of these movements, our argument is that there is a growing and palpable concern amongst activists of the recognition of, and immersion in, the material relationships we have with the resources we use, and the transformation of means of production that have been both alienating and unsustainable. In each of these material areas, while we recognize the importance of individualized and consumer action, our focus is on the development of community movements and collective institutions. There are many ways in which we are encouraged to put values into practice individually—doing fifty things to save the planet, cutting our use of air travel or fast fashion, or buying LED light bulbs and organic produce at Walmart. But even more engaged individual actions, such as buying food at farmers markets, putting up solar panels, or upcycling clothing, are not seen to address, or impact, larger problematic social and material practices and flows. Unfortunately, much of the literature on material and consumption movements is focused on these kinds of individual actions, and we address some of the limitations of common approaches, including political consumerism, in Chapter 2. Individual action may take some of our everyday life out of such flows, and so assuage our values, but such isolated statements are simply not seen by movement participants as enough to interrupt the flows of debilitating and anti-environmental industrialized practices.

In response to that realization of the limits of individual action, many individuals and movements have moved to address their concerns with more innovative, collective, and reconstructive responses to the unsustainable institutions and practices in which their lives are immersed. So rather than simply show an interest in better-quality food, or post-carbon energy generation, or fair fashion, we see more individuals, groups, and organizations developing, participating in, and enjoying the products of new food *systems*, community energy *systems*, and sustainable fashion *systems*. The institutionalization of these larger collective responses and systems—to what are seen as errant, destructive, unsustainable flows of materials—is key to our focus.

Participants in these movements and practices are often keenly aware of their own unique political motivations, strategies, and impacts, and the movements are clearly growing in numbers and scope. Academically, however, current analytic frameworks for understanding environmental movements do not adequately address this wide variety of interlinked innovations. While there are key studies of new food movements (Gottlieb and Joshi,

2010; Alkon and Agyeman, 2011), most focus on a justice-based framework for understanding these movements, while we see them as exemplifying a larger sustainable materialist concern as well. Much work on community energy focuses on the transition town movement; there, some confine themselves to offering either technical instruction or uncritical praise (Hopkins, 2008, 2011), while others are more critical (Blühdorn, 2013; Kenis, 2016). And sustainable fashion in academia has been more about how-to, which is excellent, but not part of a social movement framing. While there is a growing literature on theorizing urban environmentalism (for example, Loftus, 2012), these works do not address the relationship across numerous urban movements. Hess (2009) offers an insightful study of localist movements that address a range of these efforts, including food, energy, and the localist retail and media sectors. But while Hess focuses on these movements' response to globalization and the endangerment of the local, we think the conceptions of power and sustainability in these movements require the application of additional frameworks, including, crucially, a new materialist approach to everyday life.

## Key Research Questions and the Structure of the Book

Our goal here is to more fully engage the broad and numerous distinctive political and materialist meanings of the practices of these movements and community institutions. There are really three very simple research questions in this study. The main question, and what takes most of our focus here, is the issue of *what motivates this kind of activism?* Secondary questions follow, and have more to do with our assertions that these are unique political movements. Here, we ask, *are these movements really political?* And *how are they unique?*

In response to the first question we see four different though clearly interrelated ways of understanding and framing these movements through their motivations, visions, meanings, and obstacles. All of these motivations are related in some way to participants' understanding of, and reaction to, the flows of power and materials through the body and community. In short, these participants and movements are motivated by:

(1) a shift from the standard notion of postmaterialist politics into a sustainable materialist focus on instituting and embodying collective practices and institutions of provision of the basic needs of everyday life;

(2) a focus on social and environmental justice;

(3) a response to power, in particular the power of the material circulation of things, information, and individuals—and the way that power reproduces itself; and

(4) an ethos of a more explicit acknowledgement of human immersion in non-human natural systems, and a desire for a shift to a more sustainable set of practices that make up human/non-human relations.

These frames and motivations illuminate common themes across numerous, seemingly disparate, initiatives and movements, and make up the main structure of the book. Chapter 2 addresses the shift from postmaterialism to sustainable materialism, and the political critiques and fatigue at the heart of activist motivations. It contrasts those political and structural motivations with other attempts to theorize material action. Chapter 3 addresses the justice motivations of activists in these movements, in particular a concern with a *material* form of political participation, a response to the injustices of power, and a focus on the basic capabilities and needs of communities. Chapter 4 explores activist understandings of, and reactions to, conceptions and practices of both power and counter-power—the identification of the flows of power, the material removal of bodies and communities from those systems of power, and the construction of alternative flows of both material and power. And Chapter 5 explores the idea of sustainability in these movements; there, we examine the growing concern for sustaining the material flows of everyday life, including reconnecting to both human relationships and human–non-human entanglements. We discuss how these environmental concerns both motivate actors and help structure sustainable materialist movements in response.

The second research question comes from some of the academic *critics* of these kinds of movements, as well as our approach to them, who insist that such actions and systems can never effectively take on the *real* and entrenched political problems we face. The accusation is that such action will never really make a politics that matters, or, worse, that they are simply a simulation—a post-political set of coping practices, rather than a political counter-movement (Blühdorn, 2017). We find these kinds of critiques unconvincing, primarily because they are not based on any kind of empirical evidence, in contrast to the one hundred interviews we conducted for this project. These kinds of critiques are addressed more or less implicitly throughout the book, but we take on some of the specific points in Chapter 5, on the political implementation of new materialism.

The third research question again comes from critics—less critics of the movements themselves and more of the idea that they actually represent anything new. In the past few years of discussing the idea and progress of this study with our academic colleagues, a type of combined fatigue and fatalism about movements would often emerge in questions. What could possibly be new or different in environmental activism, they asked, that has not been done before? Again, we address this question throughout—the central claim, of course, is that sustainable materialism makes up a qualitatively different kind of environmental and social movement. But the focus of Chapter 6 is more specifically directed towards these kinds of queries; there, we address a range of movement strategies and activist virtues. The combination of a dedication to collective action, to material sustainability, and to an expansive prefigurative politics is, we argue, unique; those strategies are informed and directed by a set of participant virtues—systems consciousness, prefigurative humility, boldness in the face of massive power and injustice, and an ethic of care to human and non-human alike. These strategies and virtues tie the different focus areas and redesigned material systems we explore—food, energy, fashion—together in a new, unique, and potentially powerful way. Finally, we conclude with a reflective discussion of the broader meaning of these movements of practice, in terms of both their limitations and the real potential of movements of material practice to bring about broad change in the systems of production and consumption of the needs of everyday life.

## A Note on Method

Before moving on to explore the political motivations of movement activists in sustainable materialist movements, it is important to lay out and reflect on our methodology for this study—the method and the *point* of that method.

In the more technical sense, our analysis draws, first, on a content analysis of group-generated mission statements from coordinated groups focused on new food systems, community energy, and sustainable fashion in the US, the UK and Australia. These statements have been sourced from online content that self-identifies as a formal summary of a group's aims and objectives. A total of 135 groups (fifteen food groups, fifteen energy groups, and fifteen sustainable fashion websites from each of the US, the UK and Australia) were included in the content analysis, with a sampling frame instituted to keep the analysis workable. Content for each group was limited to a maximum of 250 words, to ensure certain aims and objectives did not outweigh others in the aggregate analysis.

Results from this analysis have been supplemented with interviews conducted with one hundred individuals from these and other organizations in the three countries. Again, it is important to note that we did not intend a comparative study of these countries, but rather chose them because of the similar nature of the emergence and growth of these new materialist movements. In terms of demographics, the one hundred interviews include forty-one in Australia, forty in the USA, and nineteen in the UK; forty-nine of those were of food systems participants, fourteen in energy, sixteen in fashion, and twenty-one working across other and/or multiple material systems. This latter group includes localist economic development, worker cooperatives, and slow money/alternative finance activists—all also linked, in some way, to food, energy, and/or sustainable fashion movements. Our gender breakdown leaned towards women, with fifty-seven female and forty-three male interviewees. We also interviewed across the age spectrum, with twenty participants under age 30, eighteen in the 30 to 40 age range, thirty-two in the 40 to 50 range, twenty-two in the 50 to 60 range, and eight hearty and active souls over 60. This data is laid out in Table 1.1.

**Table 1.1** Demographic Breakdown of Participants per Country

| Domain | Participants | AUS | | USA | | UK | |
|---|---|---|---|---|---|---|---|
| | | Number | Per cent | Number | Per cent | Number | Per cent |
| Food | 49 | 29 | 70.73 | 14 | 35.00 | 6 | 31.58 |
| Energy | 14 | 6 | 14.63 | 1 | 2.50 | 7 | 36.84 |
| Fashion | 16 | 5 | 12.20 | 8 | 20.00 | 3 | 15.79 |
| General | 21 | 1 | 2.44 | 17 | 42.50 | 3 | 15.79 |
| TOTAL | 100 | 41 | 100 | 40 | 100 | 19 | 100 |
| Gender | Participants | Number | Per cent | Number | Per cent | Number | Per cent |
| F | 57 | 26 | 34.15 | 20 | 50.00 | 9 | 47.37 |
| M | 43 | 15 | 65.85 | 20 | 50.00 | 10 | 52.63 |
| TOTAL | 100 | 41 | 100 | 40 | 100 | 19 | 100 |
| Age | Participants | Number | Per cent | Number | Per cent | Number | Per cent |
| 18 to 30 | 20 | 11 | 26.83 | 4 | 10.00 | 5 | 26.32 |
| 30 to 40 | 18 | 7 | 17.07 | 8 | 20.00 | 3 | 15.79 |
| 40 to 50 | 32 | 12 | 29.27 | 13 | 32.50 | 7 | 36.84 |
| 50 to 60 | 22 | 7 | 17.07 | 12 | 30.00 | 3 | 15.79 |
| 60+ | 8 | 4 | 9.76 | 3 | 7.50 | 1 | 5.26 |
| TOTAL | 100 | 41 | 100 | 40 | 100 | 19 | 100 |

One clear point to make about the demographics is that, even with a particular effort at making our interview population mirror the ethnic breakdown of each country, these movements are, simply put, whiter than their countries as a whole. In Australia, for example, while the country is 85 per cent white, our sample was 95 per cent white, with the remainder of Asian background—which underrepresents the Asian population by over 7 per cent. In the United States, while we interviewed participants from white, African-American, Asian, Hispanic, and Native American backgrounds, our numbers were still short of the percentage in the general population, in particular lacking interviewees from Hispanic or Chicanx backgrounds. In the UK, our sample overrepresented the country's percentage of Black residents (making up 10.5 per cent of our interviewees there, while the national percentage is around 3 per cent), while it underrepresented the Asian population (just over 5 per cent, while the national population is 7 per cent Asian). More specifics of this data are in Table 1.2. While we made sincere efforts to diversify our pool of interviewees, in particular struggling to match the general demographics of each country, we did not want to artificially deny the reality that these movements are, in many areas, still overwhelmingly white. The community energy and sustainable fashion movements are, it must be said, more white on average than food systems movements, where, particularly in the US, African-American activism has been a major impetus and supporter of food justice organizations in many cities, though they are still outnumbered by the, again frankly, whiter slow food movement.

That all said, after years of engagement with these movements—researching groups, interviewing, attending events and conferences—we do think that this demographic breakdown of our interviewees does reflect the reality of movement participants broadly in the three countries. And while our goal has been to understand the political motivations of sustainable materialist movements in the large sense, it is clear that there is an important role for work that is directly focused on the differences within the movement as it exists. We do reflect on the limitations of these demographics for the theorizing that emerges, and in particular what it means for conceptions of environmental justice, in Chapter 3.

As for our own methodological approach, again, the standard way of describing the process is that both the website text and the transcripts of interviews were coded in NVivo for the presence of various concepts relating to our theoretical frames, and systematically analysed to help identify the extent to which individual and group statements fit within, or modified, our

**Table 1.2** Interview Population and Ethnic Breakdown per Country

| AUS | | | |
|---|---|---|---|
| Ethnicity | Participants | Study % | AUS Population |
| Caucasian | 39 | 95.12 | 85.00 |
| Black | 0 | 0.00 | 1.68 |
| Asian | 2 | 04.88 | 12.00 |
| Hispanic | 0 | 0.00 | — |
| First Nation | 0 | 0.00 | 3.30 |
| Total | 41 | | |

| USA | | | |
|---|---|---|---|
| Ethnicity | Participants | Study % | USA Population |
| Caucasian | 29 | 72.50 | 76.60 |
| Black | 3 | 7.50 | 13.40 |
| Asian | 6 | 12.50 | 5.80 |
| Hispanic | 1 | 2.50 | 18.10 |
| First Nation | 1 | 2.50 | 1.30 |
| Total | 40 | | |

| UK | | | |
|---|---|---|---|
| Ethnicity | Participants | Study % | UK Population |
| Caucasian | 16 | 84.21 | 87.00 |
| Black | 2 | 10.53 | 3.00 |
| Asian | 1 | 5.26 | 7.00 |
| Hispanic | 0 | 0.00 | — |
| First Nation | 0 | 0.00 | — |
| TOTAL | 19 | | |

*Note*: Ethnic groups who make up less than 1 per cent of the overall population in each country were not represented in statistical data released by the national statistical agencies for the respective countries, and therefore do not appear in this Table.

*Source*: Australian population statistics were sourced from Australian Bureau of Statistics (2016); US data was sourced from United States Census Bureau (2017); and UK data was sourced from the Office for National Statistics (2011).

framework. We refer to both word counts and the actual substantive text of organizational websites and interviews throughout this work.

In addition to this formal work, we attended numerous conferences, workshops, gatherings, and more where the design and implementation of sustainable systems around food, energy, and fashion were the focus. These included meetings of the Congress for Community Energy (Australia), Right to Food Coalition (Australia), Business Alliance for Local Living Economies (BALLE, USA), Vermont Sustainable Food Systems Summit (USA), and the Food and Enterprise Conference (USA); we also engaged and observed at a wide variety of farmers markets, food policy meetings, community energy meetings and conferences, sustainable fashion shows and markets, and more. The point of all of this was to extend our immersion, and our listening, to those who were making, directing, and strategizing about new food, energy, and fashion systems and flows of the materials of everyday life.

Methodology, however, does not exist in a vacuum. There is a theoretical foundation for the way that we constructed our engagement with these movements and our interviewees, and it is crucial to lay out the thinking behind the methodological machinery. At the base, of course, is a recognition that all knowledge, including that of deeply engaged participants, can only be partial. The point of developing a broad framework of motivations for actors in sustainable materialist movements is that there are multiple frames and motivations working simultaneously—for some it is frustration with politics as usual, for others it is justice or power or sustainability. For many, the motivation is all of the above. We are not seeking to privilege one perspective or motivation, but rather looking to construct an integrated argument out of the patchwork nature of individual perspectives.

Crucially, this project does something a bit different than a standard qualitative interview methodology. The point of engaging so many actors, and of trying to understand the diversity of perspectives and motivations, is to understand and tap into the political and social theories that these movements are themselves making and living. This requires 'a distinct process that involves dynamic engagement with movements in the formulation, production, refinement, and application of the research' (Bevington and Dixon, 2005, p.189). As Venn and colleagues (2006) note, academics and practitioners conceptualize theories in different ways, and it is often the case that the theories made by those on the ground are left out of social movement research. For us, it is absolutely crucial to actually talk to folks about what matters to them, what motivates them, and how they describe the practices in which they are engaged. Put another way, 'attention [must] be paid to the actual voices of those who are the "object" of theorising' (Martineau and Squires, 2012, p.533).

The methodology is about tapping into the theories that these movements are themselves producing. It is not just about movement-relevant theory, but movement-*produced* theory. The interest in movement theorizing has been a long-standing part of co-author Schlosberg's academic work. Heavily influenced long ago by social movement scholars such as Epstein (1991) and Sturgeon (1995), one of Schlosberg's constant themes is the recognition and examination of political activists and actors as political theorists (see especially Schlosberg, 1995, 1999a, 1999b, 2007; Schlosberg and Carruthers, 2010; Schlosberg and

Coles, 2016). This is about understanding the political theory made and practised by social movements, and then bringing those theoretical insights and developments into academic conversation. Recognition that there is actually a theory-building capacity of movements in practice has not been the most welcome thing in the subfield of political theory that is primarily based in analytic philosophy, though that is changing. Our argument is that this approach is the only way to comprehend the way that real political concepts such as legitimacy, justice, power, and democratic participation are actually understood, embodied, and acted upon in genuine political action.

In one way, then, talking to activists about their theorizing may sound like a standard approach to qualitative interview methodology, and it is to that point. But this project also does something a bit different. We view the interview part of our data collection process as an exercise in joint learning, or of what Wolff and de-Shalit (2007, p.12) have called 'dynamic public reflective equilibrium,' which is just a complex phrase for describing how participants are actually brought into the process of theorizing. At its core is listening, dialogue, and receptivity. A number of authors working in political theory, with a good example being Bickford (1996), have written about the importance of listening to a functioning democracy. Building from this foundation, our argument here is that listening as a method is also at the core of a co-produced political theory. As Gordon (2011, p.211) has suggested, listening well involves being open to receiving the speaker as a whole person by creating a methodological space within which participants can speak their own words and meanings. Kompridis (2006, p.208) argues that the conception of receptivity is about moving us beyond simply receiving information, to engaging it. Receptivity, therefore, involves a level of accountability. Throughout this project, we worked to actively design these methodological spaces to maximize our own abilities to be 'receptive to the speaker's presence, ideas, and intentions', beyond what is often achieved in more mundane or quotidian encounters (Haroutunian-Gordon and Laverty, 2011, p.124).

In practice, what this means is that rather than simply gathering the views and opinions of our subjects, we also consulted interviewees about our project, its foci, and our initial thoughts on understanding these movements. We learned from their reflections and responses, and in the process revised and modified our explanatory approach with input, intuitions, and theories expressed by the interviewees. At multiple points over the course of the project we returned to many of our participants for subsequent conversations about the 'results' of the theoretical development, and a number of activists joined academics in a final workshop on the draft book. We do not claim that our data provides any statistically meaningful information; rather, it provides substance and reflection from which our own theorizing has grown.

In addition, the data from the content analysis supplements this process. The analytical challenge is integrating these different kinds of 'data' to facilitate theorizing that is responsive, coherent, and parsimonious. Mixing methods is traditionally advocated as a way to 'triangulate' results derived from different methods to ensure that they are consistent or corroborate each other. However, a process of 'public reflective equilibrium' must value the contradictions between different sets of data, accepting that the knowledge produced from a particular method is partial and not easily triangulated. We argue that this approach, together with a commitment to iterative, reflexive rounds of analysis, is the best way to develop theories that are responsive to the values, aspirations, and understandings of these community-based political actors.

Returning to the point about all knowledge being partial, this method also resonates with the idea of multi-perspectival theorizing; that we aim to see 'from within various perspectives, moving from one vantage point to another, inhabiting them in turn, holding them in the mind's eye at once' (Kim, 2015, p.19, emphasis in original). Using these various reflections, we aim for a form of engagement with participants that is a type of 'practice of co-production [that is] sensitive to a situated epistemology' (Chesters, 2012, p.154). In other words, it is not just the two of us as the co-authors; we have actively engaged our participants as co-producers in getting at the political theory of movement actors and groups in sustainable materialist movements. This is a kind of theorizing that movements can seldom do themselves due to resource constraints (Bevington and Dixon, 2005, p.200), but which they strongly desire; many of our conversations included reflection on what the movement was doing in other places.

Why is this point about this engaged and co-productive methodology important to this project? We offer two key reasons. The first is the more obvious one—this approach simply works to provide a better representation of the theoretical content and sophistication of the movement. For example, when we started this project, it was assumed it was going to be distinct from Schlosberg's previous work on environmental justice, and more along the lines of other examinations of the motivations and discourses of environmental movements (for example, Dryzek et al., 2003). This is why the concept of justice as a core motivation of sustainable materialist movements is not mentioned in the first theoretical paper published on the project (Schlosberg and Coles, 2016).

But once we started the actual interviews, justice kept coming up. As many of these groups identify as food *justice* movements, or are concerned with energy *justice*, it is not surprising to find a range of concerns and conceptions of social and environmental justice. But it became obvious that these conceptions are central to the self-identity of these groups and actors. On the one hand, this reality clearly demonstrates the discursive power of the idea of environmental justice in broader environmental movements (Agyeman et al., 2016)—even in these predominantly white organizations. But, on the other, it was only through the intensive interviews with community activists that we learned how integral the notions of social justice are to the sustainable materialism being developed and practised.

The second thing about this method is more political, and probably a bit more controversial. We want to contrast our method with another common approach in the academic community: that theorizing and analysis about social movements is meant to 'inform, direct or inspire' activists, a phrase in the introduction to a recent collection on food movements (Alkon and Guthman, 2017). On the one hand, we understand and support an approach that aims to educate movements with regard to ideas and political strategies; co-author Schlosberg has done exactly this kind of work on the relationship between environmental movements and states in the past (Dryzek et al., 2003). And yet, while some of the recent language of academic work on food and energy movements in particular is about generating and inspiring self-reflection in movements, some of it becomes surprisingly paternalistic, even in some feminist analyses of food and anti-capitalist activism, for example, by scholar activists who we deeply respect. In contrast, our primary goal in this work is not to 'inspire' or 'direct' these movements or activists. The point is to *identify their theorising*, to offer a framework for understanding the development of sustainable materialism as a social movement, and to bring that out in a clear and thorough way to both the academic and movement communities. Our focus is not the classic question of 'what is to be done', but rather that of 'what is being done'—and how it is understood, framed, articulated, and implemented.

## Possibilities

As we said at the outset, this is a book about possibility. In Thomas Pynchon's classic *The Crying of Lot 49*, there is a discussion about miracles and possibility between the main character, and the leader of a Mexican organization that translates as either a Conjuration or Conspiracy of Insurgent Anarchists (CIA, of course). In one of the most quoted lines of the book, the anarchist says: 'You know what a miracle is. Not what Bakunin said. But another world's intrusion into this one. Most of the time we coexist peacefully, but when we do touch there's cataclysm' (Pynchon, 2006, p.97). The point is that the anarchist is faced with the difficult realization that such radical change would truly be a miracle. And yet he is entranced by the existence of another character, the nearly perfect caricature of a capitalist—a miracle himself, 'too exactly, and without flaw the thing we fight' (Pynchon, 2006, p.97). It is, in a way, the reality of that capitalist miracle that may keep the possibility of its opposite, the anarchist miracle, alive. The activists interviewed for this work, we believe, see the world in a similar way. Not that they are necessarily anarchists, but that they fully understand what it is that they are up against; the power and the material flows of the unjust, entrenched, and destructive practices that feed, power, and clothe us are clear to them. And yet, their response illustrates the potential that alternative practices, counterflows, and new and completely different material relationships with each other and the non-human realm are possible—just as possible as our current reality. The focus of sustainable materialist movements is exactly the kind of intrusion and cataclysmic touch noted by Pynchon.

To be clear, our argument is not that such movements provide the sole—or necessarily the best—answer to the host of political, economic, and ecological problems faced in contemporary life. These movements are clearly just a small part of a broader set of political and social movements dedicated to greater political legitimacy, democratic power, social and environmental justice, and ecological sustainability. The point is simply that a growing number of activists and organizations are reframing both the form of, and justifications for, their actions along the lines of a new sustainable materialist practice and politics. They are designing, implementing, and living a set of alternative material systems and flows. To answer some straightforward questions right at the outset: Is this everything? No. Do activists think it's everything? Of course not. Is this movement towards sustainable materialism something valuable? Absolutely. Can it serve as an example of just and sustainable practices that can be replicated and spread? Yes, and one of our points is that this is already happening.

At the conclusion, we will come back to this question of possibility—and lay out some limits to our study and some suggested ways forward. First, we turn to one of the key motivations for political action on sustainable materialism.

# PART II
# POLITICAL MOTIVATIONS FOR SUSTAINABLE MATERIALISM

# 2

# From Postmaterialism to Sustainable Materialism

## Context and Introduction

We begin our analysis of the unique properties of groups concerned with environmentalism in everyday life, or what we are calling sustainable materialism, with a discussion of *why* movement actors develop sustainable materialist practices. The premise is that there are a growing number of people and groups who are working on environmental *practices* and *systems*—food movements, community energy, sustainable crafting, and fashion—and that these movements present a growing approach to environmental politics and activism.

Some activists have actually shifted from more classic political action and policy development, some have expanded to address both practice *and* lobbying/action, and some are drawn solely to the focus on practice. While much work has been done in the academic literature on this move to everyday lifestyle politics and practice, the argument here is that the current literature is inadequate in its examination of the unique *political* motivations, values, practices, and implications of sustainable materialism as a movement strategy. Absolutely key to these movements is that they are also thoroughly informed by some core political frustrations, borne out of the lack of satisfaction with mainstream political processes.

This chapter examines one of the core political motivations of sustainable materialism activists, and contrasts it with alternative theoretical frameworks of environmental and materialist activism. We begin with a critique of earlier postmaterialist analysis and then go through conceptions of material action understood as lifestyle politics, political consumerism, sustainable consumption, and postcapitalism. The argument is that the sustainable materialist actors and movements we examine are a different and unique category of movement— one that cannot be captured by these existing theories and frameworks.

We argue that the articulation of a new and sustainable materialist politics should be understood as an alternative to classic ideas or processes of postmaterialist politics, and more political and collective than lifestyle politics and other current evaluations of practice-based movements. The movements at the centre of this project are focused on replacing unsustainable practices, and forging alternative, productive, and sustainable flows and institutions. They see the creation of new material flows as a form of both political and ecological resistance. That is, no longer willing to take part in unsustainable practices and institutions, and not satisfied with traditional political processes or purely individualistic consumer action, the focus of action in such movements is increasingly on building collective responses that orient around everyday practices of material sustainability. These responses, we argue, stem from a desire to transform everyday lives, economies, polities, and to literally embody and embed values in new material relationships. The sustainable materialist movements we examine are actively transposing these values into lived experience, building the institutions to support them, and prefiguring new possibilities for more sustainable futures.

## Postmaterialism and Social Movements

The opening lines of Ronald Inglehart's (1997, p.3) initial and now classic statement of the postmaterialist thesis, *The Silent Revolution*, state clearly: 'the values of Western publics have been shifting from an overwhelming emphasis on material well-being and physical security toward greater emphasis on the quality of life'. The consistent argument (for example, Inglehart, 1989, 1997; Inglehart and Welzel, 2005) has been that the modern state, both in terms of its welfare component and level of liberal development, provides the material and political environment in which citizens can express and achieve a wide range of values and lifestyles concerned with identity and non-economic interests.

One of Inglehart's original interests was explaining social movements of the type that developed in the 1960s and 1970s, and the way that values were being expressed both traditionally, in standard electoral and legislative interest group pressure processes, and in grassroots political engagements such as protests, boycotts, and direct action. Later turning to broad comparative studies of postmaterial or postmodern values (Inglehart, 1997) and the claimed cultural shift they collectively bring, the core idea remained that political change comes from individual citizens who both hold values and insist that they be represented and addressed by interest groups and/or their representatives in democratic states. The political argument of this postmaterialist thesis is that there will be a fairly direct and linear link between the shift in individual values, a larger cultural shift, and a change in the political environment, such that policies will then be reflective of these new values. Postmaterialism is both predicated on, and assumes, a liberal pluralism open to democratic expression and influence.

In the postmaterialist conception of social movements, environmental concerns are seen as part of a range of interests that emerges only after basic material needs are met. Those values are then engaged in the political environment of a functioning liberal pluralism open to democratic expression, influence, and incorporation of non-material values.

Succinctly put, over the last forty years, the simple argument of postmaterialism has been that, as countries develop, their populations move from a concern with the material needs of everyday life to a focus on the expression of their individual values. The thesis also posits that, along with this shift in values, the public becomes more involved in, and influential over, improved democratic systems. In other words, the postmaterialist thesis posited two shifts, from material to postmaterial values in the populace, and towards a democratic opening in the liberal state that would represent and implement those values.

Our argument here is straightforward as well: neither of these aspects of the thesis holds up, and this is reflected in the values, beliefs, and actions of recent environmental and social movements. First, the assumed dichotomy between material interests and postmaterial values does not accurately describe recent movements, where the quality of the *material* in the everyday activity of life is understood as necessarily *value-laden*. Second, the motivation for sustainable materialist action comes, as activist interviews illustrate, in large part from a frustration with the lack of realization of those values through traditional forms of liberal-democratic politics. The problem, of course, is that politics does not actually work to represent values, as illustrated by the lack of action, for example, on a host of environmental concerns and policies that a majority of the populace in the US, the UK, and Australia support.

## Environment, Postmaterialism, and the Problematic Dichotomy Between Materialism and Values

A wide range of authors (including Martinez-Alier, 1995; Brechin, 1999; Mertig and Dunlap, 2001; Dunlap and York, 2008) has contradicted the basic demographic and dichotomous assertions of the postmaterialist thesis in relation to environmentalism. John Meyer asserts that Inglehart and his colleagues have 'two discrete manifestations of environmental concern: one based on the "subjective values" of postmaterialism and the other based in "objective problems" most evident in poor and more polluted countries', while actual data about the motivations of environmental action 'undermines the supposed dichotomy between (objective) problems and (subjective) values' (Meyer, 2015, pp.55–6). Similarly, in their discussion of the difference between an 'environmentalism of the rich' and an 'environmentalism of the poor,' the latter primarily in developing countries, Guha and Martinez-Alier (1997) aim to illustrate the mistaken assumption at the heart of postmaterialism—that poor people do not have environmental values.

To be fair, even in Inglehart's research, this basic dichotomous presumption that postmaterialist societies are concerned with the environment, and those still faced with objective material needs are unconcerned with such things, never held. In his own cross-cultural study of environmental protection, Inglehart (1995) found that *both* those concerned with 'objective' problems like pollution (primarily in poorer countries) and those with postmaterial values (in more 'developed' states) support environmental ends. Indeed, he notes that 'the evidence suggests that external conditions and subjective values are both important... thus, public support for environmental protection policies is stimulated by two completely different types of factors' (Inglehart, 1995, pp.65–66). Even with that evidence, the highly problematic dichotomy between value and practice is still clearly held, even in this latter interpretation.

As Brechin (1999, p.795) notes, 'while understandable as a shorthand way to describe the two major types comprising global environmentalism, such a distinction is both extremely crude conceptually and misleading'. While there may have been an important and valid point to make, and critiques to offer, about the outdoors/wilderness foci of the major environmental groups and campaigns in northern countries (Guha, 1989), when it comes to individuals and a broader range of social movement groups, the evidence is plenty that both subjective values and objective conditions are tied to support for environmental concerns in both rich and poor countries. To insist on distinguishing cleanly between rich and poor, north and south, material and value-based, simply fails to adequately describe the bases of environmental concern. Environmentalism is complex, consisting of multiple movements, driven by multiple engines (Brechin, 1999, p.793).

One of the key problems of this, now common and widespread assumption of a dichotomy between material interests and subjective values, is that it misses the reality that values actually inform the understanding of, and response to, objective material problems. It also rejects the reality that such problems clearly spur reflection and action on strongly held subjective values and ideals. This combined concern has a long history in environmentalism (see, for example, Gottlieb, 2005; Melosi, 2008). For instance, the connection between social values and the condition of everyday life has been central to environmental and climate justice movements (Schlosberg, 2013; Schlosberg and Collins, 2014). We aim to illustrate that those with postmaterial values in the US, the UK, and Australia do, indeed, have core concerns with 'objective' problems, and bring those concerns not only into the policy realm but also into material practice. Our argument here is that it is exactly this combination of material goods and subjective values—and the perception that they must be inseparable—that is at the heart of sustainable materialist movements.

In short, activists in sustainable materialist movements provide an example of an approach that refuses to distinguish material life from values, and politics from embodied action.

> The whole point is that food enables us to get the job done. Do you want a fairer economy? We can do that through food. What about a more sustainable city? Food, too.                                         (Food movement activist, UK)

> Look, I think all of us know that the work that we are doing here isn't going to change the government, but that's really not what we are trying to do . . . Fashion is everywhere, everyone literally touches it everyday . . . and the modern, industrialised fashion system is responsible for a whole host of the social and environmental ills we face. What we're doing . . . is [creating] an alternative fashion industry that is one small piece of beginning to address these ills . . . one pair of underwear at time.          (Sustainable fashion activist, Australia)

Clearly, the postmaterialist thesis is dated, and there are a variety of reasons to revisit its analysis of many environmental movements. The reality is that many movements and activists combine the interest in everyday material life with a range of what Inglehart and others would consider postmaterial values. On the one hand, as noted above, the whole idea of the postmaterialist thesis dichotomizes values and material experience, and seemingly does not allow for the reality that individuals and movements actually attempt to address exactly this relationship between value and material experience. On the other, Inglehart has long implied that postmaterialism does not simply end with values. The whole point of describing countries with higher levels of postmaterialist values as having higher environmental *activity* is that the 'process of value change seems to bring changing behaviour, not just attitudes' (Inglehart, 1995). Sustainable materialist movements, we argue, are a prime example of activisms that move beyond the inadequate dichotomies of postmaterialism, and aim to embody and embrace both attitude and behaviour, value and objective conditions. What we posit is a better explanatory framework for this approach.

## The Political Implementation Deficit of Postmaterialism

As noted earlier, there is another problematic assumption on the *political* side of the postmaterial thesis. The claim was that, along with expanding values, there was a simultaneous political shift happening in postmaterial states, where the public was being given 'an increasingly important role in making specific *decisions*, not just a choice between two or more sets of decision-makers' (Inglehart, 1977, p.3, emphasis in original). The idea is that 'responsive government is an element of human development' (Inglehart and Welzel, 2005, p.4). The political basis of the postmaterialist thesis, then, is that there will be a fairly direct link between the shift in individual and cultural values and subsequent political change. The argument is that people get materially comfortable, develop postmaterial values, participate in representative democracies to insist that public policy be reflective of these new values, and the state responds with new and improved policies.

Such an idealized picture of liberal democracy is clearly inaccurate, and illustrates that a postmaterialist reading of action-based material movements is inadequate on both values and politics. As we will demonstrate, the political frustration of sustainable materialist activists is both complex and motivating.

Crucially, citizens develop values that do not get reflected in everyday life—either in the political realm or in their everyday interactions and practices. The reality is that the celebrated postmaterial values and policies expressed by citizens are regularly shut out by governments with strong vested interests. The predicted political flow, from changed individual or collective values to the adoption of related public policies, faces an important and powerful counterflow, long noted by critics of liberal pluralism and neo-liberalism. The result is that contemporary citizens are often laden with a set of material and postmaterial, environmental, and democratic values that are simply not reflected in formal politics and policy. There is, in other words, a significant and noticed *implementation deficit*, or a *governance gap* (Stolle and Micheletti, 2013, p.10), with regard to both material needs and postmaterial values that has become increasingly obvious, salient—and frustrating. The result is a political disconnect between values held and public policy experienced, and a reassertion of the importance of everyday material acts and practice on the part of recent movements.

This frustration with traditional politics and the shift to material-based activism has been examined in some depth in the past two decades. In their overview of the rise of consumerist practices as political statements, Stolle and Micheletti (2013, p.3) begin by noting the importance of the 'decreasing trust in the representatives of democratic institutions'. They identify a strain between 'declining trust in governmental institutions and rise in demand to solutions to complex problems' (Stolle and Micheletti, 2013, p.3).

Of course, many authors have identified the drop in classic political participation and involvement (for example, Putnam, 2001; Macedo et al., 2005). There is a wealth of literature in the political field about the various structural problems of late capitalist democracy, and many arguments about the 'end of democracy' at the hands of neo-liberalism—or, more recently, neonationalist populisms. Democracies, Crouch (2004, 2016) argues, 'are declining in effectiveness, as the dominant forces in politics are not those of the democratic will' (2016, p.71). Political parties, where values were to be represented, have declined 'with the growth of the hegemonic ideology of neoliberalism and the power of political influence' (Crouch, 2016, p.71). This is the essence of Crouch's 'post-democracy'. Such critiques are longstanding—Schattschneider (1960) identified the *Semi-Sovereign People*, ordinary citizens who really do not have much of an influence on political and economic decision-making. What is growing, however, is the relationship between this decline in democracy and broader discussions of the decay in political parties, and citizens withdrawing from traditional politics such as voting and 'heading for the exits of the national political arena' in supposedly democratic states (Mair, 2013). For Mair, this leaves democracies without their demos.

For Brown (2015, p.9) blame lies mainly not just in neo-liberalism, but neo-liberalism as all-encompassing—'a normative order of reason developed over three decades into a widely and deeply disseminated governing rationality' that frames and changes all human endeavours into very specific economic acts. As such, neo-liberal rationality undoes basic elements of democracy—'vocabularies, principles of justice, political cultures, habits of citizenship practices of rule, and above all, democratic imaginaries' (Brown, 2015, p.17). Similarly, Honig (2017) notes the decimation and privatization of 'public things'—and the new reality that democracy is limited to anaemic procedures like elections, but stripped of any conception or spatial embodiment of the public good. The capture of the state by this one-dimensional neo-liberal frame hollows out the very life of democracy—undoing the 'demos' and replacing it with homo-economicus (Brown, 2015).

In addition to this political analysis of neo-liberalism, there is also the economic one—that the austerity that has come as a result of the domination of neo-liberal discourse has stimulated new movements of practice, in particular in those states hit more thoroughly with economic crisis. Bosi and Zamponi (2015) for example, see an increase in 'direct social actions,' or transformations of society by the means of action itself, rather than a more traditional politics focused on making claims to the state. Such action often directly addresses economic crisis and austerity, and is 'increasingly related to the satisfaction of material needs' (Bosi and Zamponi, 2015, p.374; also see Forno and Graziano, 2014). In a sense, austerity *strengthens* the growth of such materialist practices among those with postmaterial values (Guidi and Andretta, 2015).

The political frustration expressed by activists is often not only with the state, but also with the 'elite' organizations and interest groups—the very same groups that postmaterialist theorists argue will represent and foster into reality policies that meet the public's growing values. The voices of such groups—the mainstream environmental movements—are not delivering on their promise any better than liberal states, adding to the frustration of activists we interviewed.

The result is a declining confidence that growing cultural values will be represented and implemented; this has struck at the legitimacy of institutional political processes. Such frustration applies not just to parties, but the very ability of any political group—traditional social movement organizations included—to have an impact on political decisions and change policy. Elements of the public have increasingly abandoned those organizations as well as the state. For many of our interviewees, who we turn to shortly, it is the set of policies surrounding everyday life—in particular climate and food policies—that have driven their disappointment with this standard liberal political model.

As Della Porta (2013) has argued in her explanation of recent political movements, behind their growth is the basic reality that three central conditions for liberal democracy no longer hold: functioning and empowered political parties, the territorial nation state, and the kind of political, social, and economic equality necessary for efficacy. In this sense, it is not that people have turned against political participation in the state, it is that the current political discourse and condition of the state blocks such traditional modes of efficacious participation, and alternatives are taken. Alternatives, in this sense, are actions that are no longer oriented towards the state's adoption of a set of political values, but instead towards action itself (Bosi and Zaponi, 2015).

For Stolle and Micheletti (2013, p.33), citizen action in the material consumer realm is understood, following Beck (1997), as a promising illustration that citizens have responded to frustration and a lack of political trust in traditional processes by finding new and different political forms and ways to engage in politics. This emerging form of political action is a sub- or micro-politics that plays out at the material level in collective action. Specifically referring to the material needs of everyday life, Stolle and Micheletti note that 'activism can frequently be explained by a need to fill in governance gaps due to governments' lack of initiative and action on particular problems associated with production and consumption' (Stolle and Micheletti, 2013, p.28).

As Tormey (2015, p.7) declares, 'We might hate one *kind* of politics, repre-sentative politics, the politics of "the politicians". But other kinds of politics, particularly politics that involves us directly as actors and participants, is, if anything, gaining force and momentum...'. Or, more directly, increasingly 'politically engaged citizens don't vote, they act'. While Tormey's focus is pri-marily on oppositional street action, our research illustrates activists' sense that 'just doing' material action and practice can make a positive change where policymaking and traditional environmental lobbying and pressure have failed.

## Activist Framings of the Disconnect Between Values and Political Implementation

Our interviewees from food, energy, and sustainable fashion movements repeatedly cited the frustration and the disappointment with the political realm as their main reason for focusing their activities and practices on the everyday material realm. As one participant articulated it for us, 'the right amount of frustration is also the right amount of inspiration' (Food activist, USA). Another expresses it in similar terms:

> I think that as part of this evolution that's happening—it was happening anyway, but people maybe have been frustrated by the national political environment, having not been supportive enough of what needs to happen. I think the community is ahead of large institutions.   (Food activist, USA)

What our subjects are reporting is a frustration with a political process that is a barrier to sustainable practice. They have the values, but there are institu-tional barriers to their implementation. So rather than have individual and democratization values leading to a responsive state, and rather than just living with the resulting political and ethical frustration, we see those values leading to the demand to restructure some of the economic and environmental processes that are part of everyday life.

Among community energy advocates, for example, the lack of government support for the development of post-carbon and renewable energy economies is extremely disappointing, and motivating. Interview subjects clearly express this frustration and distrust of the political process.

[N]ot to be supporting [renewable energy] from government is well daft, and shows that they are being corrupted by vested interests and we won't stand for it.
(Energy activist, Australia)

[The] Emissions Trading Scheme getting canned, carbon tax getting cut… people were frustrated with what was happening with the government.
(Energy activist, Australia)

Then you know after Copenhagen there was just despair…
(Energy activist, UK)

I think it [the new form of activism] is broadly people's response to the despair they feel about the normal political and other aligned institutions.
(Energy activist, USA)

Such movement actors and organizations express concern that widely held values and opinions in supporting renewables are not actually reflected in their ostensibly democratic states. The values and support for sustainable policies are present, and a democratic process complete with input from NGOs and social movement organizations exists, but the latter system does not reflect the former in its outputs, resulting in political frustration. But rather than stop there with an acceptance of such faux democracy, we are seeing a turn to new material outlets for the realization of values—political action outside the bounds of liberal state policymaking.

Frustration with the disconnect between political and ecological values, as well as with everyday and large-scale political, cultural, and industrial forces, we contend, has led to a growth of new groups and movements with a different—much more embodied and applied—idea of what constitutes appropriate and necessary political action. What we hear in interviews is that when values about justice, power, and sustainability in the population meet a democratic deficit and disappointment, citizens with strongly held values move to an insistence on their material realization in everyday life. This is clearly a politics ultimately born of frustration, with our interviewees in sustainable food, energy, and fashion movements and practices all noting:

[Political] systems were creating a situation where fewer and fewer people actually felt like they had a stake in what was going on and had the ability to influence the course of their own life or their kids' lives, that I really felt the more I learnt about the local movement to really take that back, the stronger

## Box 2.1. Community Renewable Energy Wandsworth ('CREW')

CREW's mission is to make south-west London a shining example of a low-cost low-carbon energy future in the capital. They use a community-led model to deliver energy efficiency and renewable energy projects across south-west London boroughs.

As a voluntary group of committed individuals living in south-west London, CREW works to make Wandsworth a more resilient and sustainable community. By helping community groups and individuals across the borough access low-carbon solutions, they are helping to reduce the carbon emissions of the capital. They have seen significant benefits from their work, including lower carbon emissions, lower energy costs, increased awareness and education of sustainable living, and stronger, more connected, more resilient communities.

They raise funds to support these projects from a mix of foundations, grants, crowd-funding, and local investors, directly invested in programmes promoting sustainable community well-being. Their work is deeply driven by social justice, and our conversations with CREW representatives emphasized that many residents are at risk of fuel poverty across south-west London, with CREW committed to ending fuel poverty through working with communities most at risk.

I felt that that was really, ultimately at the end of the day, our best hope of making change happen.                                    (Food activist, Australia)

[T]he policy organisations are so hamstrung these days because of politics and there's so little appetite for any kind of significant policy-driven change, you know, global warming being the perfect example, that it's evident that these kinds of things have to happen at a local level and at a grass-roots level or they're not going to happen...[T]hat was really one of the driving motivations that I had...                                    (Energy activist, UK)

[P]eople were frustrated with what was happening with the government. The big question with anything, whether it's any matter of social or environmental justice, is what can you do. Sustainability is one of those things where you're undoubtedly making positive change if you actually just do something.
                                    (Fashion activist, UK)

The focus of this *doing* is on the creation of new practice-based institutions where values are viscerally felt and acted upon. The creation of new systemic flows of material goods is necessarily connected to a new discourse of what it means to live in a modern democracy, and to embody and express the necessary interconnectedness of values and material goods in a way previously unavailable to them. As Alkon (2014, p.30) argues, food activists, for example, not only 'attempt to do the work abandoned by the neoliberal state', but also 'trumpet their own abilities to do it better'.

Sustainable materialism focuses on creating the capacity, ability, and influence to establish new institutions and sustainable material flows where existing political and economic structures have failed. That some of these movements also literally embody public space—a farmers market, community garden, or collective kitchen in the food space, or a shared rooftop for a solar array in community energy—and that *community* is key to those spaces and articulations, shows a reclaiming of democratic values, practices, and space simultaneously.

My main interest is community. I come from an urban activist background and I'm interested in living in an area where there is a sense of community and where there are community things going on. One of the things I really like about the market is that it does improve community in a whole variety of ways. I know most of the market stallholders, I didn't know any of them before the market, some of them are now my friends. I eat much more local food since the market. Food swaps...in some ways are the most important food thing that goes on around here but they're not really about food, they're a social thing...So my motivation is the community, not just food really.                                    (Food activist, Australia)

There's something about growing food [in a community garden], isn't there—there is for me, and doing it together, a shared activity, a sense of doing something for the community together.       (Food activist, Australia)

So we've become like the kitchen for the community, and that I think is so far opposite to running a five star restaurant, but just as important, and even more so important, because you're getting to a broader spectrum of people— and the other really fascinating thing is that you watch children grow up— they come in with their mothers, and I've got two boys, and the next thing they are in prams, and then the next they're walking in, and the next they're putting their money up on the counter—so in the five years I've seen that.

(Food activist, Australia)

With the shutdown of the pathway to the state—ideologically, politically, and economically—values are being asserted in actions outside of traditional liberal-democratic political processes. Our argument here is not directly about the variety of causes of the rise of neo-liberalism, the demise of democratic process, or the increase in the democratic deficit. Rather, the point—and what we hear from interviewees in these movements—is that the disconnect between political and environmental values and everyday life, and the lack of authentic and efficacious democratic process and output, has fed interest in, motivation for, and the growth of community practice-based movements.

What we will also illustrate in the chapters to come are other specific political concerns, around justice, power, and the importance of prefigurative and collective political action.

## Explaining Political Action in the Material Realm

Frustration with the disconnect between political and ecological values, as well as with everyday and large-scale political, cultural, and industrial forces, we contend, has led to a growth of new groups and movements with a different— much more embodied and applied—idea of what constitutes appropriate and necessary political action. Our argument is that when postmaterial values in the population meet a democratic deficit and disappointment, we see citizens with strongly held values move to an insistence on their material realization in everyday life.

There are, however, a number of ways individuals and collective actions have approached everyday practice, and a variety of scholarly analyses of such practices and movements. Here, we want to distinguish both behaviours and analyses, to clarify the movements and activists we are examining from those documented in other conceptions and studies of material and consumptive practice. Ultimately, what we are examining is collective and self-consciously political action in the realm of everyday material practice.

## Lifestyle Movements and Politics

Inglehart (1977, p.182) originally understood individual-level postmaterial values to be reflected in 'lifestyle preferences' rather than institutional, political, or collective action. Likewise, recent analysis in this realm focuses on individual action and the concept of 'lifestyle politics'. This kind of personal responsibility-taking is often seen in the literature as a form of 'individualised collective action' (Micheletti, 2003), though we would emphasize the reality of the 'individual' focus. As Stolle and Micheletti (2013, p.41) define it, lifestyle politics is 'the choice to use an individual's private life sphere to take responsibility for the allocation of common values and resources, in other words, for politics'. Lifestyle politics is the use of ones 'personal life as a political statement, project, and form of action' (Stolle and Micheletti, 2013, p.42).

For Haenfler, Johnson, and Jones (2012), lifestyle politics is focused on individual and private, as opposed to collective action, differentiating it from social movements. Participants may see their actions as tied to others, and even believe that a wide range of individual actors, in concern, may collectively add up to broader social change. They also see such action as focused on individual identity—a quest for personal integrity rather than collective action. This clearly fits with the idea of action-taking to reconcile one's values with the lack of broader political action. The political action in lifestyle politics remains private and individual, diffuse rather than organized, and more cultural than actively political. Ultimately, the claim is that lifestyle movements 'encourage individualized participation in the private sphere rather than collective action in the public sphere' (Haenfler, Johnson, and Jones, 2012, pp.9, 12).

Others, however, see the potential of lifestyle politics as collective action. Wahlen and Laamanen (2015, p.6), for example, lay out three distinct forms of what they call 'lifestyle consumerism'. These include (1) an individualist political consumerism, where consumption is used as a political tactic by individual actors; (2) an organizational activity, which would include collective and mobilized activities 'like urban food cultivation, local exchange systems, and eco-villages'; and (3) broader mechanisms of mobilization, 'including mobilization as collaboration with more traditional social movement organizations, drawing on consumer cynicism and coping strategies, and the implications of motivating and empowering consumers to and for social change'. What is promising about Whalen and Laamanen's typology is that it allows for everyday material and consumer practice to be interpreted in a range of ways, from the fully individualistic to the more collective and broadly mobilized. What is problematic is that, by broadening the definition so widely, it sacrifices the ability to inform a nuanced analysis of what is motivating these new forms of political action *in practice*.

Joost de Moor (2016), in a similar vein, suggests that there are three basic dimensions on which we can classify lifestyle politics—individual/collective, inward/outward and direct/indirect (see also van Deth, 2014). The resulting classification scheme has six categories, ranging from individual lifestyle change—classic political consumerism—to the creation of new collective institutions, such as alternative food networks. Crucially, de Moor notes that his categories are not exclusive, and the broader trend in the literature to force an individual–collective binary onto lifestyle political activism is unable to capture the complexities of its operation in practice. New forms of lifestyle politics, he argues, have an innate conceptual ambiguity, and this 'ambiguity has essentially come to define political participation in the late modern era'(de Moor, 2016, p.15). But again, this conceptual ambiguity, we argue, results in the 'lifestyle politics' moniker falling short of the realities of everyday practice that are our focus here.

One of our tasks in this book is to make some clear differentiations between such broad notions of everyday practice and the type of action we find in sustainable materialist movements. While the conception of lifestyle politics offers one way of understanding the bridge between individual action and larger social goals, and the implementation of political and environmental values, it is still important to distinguish between the practice of an individualist lifestyle choice and more collective actions and self-defined social movements. While we agree with the ambiguity and breadth of consumptive movements noted by de Moor, that should not keep us from analyzing key differences between, and innovations in, the variety of labels, analyses, and critiques focused on these kinds of everyday practices. 'Lifestyle politics' loses its viability and value as a category as it is broadened. We aim to distinguish a very particular kind of development or expansion in contemporary environmental movements—clearly collective action on material practices, flows, and systems.

## Political Consumerism

Another approach that attempts to analyze the intersection of individual material action and collective good or impact is that of political consumerism. Here, as Micheletti argues, an individual's responsibility for the common good is expressed in the act of consuming. Such consumption is understood as an involvement part of the larger production process, demonstrating both a personal responsibility and a political motivation for consumer behaviour. Micheletti defines political consumerism as 'the practice of responsibility-taking for common well-being through the creation of concrete, everyday arenas on the part of citizens alone or together with others to deal with problems that they believe are affecting what they identify as the good life' (Micheletti, 2003, p.26).

Active engagement with processes of 'production and consumption [should] be evaluated as part of the responsibility of citizenship' (Micheletti and Stolle, 2012, p.111)—a form of 'sustainable citizenship'. In this view, citizen-consumers bring temporal, spatial, and material or ecological dimensions to the consumptive practices of everyday life. Such citizen-consumers believe that changes in consumptive practices can address past and future injustices, conditions both in their own country and on a global scale, and the human impact on (and responsibility to) non-human nature (see also Hobson, 2013).

In Stolle and Micheletti's version of political consumerism, 'corporations are the center of attention in new frameworks of responsibility-taking and a political target for activists because they can play a significant role in preventing detrimental effects on the environment and human rights' (2013, p.18). The act is about citizens using the market to 'voice their concern about production, labor, environmental, and other objectionable corporate practices' (Stolle and Micheletti, 2013, p.58). Again, this is individualized, and responsibility-based, action. However, Stolle and Micheletti attempt to avoid labelling all such political consumerism as individualized. They insist on an interplay of roles for both corporations and consumer choice in solving complex problems (Stolle and Micheletti, 2013, p.13). And they argue that the rise of political consumerism 'signals a de-emphasis on the distinction between the public and private spheres that historically have shaped the working agenda of government and business as well as the division of labor between citizens and consumers' (Stolle and Micheletti, 2013, p.13). The focus of political consumerism, in this vision, is that of consumptive practice as a pressure on the responsible party—the corporation—through consumer action.

There are critiques of political consumerism other than its emphasis on individualist action. On the one hand, a focus on consumption may simply fail to take on the detrimental impacts of capital. For Dubuisson-Quellier (2015; see also Fridell, 2007; Newell, 2008) these movements may simply become the pawns of capital, appropriated in greenwash campaigns, rather than being actors for broader change. Worse, such a focus on consumption may limit citizenship to the consumptive practice, and simply drop pressure on government and policymakers to act; Maniates, Conca, and Princen (2002), for example, ultimately see a focus on political consumerism as depoliticizing. Our participants make these critiques of their own activisms, which is one of the reasons, we argue, that they gravitate towards sustainable materialism as an alternative to a corporation-focused politics and a focus on ethical consumption alone.

While the kinds of political consumption discussed by this range of authors have certainly grown, we want to distinguish this idea of political consumerism from the sustainable materialism we have found in environmental action. The major difference, of course, is the focus on the development of new *systems* of material flows, rather than pressure on existing corporate practice (discussed further in Chapters 4 and 5). So the political consumerism at play in sustainable materialist movements is not simply about pressure on the responsible party, but a form of responsibility that aims to replace detrimental material flows with practices that are distinct from problematic corporations and products, in order to become part of a reconstructive collective practice of consumer responsibility—new sustainable flows of material goods through communities and households. The form of political responsibility is similar to the idea laid out by Young (2004, p.388) with regard to anti-sweatshop activism, in particular the recognition that responsibility lies with those 'whose actions contribute to the structural processes that produce injustice'. As such, responsibility is seen in moving beyond a classic liberal individualist framework—more focused on collective solutions to structural problems (Lavin, 2008).

Political consumerism breaks down the traditional distinction between individuals as citizens and individuals as consumers, and it is an important fusion of these clear roles that participants identify as interrelated. But what we are seeing in sustainable materialist movements is individual participation in a self-consciously *collective* project that also combines consumption, citizenship, and responsibility. These practices do not contradict or argue against the theory or practice of political consumption, but they do make up an area of collective action in a space that is consciously moving beyond that of responsible consumption as an individual political act.

---

### Box 2.2. Moonbird Designs

---

Rachel started Moonbird Designs in Sydney, Australia having become increasingly concerned about how modern society lives, and the effect this was having on our planet—at the same time as becoming completely disillusioned with the fashion industry. She decided to do something about it and Moonbird was born. Moonbird describes itself as not just a fashion brand, but a 'Revolution in Progress'. Starting as a business that produced ethical and sustainable women's pyjamas, they are now scaling out to be a complete lifestyle brand.

Moonbird has made a commitment to only produce garments in an ethical, sustainable way with fair treatment for everyone involved along the journey. Their goal is to use their business as a force for good. Their cotton garments are made using 100 per cent certified organic cotton. Always organic and fair trade, they champion the handmade and continually scrutinize their supply chain and processes to identify where they can improve. From the slums of Kolkata to the beaches of Sydney, they're passionate about empowering and educating girls to take their rightful place in the world. This passion has resulted in a number of tangible partnerships along the supply chain, including a range of Fair Trade co-operative businesses in India.

---

Our participants routinely expressed the necessity of building a relational conception of *personal* responsibility, with participants noting that the focus of activism is on answering the question of how to connect everyday action at home to larger, and more global political issues. And yet, it is clear that our interviewees focus not only on such a relational conception of responsibility, but also on collective action to build new systems. As one argues, the things activists 'individually want to see' are the same things about which they must 'collectively...act together in concert...in order to realize' (Food activist, UK). Such sentiments are more than simply position statements: they motivate and inform the structure of the new sustainable flows and institutions that our participants seek to enact.

But we can in community, and I think the broader thing is it's a political strategy. I don't really care about going off the grid. I want us to take over the grid. And we're not going to do that if everyone is looking at energy as this very individualised consumer thing. This is a community system. It's something that we have to relocalise the whole economy.   (Energy activist, UK)

[W]e need to explore change as a collective practice... if we could harness our collective resources, we could really make something of it.

(Fashion activist, USA)

[T]here was so much focus on individual action and... the dominant message from governments was just to get your own house in order. [But] I see social movements and collective action and working together as... a vital thing, not just getting your own house sustainable... [S]o how do you bridge that idea of just doing it in your own home versus this huge political, a global issue—and you know people feel totally insignificant when they act alone, whatever they do. So we have to construct the work we do to make it about community.                                    (Food activist, Australia)

The collective motivations of sustainable materialist activists suggest that the focus on individual action preferred by many authors in the political consumerism literature is inadequate to account for the kind of activism we see in new environmental movements. There is a place for a different—collective and materialist—understanding of politicized consumptive practices. We will return to this idea of collective action in Chapter 7.

## Sustainable Consumption and Practice Theory

Another major approach to recent environmental analyses of consumption is the field of sustainable consumption, which is about the clearly related intersection of sustainability and politically motivated consumption (see, for example, Middlemiss, 2018). Beyond political frustration, sustainable consumption is a response to the lack of action on environmental and sustainability issues; it is based on a realization that we need more than simply *policies* for environmental 'protection', but also wholly new collective material *practices* that do not work against the sustainability and functioning of Earth systems. The focus on sustainability as a core component of such consumption-based politics is clear. As one of our participants noted:

> For me a lot of it is just seeing the main threat to our natural eco-systems and our own population is our consumption as a species, a massive over-consumption of everything we can get our hands on…Moving toward local food and local energy systems and those kinds of things is actually trying to target that consumption a little bit. So it's trying to actually influence people's mindset around just consuming.   (Energy activist, USA)

Academically, the field of sustainable consumption 'integrates across industrial ecology, ecological design, ecological economics, sociology, psychology, science and technology studies (STS) and consumer studies' (Cohen, Brown, and Vergragt, 2013, p.2), or three key 'domains' of new economics, socio-technical transitions, and social practices. Even when there is an acknowledgement of a shift to some sort of movement, or 'communal interdependency' like urban farming or community-based energy, for many in sustainable consumption the focus is primarily on the technology that makes it possible (Cohen, Brown, and Vergragt, 2013).

There is a key difference between this kind of shift in socio-technical systems and the movements for sustainable materialism that we are discussing. There may be a related socio-technical transition in some areas, such as moving power generation from fossil fuels to renewables, and from a centralized utility to a distributed model. But what we are looking at is not only that technological transition, but the political *motivation* of the actors within it, and the structure of the *social practice of change*. Such movements do include technological shifts, but the focus for the activists we interview is on the combination of material, social, and political systems and practices.

For much of the social science in the field of sustainable consumption, the 'unit of analysis' is the individual and the practice, rather than the things or technology consumed. Middlemiss (2018) has argued for the need to put the trend towards sustainable consumption in both social and political context; her recent work explicitly critiques a singular focus on an individualist and consumerist approach to such action, while delving into social, political, and systemic structures that both construct and constrain more sustainable action. While a crucial addition to the field, Middlemiss concludes with a discussion of collective action around sustainable consumption, but limits that to examples of Transition Towns and the sharing economy. Our simple response is that the social and political context of a concern with more sustainable consumption needs further development.

As for method, the sustainable consumption literature is often informed by practice theory. This approach is used primarily to examine the intersection of materiality and everyday actions—primarily by individuals. As Schatzki (2010, p.123) lays out, the ontology backing practice theory '(1) analyzes social phenomena as slices or aspects of nexuses of practices and material arrangements, (2) recognizes three ways materiality is part of social phenomena, (3) holds that most social phenomena are intercalated constellations of practices, technology, and materiality, and (4) opens up consideration of relations between practices and material arrangements'. Materiality, in this sense, is absolutely key to social theorizing around consumption practices, as it addresses the relationship of the physical and the social, and considers the added role of nature in social life—and our analysis of it (Schatzki, 2010, p.126).

Social practice theory gives us a way to see 'innovation and stability in social practices, such as cooking, showering, or driving, as resulting from the horizontal circulation and integration of different elements of practice' (Hargreaves, Longhurst, and Seyfang, 2013, p.402). Combined with a more multilevel perspective (Geels, 2011) that looks vertically at 'niches', 'regimes', and 'landscapes', we can understand the spaces and practices of changes in both practices and different consumptive arenas.

However, there are some limitations of both practice theory and such theory as attached to sustainable consumption. On the one hand, the idea of sustainable consumption often focuses on just one aspect of the material chain—the consumptive side. And practice theory can often focus on material practice at the expense of agency. What it tends to miss, and what our focus engages, are the political questions behind shifts in such everyday practices and material flows, as well as the collective nature of such political action. The landscape of the movements we examine importantly includes the democratic deficit previously noted. Movement actors themselves articulate specifically political motivations for the shift in practice—responses to issues of power, social justice, political participation, and more. The 'niches' for changed practices are closely related to the political analyses and strategies for intervening in, and transforming, material systems and flows in that political landscape. In addition, these movements are about collective action—and it is that collective action that is our main unit of analysis. As Welch and Yates (2018) argue, practice theory has been helpful in the broad study of sustainable consumption, but it has difficulty accommodating a thorough account of the collective action at the core of movements for large-scale social and material change. At best, practice theory can identify what Welch and Yates call 'dispersed collective activity' which, to us, is more similar to the imagined collective action of political consumerism than to collective reconstructions of material flows.

These aspects of the movements we examine require a broader or more targeted theoretical frame than those on offer in much of the sustainable consumption or social practice theory literature, one that encompasses changes in collective material practice, as well as the central political and environmental values and motivations noted earlier.

Attempting to broaden the perspective of sustainable consumption, Forno and Graziano (2014, p.143) lay out what they see as five characteristics of sustainable consumption *movement* organizations. First, movements link consumption to environmental damage and instances of social injustice. Second, they contrast problematic mass production with artisanal or natural and handmade. Third, sustainable consumption movements are not just localist or parochial, but concerned with global supply chains and transnational justice issues. Fourth, these movements encourage direct relationships between consumers and producers. And, finally, sustainable consumption movements illustrate a 'diffused mutual solidarity' both between consumers and producers, and between producers. A focus on sustainable consumption as a political act illustrates the belief of participants that change can be sought through the market, and lived and promoted through individual consumption (Forno and Graziano, 2014, p.154).[1]

We agree with Forno and Graziano as to these broader aspects of movements engaging with sustainable consumption—in particular the relationship between social justice and material flows—but also see more thoroughly political motivations at their core. It is a political frustration which has pushed and motivated activists to participate in, and collectively organize, new and sustainable materialist movements. Again, this illustrates the need for a unique theoretical approach—the sustainable materialism we lay out here.

---

[1] We should differentiate between this kind of sustainable consumerist approach, which supports environment-friendly practices, from the anti-consumption and de-growth movements (Martinez-Alier, 2012; Eversberg and Schmelzer, 2016), which insist on *less* consumption as the key to sustainability. For our purposes, such movements, while intent on bringing attention to the range of materialist impacts of consumption, are distinct from the kinds of movements interested in creating more sustainable and just material flows.

## Postcapitalism and Alternative Economies

Finally, it is important to note the frameworks laid out by feminist political economists to understand materialist movements. Here, the work of the duo J.-K. Gibson-Graham (2006), along with ongoing research by Kathy Gibson and colleagues (Healy et al., 2018) on what they have recently called 'postcapitalism as an everyday politics', is key. The work of Gibson-Graham (1996, 2006), was defined first by the notion of *The End of Capitalism (As We Knew It)* and later as *A Postcapitalist Politics*. Both were ground-breaking arguments for how we might rethink and re-envision alternative economies— and both help us move away from what is clearly a masculinist notion of political action that distinguishes itself from everyday tasks, materiality, and flows. The latter book, in particular, focuses on the proliferation of political economic alternatives and practices that reference the kinds of movements and practices we write about here.

On the one hand, we owe an immense debt to this framework—this critical and feminist critique and rethinking of economic practices is, we believe, clearly reflected in the interviews with the movement actors we address here. Likewise, many of the motivations—in particular the collective community and sustainability concerns we address in later chapters—are clearly articulated in Gibson-Graham's work.

On the other hand, however, there are three key places we wish to distinguish our work, though in those areas the point is to make distinctions rather than to critique their approach. First, Gibson-Graham and colleagues often use a language common among critical theorists—that, for example, the work is about developing techniques 'specifically designed to cultivate more diverse, people and environment centered economies' so to help academics and researchers cultivate this kind of activity (Gibson-Graham and Roelvink, 2011, p.29). The idea is to foster a more 'reparative' approach to capital, 'receptive and hospitable, animated by care for the world and its inhabitants' (Graham and Roelvink, 2009, p.234). The critique is of a standard approach of social scientists to the negative impacts of capitalist practice; their contrast is an approach that is actively focused on motivating change and expanding possibilities in the world. The idea is not simply to lay out the classic 'what is to be done,' but rather to 'marshal examples of "what is already being done", thereby contributing to the credibility and strengthening of alternative economies' (Graham and Roelvink, 2009, p.331). Similarly, some analysts of new food systems see their work as being about 'inspiring' activists and academics alike to engage in new projects and campaigns, in part by illustrating and explaining current movements (for example, Alkon and Guthman, 2017, p.3).

While we fully support this interest, method, and active role for scholars, our focus here is one step back, and focused in another direction. The project is limited to an analysis of the motivations of activists taking this reparative approach—those who are actually making new economic practices and repairing alienating and damaging systems and flows. This project aims to examine the *motivations and discourse* of movement organizations. Following on much of Schlosberg's past work (Schlosberg, 1995, 1999b, 2007, 2013; Schlosberg and Coles, 2016), the interest is in *understanding the theorizing* that goes on in movements, rather than shaping or inspiring them. In fact, given the obvious readership of an academic tome published by Oxford University Press, the point here is less to inspire activists than to bring the broad, original, and empowering critiques of those movement activists into both academic frameworks and discourse about new political and sustainability movements.

The second point on which we distinguish our work from the 'postcapitalism' approach is on the role of the idea of capitalism itself. After one hundred interviews with activists, we hesitate to claim that the motivation of those in the alternative economy is about 'the end of capitalism' or 'a postcapitalist politics'—such an explicit articulation simply does not often get stated by the activists and creators that we interview. None of our participants called what they do postcapitalist or anti-capitalist. What we do find articulated, however, is quite similar to what many in the postcapitalist literature argue. As Healy et al. (2018: 33) explain, '[t]he *end of capitalism* is, in the first instance, the end of totalizing understandings that conflate capitalism with economy as such'. What we hear, then, is not really a 'postcapitalism'; rather, it is about a system that is moving beyond a capitalist singularity, the dominance of capitalism, and towards an openness to a variety of forms of organization in a community economy. This may be a minor point, but we think the discursive difference is important. Many of our interviewees are very critical of economic practices as they are—in particular, both monopolies and global systems with the power to undermine local practice and sustainability. But they are also quite explicit about how important it is to revise economic practices in ways that people can make a living. Our interviewees are less *anti*-capitalist than they are for an economy that is more informed, caring, sustainable, supportive, and attuned to their values. More simply put, we find much evidence for the kind of beliefs about, and desires for, a new economic system that Gibson-Graham and others have written about for decades; what we do not find is an insistence on the 'end' to capitalism or the development of something explicitly 'postcapitalist'.

Finally, the third key contrast with the work of this alternative economic, postcapitalist literature is the centrality of *political* frustration we outline above. As we laid out earlier in this chapter, it is not solely economic or ecological frustrations we hear from the movement actors we interview. Absolutely key to the motivations of activists in this innovative economic space is the dire state of democratic access and impact, and the inability to see core values reflected in public policy. There is a clear frustration and disillusionment with both contemporary material life on the one hand and liberal pluralism on the other. The 'doing' of new economic and sustainability practices, and the participation in new and alternative systems, stems in large part from that frustration. The overwhelming critique we hear in interviews is political; the economic critique is about *power*, rather than the fundamental logic of capital. This is another reason we see a distinction between postcapitalist work and sustainable materialism—one that can include and encompass the important critical and feminist framing of new economic practices, but that is also attentive to the everyday *political* frustrations and motivations articulated by movement participants.

## Conclusion—The Political Nature of Sustainable Materialism

What this chapter has attempted to lay out is the political nature and interests of activists in new and sustainable materialist movements. In contrast to a classic picture of the development *from* materialism *to* postmaterialist values, we illustrate a political desire for the embodiment of certain values in everyday material life. This entails a different kind of political practice for a social movement, a material practice—doing and making new products, and new systems and flows of those products. Key to the development of sustainable materialist movements is a broad frustration with the political order, and the interruption of the classic liberal pluralist idea that majoritarian values can influence that political order.

We also contrasted our approach to sustainable materialism from other contemporary frameworks for understanding lifestyle politics, political and sustainable consumption, and postcapitalism. In each of these, we argue, there is a limitation in the ability to address the broad *political* motivations and frameworks articulated by movement actors, and a limited ability to engage the consciously *collective* nature of such action. As we will argue, the political frustration we note here is not limited to the process of the liberal state. The motivation also has to do with three key values—a clear and oppositional focus on both justice and power, and a new sustainable and materialist approach to everyday needs. Ultimately, what is unique about these movements is not only these core political motivations, but also their comprehensive nature—this is not simply about lifestyle or consumption. Again, as we will develop in the chapters that follow, we see a dedication to collective action, not just individual; a focus on the development of new flows as a form of prefigurative politics, rather than one that waits for political decisions; and insistence on an engaged and systems-aware sustainability that incorporates connections with the non-human realm in which all material practice is immersed.

# 3

# Environmental and Social Justice in Sustainable Materialist Movements

As many of the sustainable materialist groups we examine identify as food *justice* movements, or are concerned with energy *justice* or *justice* to textile workers, it is not surprising to find sustainable materialist activists motivated by a range of concerns and conceptions of justice. These movements articulate, value, implement, and embody a variety of forms of social and environmental justice in their literature, actions, and reflections. We see a concern for justice repeatedly articulated in publications and in interviews with activists. Movement actors often see their work as responding to and going against large and inequitable systems of power, and the unjust nature of current industrialized and centralized food, energy, and fashion production and distribution systems. They articulate their motivation to act, and the broadly inclusive nature of these movements, in part as a response to the alienation and exclusion from these current systems and supply chains. And they articulate the importance of the organizations' contributions to the provision of the basic needs of their communities—food, energy, and clothing—but also health, economic development and stability, and social capital and inclusion.

In environmental justice scholarship, it has been widely argued that the idea of justice articulated by movement groups encompasses concerns relating to equity, social recognition and respect, political participation and procedures, and the basic needs of individuals and communities (Schlosberg, 2007, 2013; Sze and London, 2008; Holifield, Porter, and Walker, 2010; Walker, 2012). Movement groups and actors who use the idea of environmental justice articulate a plurality of justice concepts, and recognize and accept that different actors, with different concerns and in different contexts, will articulate those conceptions in various ways. These varying understandings of justice are distinct, but interrelated; they are not seen as competing or contradictory, but instead are most often understood as mutually reinforcing. In addition, conceptions of justice in the environmental justice movement are seen to apply to both individual actors and communities. For example, a lack of social respect or basic need is understood to apply to the community as a whole, and to impact the community as a whole in addition to the individuals within it (Schlosberg, 2007; Schlosberg and Carruthers, 2010).

So the 'justice' of environmental justice has been articulated and understood as inherently plural. And past research has shown that environmental justice groups and actors are accepting of this wide range of conceptions of justice; accommodating of movement actors having different concerns and priorities; and being attendant to the relationship and interconnection between various understandings and experiences of (in)justice.

This chapter asks two central questions about the idea and motivation of justice in sustainable materialist movements. First, we examine what social and environmental justice means—and does not mean—to the actors and movement organizations with a sustainable materialist focus. Of course, environmental justice as a concept came out of a very particular concern with racial and class injustices and continues as a crucial and critical way to understand core injustices around environmental conditions and relationships in poor communities, communities of colour, and other broadly disadvantaged communities. Environmental justice scholarship is being called upon to engage more with critical race theory, political ecology, ecofeminist and anarchist studies, as well as the reality of state violence (Pellow, 2017). And yet, on the other hand, there has long been a focus on bringing environmental justice into other issues and movements, and broad frameworks of 'just sustainability' (Agyeman, Bullard, and Evans, 2003), which aims to explicitly connect the social and environmental. So our first question is how the concept of justice translates as it is taken up as a discourse in movement groups with a clearly different primary focus than previous environmental justice movements.

Second, we examine whether or not the conceptual pluralism seen in previous studies of environmental justice is replicated in these new sustainability movements, as distinct from groups that orient around specific, singular justice concerns. In a more straightforward pluralistic sense, can procedural justice demands be articulated *simultaneously* with, for example, demands to meet basic needs? Further, and more thoroughly pluralistic, can sustainable materialist movements articulate the necessary *relationship* between multiple concepts of justice, as groups in the traditional environmental justice movement have done? Is a focus on procedural justice in local communities, for example, articulated as linked with more cosmopolitan concerns for justice in other places where production of food or clothing is done? And what is the relationship between the more particular demands for 'food justice', for example, and broader calls for social justice?

In short, when participants in sustainable food, energy, and fashion movements talk about justice, which they do a lot, they actually articulate a range of different conceptions of justice. The focus of these activists' idea of justice is most often around three things: the crucial nature of political *participation*, the importance of *responding to power*, and, most often, addressing a set of *basic capabilities* or needs. And in all of those, the role of *community* and *attachment* is central. Given the focus on the local in many of these movements, we find a broad and primary concern with 'community' as simultaneously a goal for movements, a subject and agent of justice, an enabling capability, and as the connective (t)issue that binds a range of concerns of justice together. In addition to this pluralistic set of conceptions of the idea of justice, what is crucial is that most activists understand and engage the relationships and linkages between these different types of social and environmental justice.

Our focus here is on movement conceptualizations of justice, its very pluralistic and inclusive nature, and the similarities and differences with other articulations of environmental justice in social movements. But as we will see, these notions both embody and differ in key ways from traditional discourses of environmental justice.

## Theorizing Environmental Justice in a Pluralistic World

The discussion begins with a brief review of the ways in which environmental justice has come to be theorized in multiple ways. Previous work on environmental justice has established that the conceptualization of justice in movement organizations is broadly and regularly pluralistic (Schlosberg, 1999b; Schlosberg, 2007; Schlosberg, 2013). Some of that work moves beyond this simple realization of multiplicity, to address the practice of a 'critical pluralism' in the movement, where differences are accepted and approached with a particular ethos that includes agonistic respect, intersubjective recognition, and inclusive, engaged participation (Schlosberg, 1999b). This is not to argue that the groups that make up the movement have all adopted and perfected such ethos and practices, but only that they are recognized, strived for, and often used to critique the practices of others.

The focus in this chapter is not this critical pluralist ethos, but rather other aspects of a critical pluralism: the inherent plurality of justice claims, the articulation of multiple conceptions of justice by movement actors, the acceptance of those different conceptions and varied prioritizations by movement actors, and the mutually reinforcing nature of the relationship between these concepts and experiences. What we have found in our interviews is not only a simple recognition of multiplicity of justice claims, but also an acceptance on the part of participants that it is reasonable to hold varied views of justice, and even reasonable to hold those varied views simultaneously.

As for the potential multiplicity of the conceptions of environmental justice to be addressed, the literature is broad. Inequity, of course, has always been primary and key to the idea of environmental justice—key is that some communities are subject to more environmental risks and bads, and receive fewer environmental goods (Bullard, 1990; Dowie, 1995). But environmental justice was never solely about inequity, as movements and scholars always engaged with the question of why some communities were exposed to such inequity. So, second, concerns about a lack of recognition and respect—a devaluing of some people and communities, as in a conception of environmental racism (Bullard, 1993)—has also been central to the movement and its analysis (Peña, 1998; Figueroa, 2003; Whyte, 2011). Such a concern ties into, and reflects, the more theoretical discussions of the relationship between distribution and recognition (Fraser, 1997). Third, procedural justice has been central to environmental justice discourse; movement groups have demanded a 'seat at the table', and that 'we speak for ourselves'. The very obvious and consistent exclusion of communities from a say in, and influence over, key decisions about the very environments in which they are immersed, has been a motivating factor for environmental justice activists across the globe.

Clearly, these conceptions of equity, recognition, and participation are closely interrelated (Schlosberg, 2007). It is difficult to participate when you are not recognized, or when you do not have the resources to participate. That lack of participation often leads to fewer resources—and less recognition from those that do make political and economic decisions. Wolff and De-Shalit (2007) call this kind of relationship 'corrosive disadvantage', where a failure to secure a basic need in one area spreads, and is related, to the experience of other disadvantages and injustices. In the environmental justice literature, many authors address a range of causes and frames of environmental injustice, and see the articulation of the plurality of mechanisms and processes of the creation and ongoing nature of environmental injustice as a key part of environmental justice (EJ) scholarship (Pellow, 2004, 2007; Sze and London, 2008). The recognition and validation of a pluralistic approach to understanding environmental justice is firmly entrenched in the current literature (see Schlosberg, 2013; Agyeman et al., 2016). Crucially, this conceptual pluralism is also encompassed in the environmental justice movement itself, with its acceptance of a range of participants, movements, and concerns.

One way of incorporating the broad plurality and relationality of elements of social justice is through the capability approach, developed primarily by Amartya Sen (1985, 1993, 1999) and Martha Nussbaum (2000, 2006, 2011). This approach has offered a way to encompass a range of basic needs, social and political recognition, and political participation (or 'control over one's environment', as Nussbaum puts it) in a broad framework with which we can understand the diversity and relationship between the various articulations of justice we see in environmental and environmental justice movements. While Sen discusses a broad set of political and economic freedoms, Nussbaum offers a set of ten basic capabilities, many of which are mirrored in environmental justice discourse. Life, bodily health, bodily integrity, affiliation, other species (and the non-human realm), play, and control over one's environment (political and material), are all relevant to, and expressed by, various environmental justice movements (Schlosberg, 2007; Holland, 2008, 2014).

As capabilities encompass a threshold level of basic needs, it addresses equity. Social recognition and respect, as well as participation, are also addressed, making the approach a comprehensive way to understand, frame, and articulate the wide, pluralistic, and related range of concerns with regard to environmental justice. Previous work has applied a capabilities approach to the concerns and articulations of the environmental justice, indigenous environmental, and climate justice movements (Schlosberg, 2007; Schlosberg and Carruthers, 2010; Schlosberg and Collins, 2014; Edwards, Reid, and Hunter, 2016).

That said, we do want to distinguish participation here. Participation and procedural justice are more broadly addressed independently in theories of justice outside the capabilities frame; this is especially the case in environmental justice literature (see Schrader-Frechette, 2005; Ottinger, 2013). So while we might consider participation and inclusion as part of a broad capabilities approach, we prefer to focus on the concept and practice as a distinct notion of justice. Given the earlier importance of procedural justice in environmental justice literature, the current articulations of the importance of the actual material practice as a participatory act, and what we see as a relational and pluralistic part of a broader conception, it seems important enough for us to keep participation distinct from a singular definition of justice as capabilities in these movements.

We turn now to the question of how this plurality of concerns with justice is manifest in new environmental movements of sustainable materialism. We organize the discussion of our findings around three distinct, but interrelated, notions of justice found in both the data and interviews. First, we found that organizational motivations centre on achieving increased participation in food, energy, and fashion production systems. Second, these groups articulate that their activities are, at least in part, a response to the power of strong industries in these sectors and a desire to construct alternative flows of both goods and powers. Third, and related, we observed that sustainable community movement organizations and activists articulate a broad, inclusive conception of justice, grounded in a capabilities framework.

The conceptions we lay out are necessarily broad, in our attempt to generalize across different movements and foci. The goal is not, however, to simply generalize the findings or emphasize the distinctions, but to examine the connections in the activist discourses. To finish, we discuss the ways that these notions of justice interrelate, speaking to the complex and relational nature of the way movement actors articulate justice concerns. We reflect on the way the activist's use of environmental justice can impact academic theorizing and approaches to the movement.

## Participation

First, participation and procedural justice are at the centre of movement concerns. We usually understand political participation as instrumentalist: we participate towards an end, protest to get a message across, or vote for an outcome. We participate, ideally, to inform or change public policy—and social justice requires that opportunity. But what we are finding in our interviews is an understanding of politics, and justice, as including a more materialist form of participation. We hear groups and interviewees repeatedly emphasize the importance of increasing community *involvement* in the production of food, energy, and sustainable fashion relative to their other aims and objectives. This is not only a demand for classic political participation, but an insistence on a sense of *material* participation and social inclusion in everyday practice.

As Marres (2012, p.xiv) argues, much contemporary discussion of material involvement in environmental campaigns is limited to ideas about behaviour change or small changes in daily practices; in some ways, this focus has been aimed at simplifying the demands on the public rather than challenging them to engage broadly as citizens on complex issues (Marres, 2012, p.5). Such an approach, Marres insists, belittles the capacity of people to make real and broad social change through material action. For Marres, material participation is not only about such small things, but also has the potential for new and complex and forms of intervention; the practice can 'trouble and challenge prevalent assumptions of social and political thought about participation...in potentially productive ways' (Marres, 2012, p.2). Her work not only legitimizes the study of the material realm as a valid topic of the politics of participation, but also engages thoroughly with the theoretical implications of such a shift.

Marres own contribution to the field, based in a science and technology studies approach to performance and practice, focuses on 'smart' devices, sustainable living blogs, and environmental show homes—material participation centred around particular objects and technologies. She offers a deep dive into practice—'the role of objects in the enactment of public participation' (Marres, 2012, p.5). Our interest here is a bit different. Rather than a deep dive into objects, our focus is on the way activists understand and define the political action of material participation, and the way that it has become part of an understanding of procedural justice—involvement and participation in the politics of everyday life.

Such a concern really gets to the core of the materialist aspect of a sustainable materialist politics. Participation is not just about voting or being 'consulted' about a policy. It is partly about *doing*—literally, in the case of food movements, getting one's hands dirty. One interviewee put it well when they noted that 'rebuilding parts of democratic participation and people's ability to have a say and actually *do* is a fundamental need of theirs...to take back [control]' (Food activist, Australia). Such a sense of material participation exists alongside a more traditional democratic sense of procedural justice. It is this mix of the more traditional political meaning of participation, alongside the more engaged and material definition, that makes these movements' concern with participation unique.

In our content analysis of movement websites, we see a traditional environmental justice concern for procedural justice. Out of the forty-five websites we examined in each area, procedural justice presents more commonly in energy groups (33/45) than it does in food (10/45) or sustainable fashion (8/45) groups. It may be the case that the websites focus on this traditional notion, while the activists in practice are more focused on material participation. Participation in this sense conforms to the theoretical view that 'democratic decision-making procedures are a core element and condition of social justice' and that justice necessarily relates to the 'rules and procedures according to which decisions are made' (Young, 1990). Groups advertise their participatory credentials to prospective members by claiming that 'everyone gets a vote' and that 'we don't make the decisions, you do'. That said, our interviews show a concern for political and material participation across actors in each of the food, energy, and fashion sectors.

Here, the notion of participation goes beyond a straightforward inclusion in decision-making, to material participation. Unsurprisingly, group statements relating to participation refer explicitly to 'increasing participation in... decentralised and locally owned' food, energy, and fashion systems. Similar language was used by movement actors in our interviews, with people repeatedly emphasizing the importance of increasing involvement in the production of food, energy, and fashion relative to their other aims and objectives.

> It comes up every now and then that repairing and making has become a political statement. It's become an atavistic statement. It's become a response to fast fashion, you know, and an atavistic political one at that. And part of what has come out of that is this disconnection that we've got to our clothing with fast fashion, no idea where it comes from, who makes it, how it's made, what chemicals are in it, or any of those conversations.
>
> (Fashion activist, USA)

Clearly, a key part of how groups articulate their response to injustice is by 'giving people a stake' in the collective benefit of local production systems. Movement actors note that this can only be achieved by 'mobilizing the community and creating a voice'. Crucially, though, this stake incorporates both political and material procedural dimensions. And we also see these concerns present in the sustainable fashion community. As one interviewee noted, 'by giving people the capacity to more intimately understand, see, and feel how the cotton on their bodies affects the world around them, we're helping them to act to make it a better place' (Fashion activist, UK).

> And we actually wanted to reconnect investors and entrepreneurs and eaters and farmers and businesses with their communities and ecosystems that they serve and rebuild a relationship economy as opposed to what Wendell Berry calls the 'one night stand economy'.
>
> (Food activist, USA)

Clearly, both the literature of the movements and the individuals within them articulate a strong desire for participation, connection, and engagement as part of their understanding of justice. Groups articulate a concern with increasing participation in the move away from ostensibly unjust food, energy, and fashion systems. That participation is both classically political, but increasingly also material. This sense of a participatory duty as an element of justice is very

## Box 3.1. FoodLab Detroit

FoodLab members are at the heart of FoodLab. They a diverse group of locally owned food businesses—caterers, bakers, picklers, distributors, corner stores, cafes—who support each other in the process of growing and improving their individual businesses, and who are committed to taking active steps together towards a more delicious, healthy, fair, and green food economy in Detroit.

Though FoodLab believes that food businesses can play a key role in growing a food system that serves all Detroiters, they know there are many challenges they can't tackle alone. Accordingly they consider themselves part of a larger movement and strive to develop new programs, projects, and services in a way that builds on the assets of organizations, public service agencies, community leaders, eaters, and businesses in other industries. They intentionally maintain relationships with allies and partners who share their values and mission.

They strive to create opportunities for FoodLab members to take on leadership roles at many levels, from helping to organize a Community Action, to facilitating a workshop, to telling their story to the press. They work to harness and coordinate the wisdom and energy of their diverse community towards common goals and to achieve the long-term goal of a fairer food system for all Detroiters.

common, broad, and strong in the discourse of these environmental movements of the sustainability of the materials of everyday life.

## Power and Resistance

The second frame we see in group literature and interviews, and yet again related in key ways to other conceptions of justice, is the way these groups pitch or articulate themselves as forging alternatives to the injustices perpetuated by powerful industries. We discuss power as a distinct motivator and strategy in the following chapter—the point here is the articulation of activist responses to power as part of their understanding and discourse of justice.

In line with the arguments in Alkon and Guthman's recent work on *The New Food Activism* (2017), for the activists and participants in sustainable materialist movements, we consistently hear that social justice requires new forms and circulations of power. Members of food groups, for example, consistently note the importance of the movement as a response to the industrialization and alienation of food systems, and to particular growers, corporations, and/or supermarket chains. Critical food and food justice scholars often draw a distinction between the slow or localist food movement which is primarily white (often linked to Michael Pollen) on the one hand, and food *justice* movements, which tend to be about alternative food *systems*, on the other (Alkon and Guthman, 2017). While we definitely see this divide in focus in our interviews, we also see a social justice concern across a wide range of food movement groups.

Simply put, for the activists and participants in sustainable materialist movements, social justice requires both a critique of existing power, and the development of new forms and *circulations* of power. This clear and distinct focus illustrates a conception or concern with the question of the relationship between power and social justice more broadly, rather than a singular focus on environmental justice.

For the activists we interviewed, there are two moments or parts to this relationship between power and justice. There is a focus on both a response to existing power structures, and an embodied and materially constructed alternative power flow. Activists in alternative energy groups, for example, understand justice in terms of both separating from the dangerous and unjust existing fossil fuel-based energy system, and also creating an energy system that is distinct from, and an alternative to, the status quo. This focus on being a response to corporate and political power is more pronounced on the websites of energy groups (30/45, versus 17/45 for food group websites and 28/45 for sustainable fashion websites), perhaps as a result of the influence of such power on public policy, in particular the lack of action on decarbonization, renewable energy, and climate change. Still, food groups, in particular in interviews, consistently note the importance of the movement as a response to the industrialization and alienation of food systems, and to particular growers, corporations, and/or supermarket chains—as an element of social and environmental justice.

> I think one of the things that people forget..., all of this work in Australia being a response to globalisation or neo-liberal power, is that we have a very unique supermarket duopoly in Australia.          (Food activist, Australia)

A fashion interviewee echoed these sentiments when she noted:

> [I]n Australia we're all very concerned about the supermarket duopoly, but in many ways the fast fashion industry is much, much worse. They've taken control of the entire supply chain, but we're fighting to take it back.
> (Fashion activist, Australia)

What we found is that contemporary movements around food, energy, and sustainable fashion are consciously responding to the power and injustice of the circulatory and reproductive power of these major industries.

On the reconstructive side, movement activists are, in part, motivated by seeing themselves—their bodies and practices—as replicating or participating in systems of power they disagree with. And they seek to replace practices and circulations of power that separate us from the creation and sharing of basic everyday needs. They insert individuals and collectives into an *interruption* of the material and power flows of industrialized food, destructive fossil fuels, and sweatshopped disposable fashion. The goal, as articulated by our interviewees and further developed in Chapter 4, is about creating counter-flows, or alternative flows of power. Those new flows of food or energy or clothing through communities is, in part, about empowerment as a kind of counter-power—one that addresses social and environmental justice. It is about the construction and flow of a just food system, a just energy system, and a sustainable and fair fashion supply chain.

The point, groups note, is to have participants step outside of the industrialized circulation of power and to create decentralized, locally owned and controlled alternatives that reconnect local producers and consumers. The ideal expressed by our interviewees is to *physically embody, practice, and replicate* a real alternative flow as part of everyday life.

> [M]y vision for the future is a local food system alternative to Coles and
> Woolworths [the Australian grocery duopoly] that actually relies on our
> local growers, and we start to build growers' networks, and we start to build
> buyers' networks and we bring the two together and we live in a community
> where we're very localized.                                (Food activist, Australia)

Another notes, 'It's not just about one producer, it's about collectively reshaping supply chains that are just as good for people as they are for the planet' (Food activist, Australia). While groups and interviewees understand the small scale of their efforts, and the ongoing power of the industries they seek to replace, their stated desire is to step outside oppressive and unjust systems of production and distribution, and to create and embody alternative and just practices and flows of power.

Across food, energy, and fashion, groups are attempting to change and replace unjust material flows by building new structures and institutions. Importantly, such groups do not view themselves as working in isolation, but rather as part of larger networks that both respond to existing power and construct new, alternative, flows and practices. Whether as part of a formal network of community energy initiatives or of a more diffuse 'food movement', the goal is to move beyond individual circulations to build new systems that are both a counterflow to traditional modes of power and a new, just flow of the basic goods of everyday life. This kind of reconstruction of flow at a local level, they argue, is one way to take on power—local, national, and global—and to address injustices at many levels.

> [We need an] understanding [of] what it takes to build a connection to
> people's values and build a sense of power and community out of the
> alternatives that we are creating here and use that as a connection to broader
> social movements and broader change.                        (Energy activist, UK)

> I think again it's people feeling connected to the land again. Kind of the land
> ownership. I don't know how you can put that—people taking their power
> back, really.                                               (Food activist, USA)

This sense of empowerment is a key point of the response to powerful industries. Put simply, our interviewees see the work of their activism and organizations as confronting the dynamics of power that have interrupted the realization of justice in food, energy, and fashion systems. The creation of counterflows of power is about shifting the locus of power back to communities to support the creation of new material systems that promote justice and sustainability in place.

Relating these comments to the broader literature, it is clear that activists articulate the work of these groups as a kind of counter-power, or counter-governmentality, in a way that not only addresses power, but also explicitly speaks to environmental and sustainability concerns (Hobson, 2013). Such ideas of counter-power in movements are apparent in other recent work, for example by Bomberg and McEwan (2012) on community energy in Scotland, Yates' (2014) work on other UK movements, and Alkon and Agyeman's (2011) work on food justice organizations in the US.

These concerns and efforts are articulated in concert with other aspects of justice, emphasizing the relationality of these concerns. In particular, materially focused food, energy, and fashion groups view the creation of these counterflows as a necessary element of achieving participatory justice—they enable 'doing'. There are both theoretical and practical linkages between power and participation, and the creation of counterflows is understood as an empowered and physical response to material and participatory injustices. Put another way, the relationship between control over one's environment and power is clear; groups respond to the perceived injustices with a focus on new material flows, but understand this participatory response as a form of challenging power. Whether or not individuals and communities can exercise material control over their environment, which is key to these movements' capabilities-based conception of justice, necessitates a focus on the power relationships involved in that exercise of control. Indeed, groups articulate the current lack of political and material control as necessarily connected to a power imbalance, and articulate their mission, in part, as a response. It is an inherent, and articulated, mode of addressing injustice.

## Capabilities, Health, and Community Flourishing

A capabilities approach to justice offers a way to bring together the way individuals and communities actually articulate a variety of related justice concerns, all focused on basic needs and broader community functioning (Sen, 1999; Nussbaum, 2011; Robeyns, 2017). A basic definition of capabilities is that the approach is not just about equity in the distribution of resources or 'stuff', but what people need to convert those resources into a functioning life that they choose for themselves. These are generally discussed as basic political, economic, and social freedoms and rights (see, in particular, Nussbaum, 2011). And they are broadly used to define indices of well-being, including the UN's Sustainable Development Goals.

It is clear that sustainable materialist groups articulate justice as sustaining certain capabilities, which, in turn, enable and support human functioning. Movement actors illustrate that a number of capabilities are crucial to the functioning and flourishing of both individuals and the community as a whole. These concerns are also articulated as fundamentally interconnected and interdependent; in both the content analysis and interviews, capabilities are articulated as an interlocking set, rather than individually. In terms of frequency, the concern for what can be labelled basic capabilities (such as food) outstrips the mention of other justice concepts in our content analysis, as shown in Table 3.1.

A capabilities approach offers a way to bring together the way individuals and communities actually articulate a variety of related justice concerns. This focus on concern for basic capabilities and their support for broader functioning is illustrated in quotes from both the content analysis and our interviews. For example, many organizations refer to their mission as being to 'promote social well-being and connectedness' or 'to nourish people, build community, and protect the climate'. Groups 'believe [their] work will help create a better quality of life … one that is more fulfilling, abundant, socially connected and resilient'. In interviews too, our subjects note that the point is to 'have a positive impact on people's lives' (Food activist, Australia), and to do 'good for their health and wellbeing' (Energy activist, USA). For those in food movements, in particular, 'local food is quite attractive … because it's generally an improvement in quality of life' (Food activist, UK). With changes in the production and distribution of foods 'a community [could] look after itself, so that's about sustainability as much [as it is] health and wellbeing' (Food activist, USA).

While there are a number of capabilities referenced by groups and the individuals interviewed, one obvious and key concern is health, which is a key capability on Nussbaum's formulation. Ruger (2010) has argued that a capabilities-based approach to health justice allows a broader assessment of

**Table 3.1** Concepts of Justice in Movement Website Material

| Concept | Number of groups articulating |
| --- | --- |
| Capabilities-Aggregate | 87 |
| Justice-General | 30 |
| Justice-Equity | 32 |
| Justice-Participation | 52 |
| Power | 69 |
| Any Justice Concept | 128 |

the attributes and conditions affecting individuals' 'human flourishing', as well as societal structures within which resource distribution occurs.[1] Similarly, health comes up a lot in our interviews, but it really is broadly defined. Comments are not just about individual health, or just physical health—though both of those are clearly articulated—but also more about a general experience of well-being or flourishing. In his examination of food justice, Broad (2016, p.6) also notes that food justice refers to an extensive set of systemic capabilities focused on 'improving the health of the eating public, marginalized communities, and of the food system as a whole'.

Our findings suggest that individuals consistently invoke the language of capabilities to refer to health and its constituent factors. Importantly, though, we find that health is more prominent in food groups (twice as common as energy and fashion groups). Clearly, food is more directly linked to everyday individual and community health than energy and fashion (though many of those groups do also have health concerns). Health has also been a long-standing focus of the environmental justice movement, which may explain why it remains in food and food justice movements. Health comments in the content analysis of such groups include that 'food is key in creating healthy communities', and that the focus is—and should remain—on 'vibrant local economies and healthy communities' and 'access to healthy food'. While the access language there links equity and capabilities, the clear focus is health; this is replicated in our interviews as well, where subjects note that there is 'a lot of interest in the fresh, the local, the healthy, the organic' (Food activist, USA), and that while community is crucial, there is also 'a selfishness on their part too because they want to be eating healthy food' (Food activist, USA). Health in energy system discourses is more focused on the health of ecosystems, including global systems, illustrating the elasticity of the concept, from individual bodies to the planetary.

In addition, the way that food, energy, and sustainable fashion groups talk about what it means to be 'local' conforms to an understanding of justice as capabilities, and as concerning both individuals and communities. Invariably, localism is connected to community economic development and well-being—the goal being the creation of 'vibrant' (17 groups), 'robust' (12 groups), 'resilient' (42 groups), and 'empowered' (7 groups) communities that can share in the benefits of a more just food, energy, and fashion system. Taken

---

[1] Health has also been called a meta-capability (Venkatapuram, 2013). In our view, the meta-capability conception of health unnecessarily expands our understanding of health—as distinct from other capabilities and functionings—and, therefore, overstates the relative importance of health to a person's capability set.

as a whole, 65—or roughly half—of the groups in our content analysis engage in this particular use of language in reference to the construction of strong local economies. This connection is made clear in much of our interview data too. Groups articulate that community food, energy, and sustainable fashion projects are about 'about community resilience [and] food resilience' (Food activist, Australia) as much as they are focused on having 'communities working together and knowing each other and being empowered to do something for themselves' (Food activist, UK). Similar empowerment-based language is a common feature of our interview data, which suggests that movement actors connect broader community development and well-being to their ability to exercise political control over their environment (one of Nussbaum's key capabilities, though expressed both individually and collectively by our participants). Localism, these movements argue, is about vibrant, resilient, and healthy economies and communities that provide for local well-being.

What is clear from these responses and interviews is that health is not seen as isolated and singular—a Rawlsian 'primary good'. Rather, we see this capabilities-based account of health embrace the interconnectedness of the broad range of capabilities. In a sense, this illustrates the idea of a positive relationship between capabilities, or a 'fertile functioning' (following Wolff and De-Shalit, 2007) insofar as some level of health is a prerequisite for effective access to other valuable capabilities. Our research also illustrates that participants in these movements do not see health—or other capabilities—solely as individual. Rather, there is a constant move from the individual to the group—individual and community health, related to individual and community functioning.

However, we should note (though it is not surprising given Alkon and Guthman's 2017 critiques) that we found much less of an explicit concern for the health of *workers* in the food interviews—and much *more* of that concern in the sustainable fashion interviews, where the health of workers in both cotton fields and in production facilities was almost always a key issue. This makes an important and crucial point about the discourse of sustainable fashion: it is not just about what our clothes are made of but also who has contact with those clothes, what is the impact of their manufacture along the supply chain, and are those impacts just and equitable. This is one illustration of how a more supposedly elitist movement—sustainable fashion—articulates more broad justice concerns beyond the local community to the health of those exposed to the production of both fibre and finished products.

---

**Box 3.2. Mighty Good Undies**

---

As the name suggests, Mighty Good Undies is an ethical underwear producer in Sydney, Australia that believes in a world of transparency and supreme respect for people and the planet. They partner with the world's best ethical factories and source the finest organic Fairtrade cotton to produce underwear that, as they put it, keeps your bottom comfy and your mind at rest.

Elena from Mighty Good Undies told us that the fashion industry is filled with noise about ethical standards, but in reality, any company can claim the use of organic materials and Fairtrade practices, so it's impossible to know if those claims are true. In response they developed and implemented their own stringent ethics model, which means their supply chain is certified by both the Global Organic Textile Standard and the Fairtrade Labelling Organization. Beyond this focus on environmental justice, their factories also carry the SA8000 social accountability standard certification—the leading international standard for meeting ethical labour standards.

The impact of this deliberate ethic is that Mighty Good Undies is able to ensure that their workers receive fair wages and work in safe conditions, and the environmental impact of their production is actively minimized. This goes beyond their supply chain practices, too. As part of their journey to become carbon neutral they now pair 1kg carbon offset with every pair of undies sold.

## Community, Capabilities and Place Attachment

Whether referring to capabilities in general, health, or localism, the concept of 'community' plays a key role in the way that groups think about and articulate justice concerns. Confirming past research (Schlosberg, 2007; Schlosberg and Carruthers, 2010), these movements do not limit their understanding of justice to the individual, as is the norm in political theories of justice. Justice in and for communities is a central part of their understanding of the concept.

In findings that add validation to some of this previous work on capabilities and community, our interviewees consistently make a connection between this kind of health and the larger health of the community as a whole. So a concern for health is not just about you or me eating better and being healthier, but also about a healthy and functioning community. For example, many organizations refer to their mission as being to 'promote social well-being and connectedness' or 'to nourish people, build community and protect the climate'. Groups articulate concerns for a better quality of life, a more fulfilling and connected community. The goal of many of these organizations is to have a clear and positive impact on the lives of individuals and communities.

For those in food movements, 'local food is quite attractive... because it's generally an improvement in quality of life' (Food activist, UK). With changes in the production and distribution of foods 'a community [could] look after itself, so that's about sustainability as much [as it is] health and wellbeing'. We see the same with the justice concerns in sustainable fashion, with one interviewee noting, 'sustainable fashion is about shifting the fashion industry away from a focus on "I" to a focus on "us". Community couldn't be more central for me in what we do' (Fashion activist, USA). Again, this concern was not just about the individual workers, but also about communities all through the supply chain, from cotton workers to the consumer. So community is primarily about community *connectivity*—and an active contestation against disconnection in liberal societies.

As Table 3.2 illustrates, 75 per cent of the groups in our content analysis link one or another notion of justice with a broadly defined conception of community. For most groups in these movements, then, there is an important relationship between calls for justice and the role of the community; this is a clear constant across the majority of groups we examined. However, movement discourse shows that the concept of community, like that of justice, is also pluralistic. The conception of community plays different roles for subjects—community is seen in two very different ways. On the one hand, community is a capability—it is something necessary for individual functioning, so it must be attended to. But community is also seen as a *subject* of justice—the thing that we are trying to keep functioning, or to improve its functioning.

The idea of 'attachments' to place has been an increasing topic in recent environmental justice literature (Groves, 2015; Schlosberg, Rickards, and

**Table 3.2** Community–Justice Linkages in Movement Website Material

| Concept | Percentage of groups articulating concept | Percentage of groups articulating justice and community |
| --- | --- | --- |
| Capabilities-Aggregate | 66.0 | 49.0 |
| Justice-General | 24.1 | 16.7 |
| Justice-Equity | 27.2 | 21.0 |
| Justice-Participation | 41.0 | 29.0 |
| Power | 47.2 | 41.1 |
| Any Justice Concept | 94.0 | 75.0 |

Byrne, 2017). This notion of attachment was quite prominent in our interviews as well. That said, we can contrast what we heard from these movement activists with what we usually see in other environmental justice movements. In most environmental justice issues, it is the act of *detachment*—or the undermining of attachment to place—that is the issue. For example, with the issue of lead in the water supply in Flint, Michigan, in addition to being unequally distributed—certainly because of race—we hear about how the toxicity in the water alienates people from place. The very place one lives and has grown up in is toxic, and that undermines a long-standing attachment to place. Such illustrations of alienation from toxic places, or the tension between attachment and the understanding of contamination, abound in the environmental justice movement and in the literature (see Schlosberg, Rickards, and Byrne, 2017).

But what we hear more in these sustainable materialist movements is that the experience of everyday life around the provision of material needs is, in its current form, alienating people from community and place. The desire—for example in food movements—is to *reattach* in some way with each other, with community and seasons, and with the non-human realm. It is the *lack* of attachment—rather than detachment—that is the focus. Yes, activists talk about how alienating current food systems are, and that they have created practices where we do not engage each other, or the farmers, or the land. But, crucially, what we are hearing is not just about this *de*tachment, but more about how food and energy justice movements are seeking to *re*attach people to each other, to specific places, and to the material and natural worlds more broadly; to build attachments, and community. In sustainable fashion as well, the justice concern is about how the current material practices of fashion are toxic to many in the supply chain, but one of the things we are hearing is that by bringing attention to these practices, sustainable fashion can both bring those practices out from the dark, and make connections and attachments between producers, consumers, and environment.

As one activist put it:

> Do we feel connected deeply to each other, to other human beings, not just our immediate tribe but to humans, all of us? Do we feel connected in a reverent way to the larger, natural world that we're a part of? All humans feel good when we do.
>
> (Food activist, USA)

And that is the point—we feel good when we are attached, and these movements are attempting that as an element of the just lives they are trying to construct. Or as another puts it, though maybe more generally:

> At the end of the day, this is really about building community and giving a shit about each other, and if we build community, like that's how we'll get through this. And community includes nature, you know.
>
> (Energy activist, USA)

Sustainable materialist movements are seeking to *re*attach people to each other, to specific places, and to the material world more broadly. These diverse linkages speak both to the relationality of the varied understandings of community and to the ways in which they are embedded within, and connected to, the plurality of other justice concerns we discuss here. And, crucially, it makes clear that activities focused on building community or rekindling place, through food, energy, fashion, and other material things of everyday life, can and should be thought of as environmental justice activism. This concern with attachment makes clear that activities focused on building community or rekindling place, through food, energy, fashion, and other everyday practices, can and should be thought of as environmental justice activism.

In addition, the analysis of group literature and our interviewees shows some quite similar and plural conceptions of community, but it also illustrates the role community plays in the provision of other capabilities. For food, energy, and sustainable fashion movement groups, community is articulated as an identity to be built—a goal in and of itself. But it is also seen as an enabling meta-capability and as a connective tissue linking different conceptions of justice. 'Building community' is an oft-cited goal, but building community to provide for health, for control over the local environment, and for stronger social relationships is also cited. Groups note that the strength to achieve goals comes with community, that by 'joining with others to demand action', having 'strength in numbers' or 'strength in community' is key— 'being community-oriented helps us achieve these goals'. Community here both provides the context for the provision of capabilities, and links the provision of a range of different capabilities. This finding illustrates the importance of understanding capabilities not only at the individual level, or the idea that community is something that provides for those individual capabilities, but also the crucial reality of the articulation and experience of capabilities at the group or community level (Stewart, 2005; Schlosberg and Carruthers, 2010).

This concern about building attachment to community, then, is one of the threads that tie together this whole range of justice concerns in these movements. And rebuilding attachment, community, community capabilities, and sustainable relations with each other is absolutely part of what the achievement of environmental justice would look like for these activists.

Groves (2015) argues that 'place attachment' is a 'capability possessed by individual agents only by virtue of their embeddedness in specific places and among particular others that inhabit them'. In doing so, he attempts to situate the concept of community at the nexus of place, identity, and agency. Put simply, he argues that the flourishing of community *in place* is a key component of justice. A focus on attachment to place, though, narrows the way that particular attachments are understood more broadly by individuals and collectives. As Nixon (2011) notes, places are also built upon a 'vernacular' landscape as they are emotionally and symbolically meaningful to people who inhabit them. It is attachment, in this broader sense, and its relationality (or the way in which attachment emerges out of interactions amongst people and within collectives), that we find resonated most with people in the course of our conversations with them (see, in particular, the earlier quotes in this section).

Put another way, while we do not disagree with Groves's general theorization, it remains clear that notions of community are pluralistic, and that it is articulated by our participants as more than simply 'place attachment'. At the same time, Groves' arguments support our broader claim that there is a place inside the capabilities approach for notions of place and community. And, crucially, such a claim gives us the theoretical tools to understand the injustice that stems from the loss of community or destruction of place. Attachment is a basic need, essential for a functioning life.

In a capabilities approach, justice occurs with the availability of all of the basic capabilities of human life. To deny or disrupt those capabilities, therefore, is an injustice. So the disruption of attachment, to others, to community, is also an injustice—and is expressed as such by numerous activists.

This question of pluralistic notions of community has been addressed by Walker (2011), who examined the concept in carbon energy governance; there, community entailed community as an actor, a scale, a place, a network, a process, and an identity. This term, he notes, is articulated in plural and flexible ways depending on a given context and the actors involved— something we also find not only in energy movements, but in food and sustainable fashion as well. Broadly, Walker finds that the 'positive associations that the term carries, combined with the distinctive characteristics typically assigned to communities as actors, rooted in places, and able to generate local engagement, support, and participation in ways that others cannot, all means that working through and with community mechanisms' is both central and productive (Walker, 2011, p.780). Similarly, Delanty (2003) argues that, when thought about in a strictly political sense, the concept of community undergirds access to justice for those on the margins of society. Community, he notes, is at the core of various types of political mobilization and radical democracy that orient around social justice concerns. On the one hand, then, community relates directly to a sense of common concern, while on the other, it speaks to the materialization of various forms of collective action and practice (for example, Williams, 1976). This plurality of conceptions of community has not yet been taken up by capability theorists in their treatment of 'community' in that framework—possibly because of the limited research within the broad capabilities literature that actually examines the articulation of subject groups on their own understandings of injustice, and the creation of more just communities.

## Pluralistic Justice

All of the above illustrates that the conceptions, and use, of justice in sustainable materialist movements are pluralistic, at least in a simple sense of having multiple meanings. Movement groups and activists express a variety of conceptions of justice, and hold them simultaneously. They are articulating a broad range of justice concerns—around procedural justice, responses to

**Table 3.3** Total Concepts of Justice Articulated in
Movement Website Material

| Total concepts articulated | Number of groups |
| --- | --- |
| 0 | 6 |
| 1 | 33 |
| 2 | 53 |
| 3 | 27 |
| 4 | 14 |
| 5 | 2 |

power, a set of capabilities (including health), and the place of community. This attention to the basic plurality of justice concerns is clear. Multiple notions appear in single interviews, in the material from single organizations, and in single group domains. As seen in Table 3.3, nearly three-quarters (71 per cent) of the groups whose literature was examined articulate two or more notions of justice in their mission statements.

As discussed at the outset, however, a critical pluralist account of justice is not only about the existence of a plurality of meanings. Our second point is that the literature and interviews illustrate that these different articulations of justice are understood not as divergent and incommensurable, but as interrelated, practically linked, and mutually reinforcing. In other words, not only do we find arguments for participation, power, capabilities, and community attachment as elements of justice, but we also find arguments for the *relationship* between them. This supports Broad's (2016, p.9–10) argument that food justice is pluralistic and, crucially, practiced as 'an ever-evolving mix of philosophy and action that takes shape through an ongoing process of co-construction, collaboration, and conflict in FJ [food justice] work'. It also confirms Walker and Day's (2012) argument about energy justice for 'affordable warmth' being about the integration of distribution, recognition, and procedural justice.

One food organization argues that its goal is 'create production and trading systems that provide a fair income to food producers and guarantee the rights of communities to access healthy and nutritious food produced using ecologically sound and sustainable methods'. Another calls for 'a healthier, more vibrant, and more ecologically sound city through financially self-sufficient urban farms that welcome public involvement and make fresh produce as widely available as possible'. These statements illustrate a concern for fair systems, health, and participation simultaneously.

Individual activists illustrate the same plurality. Many articulate a concern for:

> basic principles of...social justice [while] trying to improve conditions for people on low incomes...[J]ust how can we improve our food systems and how do we improve sustainability and all that kind of mixes together.
>
> (Food activist, USA)

> For me it's about health, it's about supporting your local economy and supporting your community, which is the people who grow your food, produce your food, process your food...Food is about community, it's about nourishment and it's about community as well.
>
> (Food activist, Australia)

So there is health, power and a new system, and community in a single quote. Similarly, a community garden activist states:

> I think again it's people feeling connected to the land again...People taking their power back, really...So I think that's helped people get into social justice once they start, because once they start to understand the connection between things...where food comes from...then it enhances their capacity to make connections in other ways and therefore they become more politically aware and just their sense of outrage or injustice actually—you know, they can actually hone that in to something.   (Food activist, USA)

Finally, another activist sums up the approach: '[F]or me social justice, equity, food security, community engagement, social engagement is all part of what I do' (Food activist, UK).

These movement groups and activists simultaneously articulate *qualitatively different* sorts of justice claims. But beyond that, groups and activists engaged in these sustainable materialist movements tend to articulate a strong understanding of connectedness of multiple conceptions of justice. While the conceptions of justice do differ, what we see in the groups we examine here—just as previously seen in the environmental justice movement—is a willingness, or an insistence, to articulate the commonalities, connections, and relationships between different experiences of injustice and arguments for just arrangements.

Beyond the theoretical attractiveness of pluralism, any attempt to reduce group statements about justice to their individual or distinct parts ignores the reality that, for groups themselves, notions of justice are fundamentally interconnected and interdependent—and linked to the place and environment in which they live. When groups articulate a plurality of justice concepts, they do so in a way that illustrates that their understanding of justice is both greater than, and different from, the individual notions from which it is constituted. Individual notions of justice cannot be treated as discrete entities of inquiry because the way in which they are articulated depends on the presence of others.

It is perhaps unsurprising, then, that we gravitate towards the capabilities approach as a way to understand this plurality expressed by movement actors. Indeed, as Walker (2009) has also argued, the capabilities approach has 'an internal pluralism, incorporates a diversity of necessary forms of justice, rather than privileging only one, and retains flexibility in how functionings and flourishings are to be secured'. We agree, but would suggest that our findings here necessitate two key additions to this theoretical position. First, individual and collective functionings are bound together, relationally, and often in place. That is, our participants understand and articulate the co-dependence of their capability sets at a number of levels, moving from the personal to the populational and, more aspirationally, to the planetary. These linkages are key. And, crucially, the normative project of promoting environmental justice requires that we come to terms with this relational complexity, particularly as activists become increasingly aware of the fact that a sustainable materialist politics is a necessarily coalitional one. Second, and relatedly, in order to properly understand environmental injustice as capability deprivation, power and resistance must be central. For our participants, the act of reconstructing sustainable material flows as an explicit act of resistance is inseparable from the project of realizing a world of mutual flourishing. The key point here is that the *relation* between power and functioning, in particular, is one that is always imminent in practice. We argue, therefore, that in order to properly understand environmental *in*justice as multiple, pluralistic and, crucially, fought against, power needs a more prominent place in our capability-based theorizations of it.

Overall, while we did not examine aspects of a critical pluralist *ethos* explicitly (Schlosberg, 1999b), we did find movement actors open to, and accepting of, a range of conceptions and emphases of justice. We see an implicit acceptance of the inherent plurality and relationality, rather than incommensurability, of justice claims, as well as the recognition of the validity that different organizations may emphasize different approaches depending on their context. Sustainable materialist groups, then, have embodied not only many of the ideas of justice raised in environmental justice movements, but also key parts of the critical pluralist approach raised in previous studies.

Importantly, one major caveat here, of course, is that we are examining the articulations and stated goals of movement groups and actors—not their actual actions and accomplishments. What happens on the ground may differ from the ideals that are stated in literature and interviews. These conceptions of justice, we acknowledge, are observed in discourse, not in an everyday observation of activities in practice. So, while participatory justice is articulated as a key concern, we make no claims about how these principles are embodied within the practices of group decision-making, for example.

That said, the conceptions of justice, plurality, and connectedness go beyond the articulated justice-based goals of these organizations, to the essence of the design of their broader practice. The movement literature shows organizations that claim a dedication to 'embody social justice and sustainability', and work to 'create a sustainable food system in a wider context of social justice'. Groups and interviewees articulate a sense of social justice that connects with environmental justice and sustainability concerns in the supply of the basic needs of everyday life and well-being.

## Conclusions

The central argument about the place of justice in sustainable materialist movements has been twofold. First, looking generally at the discourse of activists, these new social movements that are focused on food and energy and sustainable fashion are articulating a broad range of justice concerns— around procedural justice, a response to power, a set of capabilities, and a desire for community. And, second, these various concepts are seen not as competing, but as interlinked—and not only interlinked with each other, but also with a broader sense of social justice and just treatment of the environment.

These findings also raise a number of broader implications for conceptions of environmental justice in the movements that require further examination. On face value, groups that orient around sustainable materialist concerns seem to articulate notions of justice in different ways than traditional environmental justice movements. And that brings us to what is *absent* in the vast majority of these 100 interviews: while apparent in the literature and websites of groups, we very rarely heard the words *inequity* or *inequality* in interviews, meaning that the more classic notions of distributive injustice, which are core to environmental justice, were not really articulated across the board. In addition, we rarely heard comments on, or definitions of, justice that address recognition or disrespect of communities as a whole—another long-standing concern in environmental justice. While such concerns were articulated by some food activists in the US, and others note the call there for a food system that addresses racial and economic disparities and that is attentive to the contributions to such systems specifically made by low-income communities and communities of colour (Alkon and Agyeman, 2011; Alkon and Guthman, 2017), we did not regularly hear such claims in our interviews of activists across a wide range sustainable materialist movement groups. There are, then, some key differences between past work on understandings of environmental justice and current discourses of the term being used in these sustainable materialist movements.

One qualification here is that, while absent in interviews, 'equity' did appear very much in our content analysis of group materials. However, when equity appears in such group-generated content it is seldom spoken about in isolation, instead being linked with other concerns, such as participation and community well-being. More work is required to examine whether equity is mentioned in group-generated content because it is a buzzword in certain funding contexts (website text could be written with a particular audience in mind), or whether interview participants roll equity into other notions of justice when they articulate their aims and objectives in a holistic way.

Likewise, the lack of attention to cultural recognition may be because these food, energy, and sustainable fashion groups are predominantly white middle-class groups, especially in the Australian and UK contexts. On the other hand, it may also be important that the groups we are examining are more concerned with constructing new practices, and these practices themselves provide recognition and inclusion to their participants. Given the centrality of recognition in environmental justice movements and research, more work is needed to explore how such concerns may be expressed in movements focused on food and energy justice, and sustainable fashion, in both theory and practice. Our suspicion is that, in many ways, recognition is assumed by movement actors and remains implicit in the way that they articulate justice concerns. As many of these activists are primarily making arguments for constructing just practice, rather than arguments against injustice—the historical focus of environmental justice claims—these claims for recognition may not be prioritized. However, and crucially, we would caution that, without such attention, movements risk replicating recognitional injustices, including exclusionary and even colonizing discourses.

The lack of attention to, and mobilization around, issues of equity, distribution, and recognition in these sustainable materialist movements does represent a significant divergence from the more established and long-standing understandings of justice articulated in environmental justice movements. They are mostly present in food justice movements, not surprisingly given the relationship between such movements and environmental justice activism in the US. But while there are these differences—both internally across the movements we examine and between those and the more traditional environmental justice discourse, the general argument here stands—a broad dedication to justice is constantly articulated, and that is made specific in reference to the need for expanded participation, power, capabilities, and community attachments.

Still, it is clear that these movements do not articulate, in general, the kind of intersectional multidisciplinary understanding of a broad critical environmental justice such as key scholars like David Pellow (2017) or Laura Pulido (2015) have recently offered. We do hear a lot about power, and references to ideas that could be found in political ecology and ecological anarchist literature. There are certainly critiques of the power of corporations and of the state—and of their collusion in undermining both environment and community autonomy. But it was rare to hear anything on race—outside of black-run food justice groups in the US that referred to environmental justice and the Black Lives Matter movement. Similarly, activists were rarely explicit on feminism or gender, or on state violence. We heard nothing on decolonizing or recognizing complicity in settler colonialism—all aspects of a more critical environmental justice that are becoming more central in both theory and practice. Activists in sustainable materialist movements were much more likely to talk about species interdependence, and reconnecting with the non-human realm, than about race or colonialism. Clearly, these are primarily, if not exclusively, white-led movements—and movements that are not explicitly thinking as active allies with other movements.

So we are left with a real disconnect between the necessity and importance of critical environmental justice in theory, in the academy, in our understanding of the structures that build and maintain a whole host of oppressions on the one hand—and the way the term is used on the ground in increasingly less critical ways. One of the key questions is whether all of these movements—these quite empowered and empowering movements creating new systems for the flow of materials through communities in just ways—can actually achieve what they hope to. Can we have just material systems without sustained public attention to a broader range of systems of oppression?

Still, and we would argue very importantly, these findings demonstrate that the broad discourse of environmental justice is alive and well in movements around the basic needs of everyday life. The conception of justice is rich, engaged, linked, and vibrant—illustrating the strength and influence of the idea and discourse of social justice generally, and environmental justice specifically. These 'next-generation' environmental movements remain closely wedded to notions of social and environmental justice—even if those definitions differ from both past and more critical uses of the term. There is no doubt that these concerns manifest in different ways than they did in earlier activism, but the point remains that the conception and discourse of environmental justice is core to the motivations, strategies, and identity of sustainable materialist movements.

# 4

# Material Practice and Resistance to Power

This chapter examines conceptions of power in environmental movements focused on sustainable materialism. Interviews with activists in food system, community energy, and sustainable fashion movements illustrate that participants articulate these movements as responses to power. As initially discussed in Chapter 3, movement activists report being motivated, in part, by not wanting their own bodies and practices replicating or participating in systems of power they disagree with. Rather than simply objecting to, or making a statement about, such physical and material collusion with power, and not seeing product boycotts as enough of a form of resistance, these movement groups posit, create, share, and participate in alternatives to powerful, destructive, and unjust system flows. For example, rather than purchase food in a supermarket system that is alienating to producers, consumers, and the natural world, the idea is to physically embody, practice, and replicate a real alternative flow of food—a separate, sustainable, and dynamic food system, in everyday life. Such an understanding of practice as both resistance and rebuilding of power illustrates how these sustainable materialist movements respond to power in both innovative and highly political ways. We posit that the relationship to power articulated by these sustainable materialist movements is different and unique from those outlined in existing theories and frameworks of social movement action.

We structure the chapter around three key ways that these critiques of power, and the building of alternatives, are a central element of new materialist practice. First, power is understood as a form of material resistance, where activists remove themselves from problematic flows of the goods of everyday life. Second, power is embodied as the creation of counterflows of both material and power. And, third, movements embrace a broader and collective element of these relationships in total, and understand how such counterflows can become a mega-circulatory system.

## Power and Resistance in Social Movement Organizing

Foucault has often been used to illustrate the way that social movements serve as resistance to power—and how many such movements, and the way they understand the world, are subjugated simultaneously by both classic state power and a more subtle form of power/knowledge (Foucault, 1980, 2009). Our analysis overlays a Foucauldian framework in a unique and additional way, to examine how some movements are implementing institutionalized counter-circulations of power. The focus here is on the role both the maker and consumer play in displacing undesirable flows of both materials and power and, crucially, embodying new and more, local, productive, and sustainable flows of goods and power in wholly new institutions. One of our participants put it well when they noted that:

> It's simple, really, isn't it? They [the Australian supermarket duopoly] have all the power, and we're going to get nowhere while that fact remains true. My hope is that the work we are doing at different parts of the supply chain helps to relocalise part of the food system here in [Tasmania]... and that we can get people to get excited about healthy and affordable food on their doorstep. That's the whole point of the [farmers'] market.
>
> (Food activist, Australia)

This clearly resonates with Foucault's account of power as more about circulation than about enclosure. In this view, power insinuates itself through practices, institutions, norms, and the day-to-day behaviours of everyday life. Power does not simply dominate, but also produces and proliferates particular circulations in ways that maximize flows that generate and reproduce power. As Coles (2016, p.193) notes, 'neoliberal capitalism is organised to deploy and utilise shocks with increasing frequency and effect; our bodies are awash in and proliferate megacirculatory powers of governmentality'. These powers, Coles notes, are deeply imbued with political power. Politics and governmentality are inseparable, a point with which our participants agree when talking about the dominant players in their sector:

> Big fashion knows how to play the game... and if you track their rise over the past century it is clear that, if sustainable alternatives are to take root, we need to understand how the [dominant] industry have shaped the status quo we have to deal with.                                 (Fashion activist, USA)

Australians like to complain about energy prices, and with reason, but just look at the energy sector we have in this country: it's a cartel with the government in its pocket. Consumers have so few options...voters have so few options...it is all connected.            (Energy activist, Australia)

Yet, circulation is not merely a context for the apparatus of security; rather it becomes integral to the operation of this new mode of power. Governmentality works with, insinuates itself into, juxtaposes and utilizes circulations. Security operates by infiltrating, influencing and utilizing flows of criminals, goods, grains, unemployed, illegal immigrants, disease, trade, and so on, in order to achieve macro outcomes that are deemed power enhancing and thus desirable. Moreover, institutions of securitized power function not only by infiltrating, but also by producing and proliferating circulations in ways that tend to reconstruct the world and human beings in order to maximize flows that generate power.

While the increased circulation of grain in the eighteenth century is among the conditions that spur the development of governmentality, Pollan's (2007) discussion of the circulation of a global 'river of corn' illustrates the extreme form such power takes today—to which new food movements reply. The human body has a relatively limited capacity to absorb food, but the industrial food circulation complex has increasingly overcome this limit by, for example, adding high-fructose corn syrup into what we eat and drink, thereby overriding biological mechanisms which otherwise shut down hunger. Our bodies, desires, and lifeworlds are being *materially* reworked daily to transform us into 'industrial eaters'. Thus three-fifths of the US population is now overweight and increasingly plagued by numerous associated diseases. Americans, Pollan argues, even have particular isotopes in their bodies that mark the flow and power of the corn-based industrialized agriculture industry in their country. 'So that's us: processed corn, walking' (2007, p.23). Berry (2010, p.146) poignantly summarizes our situation: 'The ideal industrial food consumer would be strapped to a table with a tube running from the food factory directly into his or her stomach'—an image even Disney illustrated in the animated film 'Wall-E' (Stanton, 2008). The economic circulation of corn represents and exemplifies the material embodiment and functioning of contemporary power.

In addition, it is important to note the material aspect of this power and its impact on individuals and communities. The idea of power actually flowing through and with material flows was quite common across all of the movement sectors we examined—food, fashion, and energy. Such an idea seems most obvious in the material flow of food through our bodies:

Of course, but food makes us, doesn't it? It makes our bodies. It makes our children. So there's a moral and an emotional aspect to it, again, where you start going, 'Do you know what? This is not good. It's causing digestive disorders.' People are beginning to move away from it. Of course that's all about power.                                               (Food activist, UK)

While such a focus on the material power of food has become more common, we see the same kind of attention to the flow of power through the body among sustainable fashion activists, who often note the power of the chemical industry in both the development of textiles and the impacts of conventional products on the bodies that wear them. To bring the issue into the public eye is a key goal. '[There are] chemicals in our body and there's chemicals on our skin. That is a conversation that still hasn't fully happened...' (Fashion activist, UK). For energy activists, this idea is understood both in relation to the impacts of conventional carbon-based fuels on polluted communities, and the reality of climate change on everyday life. Such concerns follow those of activists in environmental justice, of course, who have addressed the impacts of energy refining and other impacts on the creation of toxic bodies and communities—from increasing rates of asthma to toxin-related diseases (Sze, 2006; Di Chiro, 2010; Gabrielson and Parady, 2010). Resisting power, in this sense, is resisting the material nature of that power, and its infusion into the very body.

The argument here is that contemporary movements around food, energy, transport, and basic needs are consciously responding to this type of circulatory power and its range of impacts. The focus of these movements is to resist and replace practices and circulations of power that not only harm, but also separate us from the creation and sharing of basic everyday needs. This fashion activist makes clear this concern with circulations of power along the supply chain:

I make clothes that people will love to wear, because they look good... but where your crappy shirt from H&M has very likely made the planet a worse place, here at [fashion label] we think deliberately about all the small details that go into producing each of our products: how can we ensure the preservation of waterways? How can we ensure that women in our supply chain are treated with dignity and respect?... These are the questions I am passionate about finding answers to.                     (Fashion activist, UK)

This quote makes evident a key point we are stressing about sustainable materialist movements. Activists in these movements see themselves as inserting individuals, collectives, and their material practices into an interruption of power flows of industrialized food, destructive fossil fuels, and sweat-shopped disposable fashion. While part of the attraction is the aesthetics, ethics, and experience of the products themselves, especially in sustainable fashion, the focus here is on the role both the maker and consumer play in displacing undesirable flows of power and, crucially, embodying new and more local, productive, and sustainable flows of goods and power in wholly new institutions (see also, Coles, 2012).

These findings resonate with other work on the movements that we are examining. Bomberg and McEwan (2012, p.440), for example, also found that community energy mobilizes around resistance, 'seeking to counter hegemonic forces' and 'mobilizing for access to decision making structures that currently exclude them'. They also note how the physical infrastructure of community energy projects—big turbines, in particular—have emblematic power, driving the circulation of new political ideas and meanings along with energy itself. Relatedly, Yates (2015) makes the case that social movement politics involves, at its core, the imagining, production and circulation of new political meanings. Material circulations are laden with the concerns, interests and values of groups that practice a politics of everyday life. This focus on meaning is also evident in the work of the movements we examine:

> The whole point of the work we do here is to show that another way is possible. Do I think we're going to bring down the corporate food system overnight? No, but look what we've done here with one co-operative supermarket that partners directly and deeply with local producers, who have helped increase healthy food intake for the most disadvantaged. If we can do it, others can too. That is the whole point.          (Food activist, USA)

Similarly, in discussing the food justice movement, Alkon and Agyeman (2011, p.349) note that 'Supporters of food sovereignty advocate for the dismantling of the monopoly power of the corporate food regime in favor of democratically controlled, regionally based food systems in which peasant agriculture can create a greater distribution of wealth while relinking agriculture, citizenship, and nature'. Sbicca (2018, p.161) adds that 'food justice can universalize struggles around a commitment to equity to broaden the horizon of food politics'. He goes on to add that 'food justice requires a resolute commitment to identifying the structural inequalities undergirding capitalism and institutional racism...to achieve socially just outcomes for eaters and workers alike' (Sbicca, 2018, p.164). Kurtz (2015, p.861) concurs, noting 'food sovereignty calls into question the nature and extent of corporate control of food systems and the modalities of power that shape industrial food production at the expense of millions of smallholder and peasant farmers'. Kurtz adds that '[the] struggle over food sovereignty is deeply biopolitical, that biopolitics are inherently spatial, and that biopolitics can be fruitfully understood as politics of scale' (Kurtz, 2015, p.870). The political power of such movements is bound with their ability to circulate materials in more productive, just, and sustainable ways.

Key to this focus, and another element that connects energy, food, and other materialist efforts to questions of power, is the concern for place. Dirlik (1999, p.171) notes that 'if any kind of resistance to this new form of hegemony [centralized power, globalization] is possible, it seems to me that the assertion of places . . . is a crucial starting point'. These social movement actors are learning how to govern the world in a manner that fundamentally redesigns the way power operates (Maeckelbergh, 2011). This process constitutes prefigurative strategy in which movement actors pursue the goal of transforming global politics, not by appealing to multilateral organizations or nation states, but by actively developing the alternative material practices and flows as the political structures needed to transform the way power operates. Their places are reclaimed and redesigned with attention to these flows of power and material. This point is also made well by Yates (2015, p.3), when he notes many social movements '[have] ambitions to build "community"—experiment with social relations and construct . . . counterinstitutions and counter-power in the course of their social movement organizing'. Our interest is in the intersection of this counter-power with the construction of new material flows in the movements we examine.

## Resistance and the Creation of Counterflow

It is no surprise that community activists and social movement participants see their actions as a form of resistance to power. Social movements have long been about pointing out oppression and abusive power—and reclaiming that power for communities. Sidney Tarrow's (1994) classic work on social movements is called *Power in Movement* for an obvious reason. It is also clear that many environmental and consumer movements have focused on addressing power, in part, by refusing to reproduce or recirculate power—boycotts and buycotts, for example (Stolle, Hooghe, and Micheletti, 2005). What makes sustainable materialism movements unique is that the specific kind of resistance identified by activists is material and circulatory resistance. These forms of resistance come from refusing everyday things that are infused with power, and with making and circulating things in a way that both deny power to oppressive forces and create *counterflows* of power at the community level.

These concerns are articulated as fundamentally interconnected and inter-dependent; in both the content analysis and interviews, these power concepts are articulated as an interlocking set, rather than individually. In our content analysis of the web-based materials of 135 activist groups, the general concern for power as we have outlined above is clear. Resistance, the power of systems, and power as participation are the most frequent concepts raised, as shown in Table 4.1.

The focus on being a response to corporate and political power is more pronounced in energy groups (noted in 30 of 45 websites examined), versus sustainable fashion groups (25 of 45) and food groups (17 of 45), perhaps as a result of the influence of such power on public policy, in particular the lack of action on decarbonization, renewable energy, and climate change. Still, food groups, in particular in activist interviews, consistently note the importance of the movement as a response to the industrialization and alienation of food systems, and to particular growers, corporations, and/or supermarket chains. Importantly, groups articulate this response as going beyond simple resistance, to include the construction and replication of new modes or circulations of power that interrupt and replace problematic industrialized and power-driven prac-tices. The stated focus is on interrupting undesirable flows of power and, crucially, creating and embodying new and more local, productive, and sustain-able flows of goods and power in wholly new flows, institutions, and systems.

Interviewees, when asked about their motivations for involvement in material movements, consistently used phrases like 'taking back the power' or 'people taking their power back'. This was the case across the board, from activists in food, energy, and fashion movements in the US, the UK, and Australia.

**Table 4.1** Concepts of Justice in Movement Website Material

| Concept | Number of groups articulating |
| --- | --- |
| Power-General | 72 |
| Power-Resistance | 39 |
| Power-Systems | 41 |
| Power-Political Participation | 54 |
| ANY POWER CONCEPT | 99 |

Interviewees in each of the sectors noted those with power in their respective sectors and countries. So, for example, it was common for food activists to comment on the power of industrialized food systems. In Australia, where there is a very strong duopoly with the two main grocery chains controlling over 70 per cent of the market for fresh fruit and vegetables, activists' comments would address that reality, noting that 'There's a certain section who see the supermarkets as just having too much power and they want to support local farmers' (Food activist, Australia). Alternative practices and flows, they note, are '[n]ot only [about] growing your own food, but it was also social resistance' (Food activist, Australia). Similarly, a sustainable energy activist responded to a question about motivations in the movement by noting how it is about 'really kind of seeing how our current industrial economy and the centralization of wealth is fuelled and empowered by very, very centralized, concentrated control of our energy system' (Energy activist, Australia). In movements focused on community renewable energy systems in the US, the UK, and Australia, the focus of movement groups and activists was on resistance to the centralization of energy systems, the removal of power—in both the political and the electrical sense—from communities, and the more general implications of political power that come with energy infrastructure.

The relationship between resistance and becoming a *counterflow* of power is put well by this interviewee from BALLE, the US-based Business Alliance for Local Living Economies:

> Our work, BALLE's work, humanity's work, is to resist corporate rule, to liberate ourselves from servitude to Wall Street corporations and financial markets, and to live into being a planetary system of community-based, local, living economies that work for all. Truly work for all.
> (Alternative economy activist, USA)

Energy activists see alternative distributional models of power, moving from centralized utilities to distributed energy generated on rooftops and in communities, as a very specific counterflow to the power of the fossil fuel industry. The counterflow, and what it can produce, has to do with much more than just energy:

> We see clean energy and a distributed model of energy bringing that physical power back into the hands of communities. How does that start to...empower the conditions for more democratized innovation, entrepreneurial opportunity, wealth, and translate into political power and local control?
> (Energy activist, Australia)

---

### Box 4.1. BALLE

---

The Business Alliance for Local Living Economies, BALLE, represents thousands of communities and conveners, entrepreneurs, investors and funders who are defying business as usual.

Their mission is to create local economies that work for all. They recognize that creating an economy that works for all is challenging and complex. While current systems are breaking down, there is an emergent ecosystem of models and successes to build on. BALLE works to highlight those stories and the people, places, businesses, and organizations that are bringing the new economy to life. BALLE's capacity-building program, the Local Economy Fellowship, supports a unique community of localists, who are transforming their local economies from the ground up and are challenging the status quo by showing how it is possible to build new food, energy, fashion, and economic systems.

For fifteen years BALLE have been imagining, incubating, and refining new systems, and then moving beyond them. BALLE actively works to shift dollars from destructive and extractive 'business as usual' to models that are healthy, equitable, and generative. Their vision is a global system of human-scale, interconnected 'Local Living Economies' that function in harmony with local ecosystems, meet the basic needs of all people, support just and democratic societies, and foster joyful community life.

---

The empowerment of communities, or the counterflow of power running through communities rather than corporations, is another often-mentioned benefit of collective power generation and flow. The response to flawed and failing everyday practices, embedded in steady flows of contemporary power relations, is to take direct responsibility for interrupting and replacing such flows, and to re-localize much of what has been taken away from communities.

The goal is not simply resilience against current flows, but a transition away from them.

> Personally for me, what I like about it is that it's about empowering communities and also it gives them their own energy which they can then use however they see fit and their own money pot as they can see fit... [to] bring communities together by using energy as the catalyst for system change.
> (Energy activist, Australia)

> So while they're creating alternative supply chains, which are designed to feed into the local economy, and that's not just about what you grow, but how it can be processed and transported locally, how we deal with the waste—can that be used to produce anything of value? There is so much more to do to build the connections we have with each other so that feasibly we could compete with the duopoly here in Australia. That's not cynicism, I'm actually very hopeful—if you look around at the Australian food movement it is increasingly clear to me that we are doing systems work that really has the power to improve the lives of Australians.   (Food activist, Australia)

> Much like in food, the skills in crafting garments and fashion have been lost by younger generations. Whether or not you think that is a good or a bad thing, the reality is that we have become reliant on others—on industry, on fast fashion—to fill a gap in our own skills and capabilities. The work of [organization] is about building self-reliance in the community... and about building connections between makers and people who want more control over what they put on their bodies.   (Fashion activist, USA)

Again, one of the unique aspects of the conceptions of power that we hear from these interviewees is about the relationship between this kind of resistant counterflow of power at both the community and the bodily level. On the one hand, multiple activists, across all of the movements we engaged with, talk about their motivations being about both community and power. But, in addition, there is an almost visceral sense of the flow of a different form of power through the body, based in the material actions and products in these alternative flows.

> Literally, there is so much power in clothing. It can empower the people that make it and the people that wear it, it can connect them, and it can do all that while looking good.   (Fashion activist, Australia)

> I can take it in my own hands, I'm in control of it, I've got the power and I can make it happen.   (Energy activist, UK)

I think a lot of people feel disempowered, but there's a great satisfaction in being able to viscerally participate in this healing process.

(Food activist, USA)

People can really be more in the role of creators and managers of the energy system as opposed to solely consumers. That's the basics.

(Energy activist, USA)

There are both theoretical and practical linkages between power and participation, and the creation of counterflows is understood as an empowered and physical response to material and participatory injustices, as discussed in Chapter 3. Put another way, the relationship between control over one's environment and power is clear; groups respond to the perceived injustices with a focus on new material flows, and understand this materially participatory response as a form of challenging power. Whether or not individuals and communities can exercise *material* control over their environment, which is key to these movements' capabilities-based conception of justice, necessitates a focus on the power relationships involved in that exercise of control. Indeed, groups articulate the current lack of political and material control as necessarily connected to a power imbalance, and articulate their mission, in part, as a response—a counter-power.

This is also an inherent, and articulated, mode of addressing participatory power and injustice. The key here is the link between disempowered and being structured out of the decision-making process, or having the ability to determine what matters to you. Rectifying that injustice is linked to bringing power back into the fold. And, again linking to the discussion of justice in the previous chapter, these concerns and efforts are articulated in concert with other aspects of justice, emphasizing the relationality of these concepts.

## Sustainable Materialism and the Rise of Mega-circulatory Resistance

### Community Power

Beyond the use of materialist action as both resistance and as a counterflow to power, there is a wider understanding of such action as part of a broader, mega-circulatory resistance. Here, both resistance and empowerment are seen in the construction of new material and circulatory *systems* to meet basic everyday needs; such systems begin at the level of community, and are seen to either scale up or expand geographically.

**Table 4.2** Systems/Community–Justice Linkages in Movement Website Material

| Concept | Percentage of groups articulating concept | Percentage of groups articulating power and community |
|---|---|---|
| Power-General | 52 | 40 |
| Power-Resistance | 22 | 16 |
| Power-Systems | 27 | 20 |
| Power-Political Participation | 40 | 28 |
| ANY POWER CONCEPT | 80 | 68 |

At the community level, for example, in both food and energy groups, activists commonly note that they are attempting to 'close the loop' by 'building new structures and institutions that ensure revenues stay within the local community'. As one interviewee represented the argument, the vision is of a system where

> we start to build growers' networks, and we start to build buyers' networks and we bring the two together and we live in a community where we're very localized.                                    (Food activist, Australia)

As Table 4.2 illustrates, 68 per cent of the groups in our content analysis link one or another notion of power with a conception of community, systems, or flows. For most groups in these movements, then, there is an important relationship between calls for the creation of counterflows and the role of the community; this is a clear constant across the majority of groups we examined.

These dynamics are persistent across sustainable materialist groups focused on rebuilding food, energy, and fashion systems. This focus on community, systems and flows is one that recognizes that sustainable materialism is not an atomized form of activism. Present across each of these organizing theoretical frameworks for sustainable materialism that we discuss in this book is an awareness and embrace of the relationality embedded in the practice of these new forms of environmentalism. Alliances, community, and connection are all seen as key to achieving change.

## Beyond the Local to the Mega-circulatory

In addition, and beyond the level of one's own community, larger alliances are viewed as key in forging mega-circulatory counterflows of power that have the active capacity to perturb and reshape the existing systems that surround individual sustainable materialist projects. As illustrated here, groups do not view themselves as working in isolation, but rather embrace their networks both to respond to existing power and to construct new, alternative, flows and practices. Some see themselves as part of a more formal network, such as those of Transition Town Initiatives; others see a more diffuse but countercirculatory force, such as the broad 'food movement'. Either way, the goal is to move beyond individual circulations to build a new food system, a community energy system, or a sustainable fashion supply chain that is both a counterflow to traditional modes of power and a material realization of a new, just flow of the basic goods of everyday life.

Crucially, this broader idea of systemic relationality is found in the vast and interdependent nature of the motivations and concerns that orient sustainable materialism, as is evident from the quote below:

> So I think there's a huge opportunity right now for all of us to come together—those who have been organising for political power, those who've been building new economic models, those who've been in the fight for economic justice, for environmental justice, to recognise that it's money or life, you know. Are we all going to be okay? Do we recognise that everyone matters? The context of our work here—our work to build a global system of local living economies—is an epic struggle between money and life, for the soul and fate of humanity and our Living Earth Mother.
>
> (Food activist, Australia)

The idea that there is a collaborative potential across these material movements—a convergence possible in the construction of new and broad circulatory flows of both material and power—is a common theme in the motivations of interviewees. The goal is to, as one participant put it:

> [b]uild a connection to people's values and build a sense of power and community out of the stories and life experiences that people actually have and use that as a connection to broader social movements and broader change.                                                                    (Food activist, UK)

Another echoed this position noting:

> [t]he potential and power for the convergence of movements; of people recognising that it's really about community control over our futures versus corporate control of our futures.                             (Energy activist, UK)

Inherent in this discussion of mega-circulatory resistance and community is a critique of the politics of scale. While, of course, many sustainable materialist activists are concerned with macro-system change, they also recognize that producing system models that can be replicated across different places, spaces, and industries is the more effective way of reshaping conventional power relationship. As one participant put it:

> So often the industrial system compromises everything righteous for the sake of scale, and one of the beauties of some of the work in this movement is that we can attempt to reinvent what it means to scale, so we can achieve it with integrity.                                                     (Food activist, USA)

Similar points were made across the diverse group of activists we spoke to as part of this project, all of whom recognized the capacity of local, replicable, sustainable, materialist systems as way to achieve political and material change in their societies. We heard from numerous participants that they were wary of the orthodox economic logic inherent in notions of 'scaling up' sustainable materialist solutions beyond the local, and spoke instead of spreading and replicating.

Many, in the food movement in particular, expressed that economies of scale usually hamper or squash niche innovators unless they are willing to compromise on ethics, a point that is antithetical to the broader project of food system reform. Consider the following quotes:

> Local is used as a pejorative term by policy makers—when we use the term, we mean something else entirely. Local, for me, means nothing more to be than something that is here, that is present, that I can touch and feel, and see the changes I affect.                                             (Food activist, UK)

> The food movement ... is willing to face the huge set of challenges that all the other environmental movements wanted to kind of limit and to draw a circle ... around how much they would take on because it's too hard. A focus on rebuilding food systems gets beyond that because it says we're about a place. We're about local. We're about a community of people. So, it's our relationships and it's our ecosystem that we need to work with.
>
> (Food activist, Australia)

The key point here is that food locates power and possibility, not in the state or market but in local places and communities—and through the (re)creation of material flows. It is about the creation of circulations of power that are diffuse, democratic, and rooted in people's collective agency, emerging from the bottom up.

Much of the food movement is therefore engaged in building a politics of the present at a local, human scale—but not necessarily an ever-growing

## Box 4.2. Harvest Market Launceston

Starting with 24 stallholders and 1,500 patrons braving the elements to now hosting between 40 and 60 stallholders and with 5,000 patrons showing up every Saturday morning to buy their local produce, Harvest Market Launceston is one of the largest farmers markets in Australia, and a cornerstone of the Launceston community.

Harvest Market is more than simply a way for the local community to source local produce, it has actively reshaped the dynamics of the City and empowered producers, retailers, and eaters. When it started in 2011, Launceston was feeling the tsunami of the global financial crisis, the forestry industry was on its knees, and businesses were closing or downsizing. The innovation, inspiration, and capacity building that Harvest has helped facilitate have resulted in a range of new businesses that has contributed positively to the local economy. Harvest has also created a positive social space for the community to come and connect each week.

Harvest is a place where new relationships and new products have been formed, new producers have tried out new products and market-tested new ideas and opportunities.

Businesses involved with the market talk about how Harvest has allowed them to sell direct to their customers, removing the costly middle man, with others crediting Harvest for having reached new markets and achieved critical mass. The market continues to evolve, and is at its heart about building community and a local food economy made up of local farmers, producers and makers, and cementing this new sustainable system as a core part of the Tasmanian economy now and into the future.

geographic one. Where the local is commonly seen as a geographic constraint to be overcome or transcended, this particular politics of scale is embedded in daily, material life and practice—based on a dedication to the making of tangible, clearly expressed, and practical visions of the local. And, importantly, if one can deal with 'global' concerns at the 'local' level, and then work with alliances to replicate the model, practice, and system, then the difference between one's own focus on a local or global scale disappears. The distinction only remains through a description of a singular entity, rather than the broader countercirculatory system.

## Challenges

Such sentiments are often heard in social movement protests, and in simplistic sloganeering. But many of the actors in this realm are thoroughly immersed in counterflows, and articulate the challenges to the complexity of such mega-circulatory resistance within their specific areas clearly and succinctly:

> It's insurance; it's distribution; it's how we construct business. You know, for example, a fast food place that has an extremely simple menu that only uses a couple of components of plants and animals, for example, and so producers like us have to find markets for all the rest of the critters. The point is that the industrial food system that we have now from regulation to insurance to workplace requirements to all sorts of things are prejudicial against innovation. They're very protective of the current big players, whether it's farm subsidies or regulatory requirements or whatever, and so those of us who are trying to find a place at the market table, we're having to pass our little prototypes through this industrial systemic sieve that's very, very difficult. So the point is that we can't just focus on food as one tiny little lever, we have to focus on rebuilding the entire food system from the ground up.
>
> (Food activist, UK)

There are, of course, significant challenges to implementing the alliances and connections that underpin mega-circulatory structures in practice, as our participants note:

> Undoubtedly it is difficult. One of the major challenges is simply that, for all the rhetoric, the sector is very bad at collaboration. We need a solution for ego and for folks being so territorial before we are going to get one for the broken food system.                                    (Food activist, Australia)

More broadly, the activists we spoke to routinely cite the difficulty of achieving these aims and objectives. The key point here, though, is that this awareness does not manifest as fatalism. Instead, activists exhibit a deliberate reflexivity that enables a fuller engagement with the complexity of creating mega-circulatory flows. As our participants note:

> [Fashion is] such a complicated industry on so many levels. You know, that's why it's taking us so long for us to kind of unravel, unpack it, to try and come up with a new system that's going to work. I just think it's such a complicated issue.
>
> (Fashion activist, USA)

> And so the biggest obstacle I think is just apathy, but the second obstacle is ... the system as it's designed—and it's not just government or regulatory.
>
> (Energy activist, UK)

## Contexts and Conclusions—Power of and in Movement

A focus on mega-circulatory resistance and reconstruction is evident in the focus that sustainable materialist groups place on approaching their practice from a systemic perspective and on the value placed on alliances in achieving that end. Systems thinking, in its technical sense, describes attempts to understand a system holistically. The systems thinking approach ' ... puts the system in the context of the larger environment of which it is a part and studies the role it plays in the larger whole' (Gharajedaghi, 1999, p.15). Importantly for sustainable materialist activists, understanding a system holistically through systems thinking allows the greatest opportunity to leverage change within it (Meadows, 1999, p.3; Seddon, 2008, p.68). A systems approach is particularly relevant here, as many of the existing systems that sustainable materialist activists are seeking to replace are antifragile. The concept of fragility emerges from the interdependencies within a complex system. In his seminal work *Antifragile*, Taleb (2012) argues that while some systems can be fragile and break under stress, other systems—antifragile systems—can benefit from shocks. Antifragile systems adapt and get stronger under the 'right amount of stress', disorder, and volatility (Brafman and Beckstrom, 2007, p.6; Taleb, 2012, pp.5, 17). The modern capitalist system, and the cycles of food, energy, and fashion that flow through it, are undoubtedly antifragile, and this is one of the major challenges that sustainable materialist activists face in achieving system change.

Of course, these 'whole-of-system' (Levkoe, 2011) or joined-up approaches to rebuilding systems, such as food systems, have been discussed elsewhere. As Levkoe (2011, p.692) argues, it is impossible for food movement actors to achieve systems change, if, at the same time, they retain 'focus on isolated issues while ignoring the interconnected nature of problems'. As an example of why a whole-of-systems consciousness and strategy is necessary, he outlines why, in the Canadian context, a siloed mentality has hampered the development of a collaborative and, therefore, transformative food politics. A whole-of-systems approach, in contrast, brings together production, consumption, distribution, waste management, and policy to work across the system and supply chain for desired ends. Levkoe's call to arms has undoubtedly been taken up by many of the sustainable materialist activists we spoke to, particularly those focused on food.

These reflexive perspectives of our interviewees resonate with other empirical work on such movements. Numerous examiners have each shown that food movement actors, for example, approach social change in a reflexive way to just 'get on with it' (Levkoe, 2011; Andrée et al., 2014; McClintock, 2014). But there is confusion here over the distinction between strategies that are reflexive and the *ethos* that informs the choice of particular strategies to build these new mega-circulatory systems. Andrée, Ballamingie, and Sinclair-Waters (2015), for example, show that many food activists in Ontario pursue incremental and systemic change simultaneously, but they do not engage directly with movement actors to understand what motivates this particular choice of prefigurative strategy. McClintock (2014, p.147) sees no *theoretical* reason why we cannot come to understand the contradictions of building a new system inside or in parallel to the old 'as internal and inherent', but goes no further. What these perspectives from our participants add are detailed insights into the lived experience of what it actually means to be simultaneously against and beyond the capitalist present, while at the same time dealing with being very much in it, as they go about interrupting orthodox flows of power through the creation of mega-circulatory counterflows. As Schlosberg and Coles (2016, p.17) suggest, movements 'work creatively . . . to overcome [these] assimilative challenges' adding that the capacity to achieve 'new materialist futures will depend significantly on the capacity of grassroots organisations to interweave resistance with supple and creative power'.

On the question of community and the role of place, arguments made by our participants often challenge those in academic discussions. In some movement scholarship, for example, the precise definitions of place and scale have often been ignored (Casey, 1993, 1997), theories of globalization have sometimes resulted in a significant and ongoing discursive erasure of place (Dirlik, 2000), and anthropological thought has often wielded a scepticism of place and placemaking. Yet the fact remains that place is important in the lives of our participants, particularly if we understand by place the experience of a particular location with some measure of groundedness (however unstable), sense of boundaries (however permeable), and connection to everyday life, even if its identity is constructed, traversed by power, and never fixed.

And on the central issue of scale, what is intriguing for the purposes of our larger project is the way sustainable materialist activists conceptualize their mega-circulatory project as bound up with a critique of a particular politics of the concept. Scale, for sustainable materialist movements, is about the replication of models that achieve certain political and material objectives, and the creation of models that embed sustainable flows of material and meaning in particular places. This is a distributed scale, one of replication, where a particular vision of politics is born out of and embodied in the practices of creating a real alternative flow of power for and by multiple communities and sectors. This is not just a practical vision of a localist economic project; it is inherently a political vision about wresting control from larger structures of power. Returning to Coles (2016, p.114), this project is one that works against instrumental or technocratic understandings of power, to create mega-circulatory alternative flows that take seriously 'questions of political power, disruption and contestation' in their emergence and operation. Our point here is that we hear these sophisticated, engaged, and broadly critical political projects about power articulated by activists in a range of sustainable materialist movements.

The central argument here is that in all of our data, these sustainable materialist movements move beyond critique and seek to replace practices and circulations of power that have devastating consequences for human health and ecological sustainability, generate vast inequalities of power, and separate us from the co-creation and sharing of basic everyday needs. They attempt to unplug individuals and collectives from the flows of industrialized food, destructive fossil fuels, and sweat-shopped disposable fashion in order to interrupt one form of power and construct another. These new materialist movements illustrate a growing resistance to participating in the flows of power that reproduce practices that dominate political processes, create a range of injustices, and, as we will turn to in Chapter 6, damage the sustainability of ecological systems. In embodying new forms of power, and being part of more sustainable flows of food, energy, and other everyday needs, these movements simultaneously express forms of resistance and empowerment.

Yet, clearly the most important critique of such efforts is their vulnerability to the very structures and practices of the rapidly intensifying circulatory power they seek to replace. Two potentially interactive factors are particularly salient in this regard. First, dominant modes of circulation are increasingly assimilating alternative visions and practices in ways that draw new materialist flows and desires back into mega-circulations of power. In the food space, to use just one example, Whole Foods Market has pioneered 'corporate organic' in ways that are often greatly at odds with the democratic flows of sustainable materialism (Pollan, 2007; though not always—see Bonfiglio, 2012). Predictably, the corporate (often semi-) organic industry that contributed to this model has moved aggressively to colonize regulatory boards that set the standards regarding what is considered organic. They have displaced smaller independent firms; colonized seats that were designated for consumer representatives; placed corporate staff who are not farmers in the seats designated for organic farmers; filled other seats with representatives of corporations that are only partly organic; and advocated for genetically modified organisms, myriad synthetic substances, and practices that are considered anathema by most in the food systems and food justice movements (Strom, 2012).

Second, and simultaneously, some articulations of the movement for sustainable materialism can present themselves primarily as a new 'yes', a new system in which to immerse, that can avoid more conflict-laden aspects of change. Such articulations may tend to diminish the critical vision, energies, and will to engage in agonistic political actions that are also necessary to supplant problematic and targeted circulations and institutions. We will return to these political implications of sustainable materialism in the following chapters.

The Detroit food justice movement provides an example of contestations that are likely to emerge more frequently as the politics of sustainable materialism develops. The growing success and promise of the movement has begun to draw corporate interest and potential investment in large-scale agricultural designs for Detroit—in ways that may undermine grass-roots initiatives. In the eyes of many in Detroit's grassroots urban gardens movement, the symbol of this corporate governmentality strategy to assimilate, capitalize on, and undermine community-based initiatives is Hantz Group, founded by one of the richest men in Detroit. Community leaders of urban agricultural initiatives across the city contend that Hantz Group has non-collaboratively formulated its designs and negotiated a substantial incentives package with the mayor behind closed doors, while the city has refused to offer comparable arrangements with community groups who have been engaged in grass-roots urban agriculture for years. The result, they claim, is a potential 'land grab' that will generate wealth for a few white men, undermine the autonomy and initiatives of African Americans (82 per cent of the city's population), create gentrification on the edge of farms, and threaten the viability of the delicate social and ecological systems that are beginning to re-emerge from the bottom up. Grassroots leaders, inheriting Detroit's long histories of civil rights, black power, and union struggles, have organized strong opposition to the corporate model, favouring instead a vision of a community-based land commons (Carr, 2010). Nevertheless, Hantz Group currently appears to be gaining the upper hand, acquiring large acreage at extremely low prices (Reel, 2014), and challenges to the local, independent, largely African-American food system movement continue.

How community-based and corporate-driven materialist initiatives may develop, radically contest one another, coexist uneasily as part of a complex polyculture, or manage to form unexpected strategic alliances is still unclear. New sustainable materialist futures will depend significantly on the capacity of grassroots organizations to interweave resistance with supple and creative power in relation to a corporate–municipal complex that is likely to pose great challenges to the radical possibilities of such materialist movements. Those in sustainable materialist movements who are insufficiently attentive to power and allergic to contestation may be ill-prepared for challenges that will almost certainly emerge. The key question is whether these movements can resist these challenges and pose an authentic challenge and counter to current flows of power and goods. While opposition to sustainable materialist shifts and systems is real, it is also clear that the movements we examine are reflexive and strategic about their own challenges to power.

# 5

# Sustainability and the Politics
# of Materialist Action

The argument so far is that while we are seeing a wide range of environmental groups, communities, and innovators focusing on the realm of everyday practice, there are also similarities across the political and social motivations for such action. Localist food movements, community energy, and sustainable fashion—while all increasing attention to the environmental and social impacts of supply chains in the provision of a variety of needs of everyday life—offer an environmentalism of a very different kind, and political motivations that are unique from those we see represented in more mainstream and policy-oriented organizations.

These movements exemplify an explicit focus of an environmentalism of everyday life, a sustainable materialism; they illustrate a unique and potentially vital approach to environmental political analysis and practice (Chapter 2), broad issues of justice (Chapter 3), and both a critique of power and the development of a systems-based understanding of power in material flows (Chapter 4). In this chapter, we more thoroughly explore how these movements understand the relationship between material practices, environmental sustainability, and broader issues of human/non-human relations in entangled material systems. In other words, the focus is on what, exactly, is the meaning of the *sustainable* in sustainable materialism.

In short, we develop the argument that when people in various movements focused on actual practices of environmentalism of everyday life talk about sustainability, which they do a lot, they do not limit themselves to mainstream notions of 'sustainable development' (Brundtland, 1987), traditional ideas of 'limits' (Meadows et al., 1972), or even the more recent interest in 'planetary boundaries' (Rockström et al., 2009). What we see is a concern for sustaining the material nature and flows of everyday life—and not just human lives, but our relationships and entanglements with the non-human realm as well. We argue that these movements illustrate a particular political implementation of key ideas of a new, vitalist, and above all sustainable materialism.

Movement actors with a concern for the human/non-human relationship, or its dysfunction, have articulated a very particular way of thinking about the connection between specific human material needs, the practices we use to produce such things, and the impacts of such practices on the human and non-human systems. The 'sustainability' part of the sustainable materialism we are examining is a concern about the relationship between the everyday flows of basic needs like food, energy, and clothing and the functioning of the non-human beings and ecosystems that provide for them. Overall, we argue, the focus of these activists' conceptions of sustainability concerns three core ideas and practices: first, the crucial role of such movements and actions in rebuilding *connections* with the materiality of the natural world; second, attention to *flows*, *systems*, or *circulations* of materials through human and non-human communities; and, third, the importance of ethically informed material practices as a form of *political action*.

The upshot of this part of the examination of environmental movements of everyday life is that it illustrates not only an understanding of the link between material life and sustainability—the core of our notion of sustainable materialism—but it also helps us understand how more academic thinking about new materialism, or the vitality of the non-human realm, has actually been politicized and practised. There is, yet again, a useful comparison to be made between developments in the theoretical realm and those on the ground. On the one hand, such explorations help illustrate what a new, active, sustainable materialism looks like in practice, and how activists understand it. On the other, such practice helps to understand the limits—and mistaken assumptions—behind academic critiques of new materialist ideas and practice, in particular the notion that such materialist practice is apolitical or post-political (Washick et al., 2015; Blühdorn, 2017).

This chapter starts with an overview of new materialism in theory, including the understanding of, and relationship between, human practice and the non-human realm at its base, as well as the *political* nature of this materialist focus. We then turn to the similarities between these ideas and the meaning of the sustainable materialism embraced and embedded in the discussions with activists working in environmental movements of everyday life. Finally, we use the empirical evidence of these interviews and articulations of activists to challenge two different claims that new and sustainable materialist concerns and actions are insufficiently political.

## New Materialism: Theorizing a Vitalist Ecopolitics

The theoretical realm of new materialism—a vital and, we would argue, an ecological materialism—has been explored and developed over the last decade. Here we want to introduce a range of concepts from this literature, as well as some differences that have emerged around theory, application, and the political implications of the ideas.

While ecological feminisms have long engaged the reality of material life (for example, Salleh, 1995; Sandilands, 1997), a focus on materiality in social theorizing was revitalized with the publication of two key collections in feminist studies, Alaimo and Hekman's (2008) *Material Feminisms*, and Coole and Frost's (2010) *New Materialisms: Ontology, Agency, and Politics*. The political side was furthered by the popularity of Bennett's (2010) *Vibrant Matter: A Political Ecology of Things*. The original goal of these efforts to develop a new or vital materialism, as stated by Alaimo and Hekman (2008, p.1), was to 'bring the material, specifically the materiality of the human body and the natural world, into the forefront of feminist theory and practice'. The effort was a response, they argued, to much feminist theory (and social theory in general) being focused for so long on the realm of discourse. It was an explicit effort to shift such theory towards a re-engagement with the material world. As crucial as discursive studies had been in bringing attention to the relationship between language and discourse on the one hand, and power and institutions on the other, and as much as it critiqued unnecessary and gendered dualisms (such as nature/culture), the accusation (unfortunately forgetting the earlier ecofeminist contribution) was that the material realm was left unattended. The argument was that the one-sided focus on discourse tended to reinforce a key and problematic dualism—that between discourse and material life.

This literature has spurred two crucial contributions to academic thinking about everyday life. It has clearly reawakened a focus on the material reality of such lives, and the centrality of the flows and entanglements between the human and the non-human world. And the best of it has insisted, along with Barad (2007) and Haraway (2016), on ways of understanding the 'intra-actions' (Barad, 2007, p.141) 'between phenomena that are material, discursive, human, more-than-human, corporeal, and technological' (Alaimo and Hekman, 2008, p.5). This intra-active approach has not only revitalized both feminist thought and new materialism, but has also given rise to further theorization of human beings, their communities, and their practices as 'biocultural'. Such a focus 'requires consideration of the multi-scalar interdependencies and inter-species communities through which humans persist in their existence' (Frost, 2018, p.556). For Coole and Frost (2010, p.2) 'foregrounding material factors and reconfiguring our very understanding of matter are prerequisites for any plausible account of coexistence and its conditions in the twenty-first century'. This includes addressing core questions of 'the place of embodied humans within a material world... [and] attending to transformations in the ways we currently produce, reproduce, and consume our material environment' (Coole and Frost, 2010, p.3). New materialism, then, refocuses on the everyday, on practice, on the flows of the stuff of life—while remaining attentive to the power and meaning of such practices in an ecological, biocultural space.

While the themes and issues in this new materialist literature are quite broad, it is well represented in three clearly interrelated themes laid out by Coole and Frost (2010) in their field-defining collection. What was striking to us is that these same core themes, noted in theory, were mirrored and expanded in the conceptions of materialism and sustainability articulated by our interviewees who are based in new and sustainable environmental practices.

For Coole and Frost, the first theme of new materialism is a *vitalist* approach, which recognizes—or extends—a concept of agency that includes non-human entities; we could also frame this as deprivileging a particular notion of liberal individualism. This view is 'posthumanist in the sense that it conceives of matter itself as lively or as exhibiting agency' (Coole and Frost, 2010, p.7), and was explored and popularized, among the academic set, in Bennett's (2010) work on vital nature. Related to the vitalism and agency of the non-human, and against the more simplistic notions of a 'post' human critique, human agency is increasingly understood not as isolated and individualist, but as thoroughly networked into, and with complex and dynamic systems and assemblages across, the human/non-human divide (see also Bennett, 2010; Khan, 2012).

Second, for Coole and Frost, the reality of this immersion—or the recognition of the immersion—raises some crucial *ethical* issues of human/non-human relations. Simply put, once we value the agency of non-humans, and recognize that human beings and their needs are tied to a whole range of ecological entanglements, we open up a range of ethical questions about human engagement with, and responsibility for, these broader material assemblages and flows. These ethics range from recognition and respect (Schlosberg, 2007), to cooperation and reciprocity, to conceptions of multispecies justice (Haraway, 2016; Heise, 2016); they are also informed by particularly feminist and ecofeminist themes such as care—through a type of care tied to political action, citizenship, and 'embodied relatedness' (see MacGregor, 2006; Phillips, 2017).

The third theme focuses on the question of how we organize economic, political, and cultural processes and institutions. Coole and Frost (2010, p.7) insist that 'new materialist scholarship testifies to a critical and non-dogmatic re-engagement with political economy, where the nature of, and relationship between, the material details of everyday life and broader geopolitical and socioeconomic structures is being explored afresh'. Such explorations, of course, illustrate both material practice and the political and economic structures and institutions necessary to support them.

While we do not want to get into the realm of arguing over the meaning of the onset of the 'Anthropocene' (Dryzek and Pickering, 2019), or the impact of particularly human practices, institutions, and systems on the functioning of planetary processes (Steffen et al., 2015), it is perhaps the case, as Mansfield and Doyle (2017) note, that the spread of the idea illustrates the attraction of finally moving beyond the dualism of human versus non-human in both theory and practice. The broad acknowledgement of, and engagement with, the very notion of the Anthropocene is an acceptance of the interconnected nature of human/non-human systems. The ontological issue here is that the 'dualist, essentialist separation between humans and nature (or inhuman) is false' (Mansfield and Doyle, 2017, p.23); the key benefit is seeing 'humans and environment as always interconnected, to see the world as relational, processual, emergent, and becoming' (Mansfield and Doyle, 2017, p.23). This gives us an opportunity for 'retextualizing' the human in the larger natural world (Gibson-Graham and Roelvink, 2011, p.5). As Tsing (2015, p.29) argues, 'survival always involves others'. Any change comes 'through our collaborations both within and across species. The important stuff for life on earth happens in those transformations, not in the decision trees of self-contained individuals' (Tsing, 2015, p.29).

Importantly, Frost insists that such a realization of humans as biocultural and connected ecological beings transforms what counts for politics—and political agents (Frost, 2018, p.558). Likewise, for Haraway (2016, pp.18–19), the current period is one where we recognize that more-than-human relationships, or multispecies relationships, are teaming up to make something new; 'sympoiesis', or the idea of making-with, is both a key ontological realization and political practice. This 'making-with' is at the heart of Gibson-Graham's feminist conception of new economies—illustrating the link between agency, ethics, and political economy in new and sustainable materialism.

We humans are neither masters nor caretakers of the environment and other species; the more-than-human world is an active participant in diverse economies. Consider the diverse exchanges, labour and surplus appropriations that involve rivers, soil profiles, animals, biota, minerals and atmospheres that contribute to economic well-being. Our task now is to rope ourselves up to the contributions of the environment and other species and to recognise the transactions we make with this more-than-human world.

(Gibson-Graham and Roelvink, 2011, p.32)

Such a shift in focus brings a materialist element to the recognition of systematic changes to planetary systems; it requires an examination of the dualist ontological split between 'humans' and 'nature' on the one hand, but also a challenge of 'systems of energy, food, transport, economics, etc. that facilitate the methods of exchange between material, goods, ideas and people' (Martindale, 2015, p.2). A new materialist approach brings both this ontological recognition, as well as a focus on the specific political, economic, ecological, and material changes necessary for more sustainable material flows and systems.

As Coole and Frost (2010, p.7) note, 'humans, including theorists themselves, [must] be recognized as thoroughly immersed within materiality's productive contingencies'. The new materialist call to theorists is 'to be more attuned to the specific and multiple ways in which non-human entities and materialities participate in the formation and deformation of social and political realities' (Knox and Huse, 2015, p.8). Of course, we argue here that activists are theorizing this very relationship as well. For Latour, such re-engaged movements see 'the process of human development as neither liberation from Nature nor as fall from it, but rather as a process of becoming ever-more attached to, and intimate with' the non-human (Latour, 2011, p.17). As Whiteside (2013, p.203) argues with regard to Latour, and as the movements we discuss embody, the point is 'making vigilance over the life-sustaining capacities of our biophysical surroundings into a matter of constant concern'. This attunement and attention to immersion, connectivity, co-production, and systems flows are key tenets of both theories and practices of new and sustainable materialism.

## New Materialism and New Movements

Surprisingly, some proponents of new materialist movements and practice write little on the question of sustainability and non-human nature (for example, Simms and Potts, 2012). In contrast, others have clearly noted the connection between a conception of new materialism and the politics that would flow from it. Meyer (2015), for example, writes on the important shift to 'engaging the everyday' in environmental movements. Mansfield and Doyle (2017, p.24) note that these kinds of 'nondualist perspectives' are prevalent in numerous practices and movements, from alternative food movements and backyard chickens to new urban homesteads and perspectives on health. The spread of such movements represents, for them, a normalization of the idea that humans and nature are, indeed, interconnected and relational. For Gibson-Graham and Roelvink (2011, p.5), the ethic of 'attunement to vibrant matter' can produce an 'experimental mode of assembling'. The view is:

> a mandate for experimentation [that] opens up new possibilities for under-standing the world by undermining and exposing established food, trans-port, economic, conservation systems to new ideas and alternative formations which are characterised by a hands-on material transformation.
> (Gibson-Graham and Roelvink, 2011, p.5)

These movements embody the idea of hybrid arrangements—actively con-structed, attentively, by participants looking for a different and more sustain-able way of both material and political life.

Other evaluations of such movements are more pragmatic, but do illustrate aspects of a sustainable materialism. For example, Piso et al. (2016) examine a set of self-identified sustainable farmers who, after noting the importance of economic efficiency for the basic survival of their enterprise, reveal key sustainability values of community connectedness, ecologism (or ecological connectedness), stewardship, and social and environmental justice. A number of authors (including Seyfang and Haxeltine, 2012; Martindale, 2015) examine the innovations of the transition town movement, which we can see as one embodiment of new materialist values and practices. Such movements embody innovations, especially those that include the development of new systems for the delivery of everyday needs (in particular, food and energy). Many of these evaluations, however, note concerns about the politics of such movements that are quite similar to the 'post-political' concerns of critics of new materialism which we return to below.

One of our claims is that the sustainable materialist movements that we examine, and the activists we interview, illustrate a keen resistance to a human separation from non-human entities and processes. The focus of movement actors we interviewed is often specifically tied to environmental impacts and relationships, and much of the motivation for action is about material damage to global systems such as climate, local and regional ecosystems, as well as the individual bodies and everyday lives of human and non-human beings and systems. In response, the conscious and deliberate design and construction of new systems and flows of material needs—food, energy, clothing—are clearly illustrative of the idea of 'sympoiesis', celebrated by Haraway (2016). These movements and activists are attentive to, and theoretically reflective about, their role in their various materialist relationships with each other and the non-human realm. Our focus on such movements is about the aim to actively replace a politics of separation with one of immersion, a politics of the domination of nature with one that recognizes human beings as animals in embedded and entangled material relationships with ecosystems and the non-human realm.

Overall, we see the discourse of these movements focused on transforming the ethical and material relationships between beings in the human and non-human realms. The idea is a sustainability that critiques and replaces practices that devitalize, dominate, and destroy ecological processes and flows with those that understand human action as embedded in material relationships with ecosystems. The stated goal is the development and support of co-productive and sustainable institutions that rethink and reconstruct everyday material human practices and interactions towards an end of sustainable flows and relations across and with the rest of the natural world.

## Connections and Flows: Sustainability in Materialist Movements

So how do the movement actors we examined understand the ideas of materialism and sustainability in their work? In this broad study of a variety of materialist movement organizations, it is not unexpected that some aspect of environmental concern (including climate change, sustainability, and/or stewardship) appears in the mission statements or websites of a vast majority—118 out of 135—of the groups we examined (see Table 5.1).[1] In simple aggregate word counts, 'sustainability' comes in fifth, after nominal terms like 'food', 'energy', 'community', and 'local'—none of which are surprising given the focus on local community food and energy movements. We also hear these terms in interviews across the range of food, energy, and sustainable fashion activists and

---

[1] The numbers in Table 5.1 do not total 118 because the categories have not been coded as mutually exclusive.

**Table 5.1** Environmental Concerns in New Materialist Group Websites

|                | Sustainability | Environment | Climate change | Stewardship |
|----------------|----------------|-------------|----------------|-------------|
| Energy Groups  | 28             | 35          | 35             | 17          |
| Food Groups    | 24             | 20          | 5              | 11          |
| Fashion Groups | 27             | 20          | 15             | 5           |
| TOTAL          | 79             | 75          | 65             | 33          |
| Aus Groups     | 24             | 23          | 24             | 6           |
| UK Groups      | 23             | 32          | 22             | 11          |
| US Groups      | 32             | 21          | 19             | 14          |
| TOTAL          | 79             | 75          | 40             | 33          |

participants. The idea of sustainability is a deeply present concern for these groups and individuals, and central to their self-identity.

But this focus is not simply about a vague notion of sustainability. For the purposes of the movements we are discussing, the idea of sustainability means a focus on changing the actual material process of the meeting of everyday needs such as food, energy, and clothing. The qualifier 'sustainable' is a key and integral part of this attention, as the materialist focus of these movement organizations is on the human place within, and impact on, flows of materials out of the non-human realm, into products, through the human community, and back out to the non-human realm through waste streams. The focus is on materials and flows alike. However, this is not just about supply chains, but rather the various impacts of those chains on human and non-human relations, communities, and functioning.

Two key concepts about sustainability are repeated across our interviewees. First, we see much in the movement—and hear in the interviews—a recognition of the absolutely crucial place for a rebuilt *connection* between human and non-human (or more-than-human) worlds. Second, our interviewees understand those connections not as simple two-way relations, but as systems, flows, and processes.

## Connection, Disconnection, Reconnection

The central concern is that key to the sustainability question is a critique of a current *disconnection* with the non-human realm. So 'reconnecting people to the natural world' is a key focus, exemplified in the idea that 'with respect for the connectedness of living things, we find active ways to promote an ecologically and socially just future' (Food activist, USA). The reality that 'the

## Box 5.1. Tanka Bar

Before buffalo were nearly driven from the Great Plains forever, the Lakota people relied on this sacred animal—Tatanka—to meet their basic needs for food, shelter, clothing, and ceremony. In this way, the buffalo sustained American Indian people for thousands of years. Tanka Bar is an indigenous-led social enterprise in South Dakota that is focused on creating a family of nationally branded buffalo-based food products that are delicious and that promote a Native American way of wellness that feeds mind, body, and spirit, as well as helping to return buffalo to the Plains.

Founded in 2005 on the Pine Ridge Indian Reservation, owners Karlene Hunter and Mark Tilsen imagined a world filled with healthy foods that add to the restoration and preservation of Native American lands and ecosystem—a world without the pain of starvation or obesity. The world they imagine embraces the lifestyle that Native American people lived just over a century ago. By adding value to traditional Native food products, using modern scientific methods and the least amount of processing possible, Tanka aims to produce innovative value-added products for the US consumer marketplace.

The vision at Native American Natural Foods is not to go back to a traditional way of life but to bring the heritage of wisdom from the Native American traditional healthy lifestyle into the twenty-first century and into the lives of those who share that vision.

environment isn't just the atmosphere that surrounds us, but includes all of the people and life that we interact with on a daily basis' (Fashion activist, UK) illustrates the dedication to the idea of building connection between human and non-human lives.

Activists focus on what they sense as an alienation from natural connections and entanglements. So one states that the problem is that 'we have lost that connection with nature and this is part of the whole problem and it's part of everything that's going on' (Food activist, USA). Another notes that 'the way modern life has gone, lots of people have lost touch with nature, don't understand that they are part of nature and nature is part of them' (Energy activist, Australia).

Many link this disconnection and alienation from the non-human with our common lack of relationship with each other.

> it's a kind of innate belief in the fact that there's a real disconnect between people and their surrounding environment. And I don't just mean the sort of natural world. I mean each other as well. There's a disconnect between the things that—the sort of processes and the values that make us human and our day-to-day activities.                     (Food activist, UK)

The analysis of the disconnect is common to activists across the movement areas, and countries, we examined, and often mentions the impacts and meaning of the larger disconnected set of practices in which we are immersed. '[O]ne of the ways that we have allowed these incredible hurtful things to happen on the planet is by othering' (Food activist, Australia).

> I think we've created this thing called an economy that somehow is largely divorced from the reality of the health of our planet...and the well-being of people and other beings on the planet...[H]ow do we take this opportunity, this perhaps dire moment, but also this incredible opportunity and help organise to create something that works better for ourselves and other species.                     (Fashion activist, USA)

Our interviewees commonly linked this larger sense of social disconnection and environmental alienation to the particular material focus of their activism or group focus. So, for example, a food justice activist states that 'we have a perilous separation right now in not knowing where our food comes from before it ends up on our table, or how people are treated through that food, or where does waste go at the end of the meal' (Food activist, Australia). And one of our sustainable fashion interviewees notes that '[there is] this disconnection that we've got to our clothing with fast fashion, no idea where it comes from, who makes it, how it's made, what chemicals are in it, or any of those conversations' (Fashion activist, Australia).

The obvious response to this analysis of the blindness to connection with the non-human realm is a focus on reconnection. So a food activist offers a representative justification for their action: '[W]e actually wanted to reconnect investors and entrepreneurs and eaters and farmers and businesses with their communities and ecosystems that they serve and rebuild a relationship economy' (Food activist, USA). Another notes that the goal is to interconnect, to add 'things all up—connection to self, to others, the natural world and the experience of generosity between us—that is interdependence. That is interconnection' (Food activist, Australia). And another: 'We have a big vision to create within a generation a global network of interconnected local economies that work in harmony with nature to support a healthy, prosperous and joyful life for all people' (Food activist, USA). Again, the analysis of reconnection is quite thorough and involved.

> I like the word connection. I guess I think of community generally as your connection to others—other people, other living forms... Understanding your connection to the natural systems. Understanding your connection to the financial system. Understanding your connection between the choices that you make to the world that you're part of.          (Food activist, USA)

Another states that:

> [W]e live in a time where there's a kind of a segregated mentality, you know, that I can do my thing and it doesn't affect anything else. And we're realising that that's not really very accurate, that all that we do affects something. And so trying to connect those dots is a big deal.          (Fashion activist, USA)

Such connection is often conveyed in language familiar to new materialist language, and it illustrates attention both to the idea of the materiality and vitality of things in everyday life, and to the centrality of the sense of reconnection with the non-human. On the one hand, some of the ideas are quite straightforward, in particular on food and its impact on human health and well-being; it was common for people to note that 'food makes us, doesn't it? It makes our bodies' (Food activist, UK). This attention to the flow of materiality is quite apparent in the sustainable fashion realm as well. In addition to discussions of the state of both landscapes and farmworkers on intensively farmed cotton fields—and the workers in sewing factories—we heard much about the impact of the flow of chemicals in everyday products.

> [Y]ou're talking about the single largest organ in your body, and we absorb as well as excrete through our skin, and we cover it in chemical-laden textiles from the minute we're born to the minute we die and it plays an important role in the most intimate moments of our life.   (Fashion activist, Australia)

These comments illustrate concerns very similar to those in the environmental justice movement, and feminist analysts of the movement, where a focus on the circulation and infusion of toxins into the bodies of women, children, and people of colour has long been a concern (Sze, 2006; Di Chiro, 2008; Gabrielson and Parady, 2010).

This material attention extends over time in sustainable fashion as well, in particular in response to the waste and disposability of fast fashion. One interviewee illustrates a link between the vital nature of things and systems flows with a comparative material history:

> You know, I know who made this. I know what it was before it was a bag. I know it had a hard life. I know the name of the farmer whose farm it was on. I know the designer and I know the place she had it made into a bag. I know where some of these stains and holes have come from because they're mine and I personally have mended it and patched it. There is such a different connection to this bag than some cheap piece of crap I bought and it gets a hole and I throw it away. And that's part of the value ... It's that reconnection back to the real value of the materials, and that's an entirely different thing than buying a £5 top for one night out in a club because it looked cute on a whim and it didn't cost any more than your cappuccino.    (Fashion activist, UK)

In the food movement, this material attention works in multiple ways—the attention to the material relations; many farmers and urban growers focus on what they can learn from such attention to the material relations and entanglements:

> So, you know, from a most practical level on our farm ... we looked at nature as a template and said, How does nature build soil? How does nature hydrate landscapes? How does nature sequester carbon? How does nature do these things?    (Food activist, USA)

This is the essence of practice that comes from one of the most famous of these new attentive farmers, Joel Salatin, and his Polyface Farm (Salatin, 2011). It illustrates that a core aspect of a sustainable materialism is attention to both vitality and relationality—the connected nature of agents in a material system. As another sustainable fashion activist relates:

> We all know deep down that the world exists as a web of life, but consumer society has taught us to think in atomistic ways. This dress has travelled the world, and has touched, and been touched by, many lives along the way, whether directly—the hands of our workers—or indirectly through the positive chemical-free impact it has on wetlands and the life that they contain. A web of life, it's that simple.    (Fashion activist, USA)

## Box 5.2. Sustain UK

Sustain is the UK's alliance for a healthy, fair, and sustainable system for food, farming, and fishing. Established in 1999, the alliance works with around 100 organizations at the national level and hundreds more at the local level, and helps to run a network of over fifty towns and cities, taking collective and coordinated action to tackle food poverty, reduce unhealthy food provision and marketing, and to increase the supply of healthy and sustainably produced food. Sustain takes a holistic approach to change—working on system-wide issues such as agricultural policy and fiscal measures, as well as technical and thematic issues such as climate change, sustainably caught fish, and junk food advertising regulation.

Sustain was instrumental in establishing the London Food Strategy and has for over a decade, and working with three successive London Mayors, assisted in running implementation activities. This has included support for local authorities to improve their food procurement, make land available for community food growing, and to take a joined-up approach to tackle the root causes of food poverty.

Sustain recognizes that food is fundamental to healthy lives and well-being and our relationship to the natural systems that sustain us. Having spent twenty years establishing the rationale, evidence, standards, and mechanisms for systems change, the Sustain alliance is becoming ever more determined to stimulate that change to happen. In 2018, Sustain launched the Right to Food project, seeking legislation that would allocate responsibilities across government, local authorities and agencies for cultivating the step-by-step journey towards a healthy, fair, and sustainable food system in which everyone can live, work, and eat well.

## Flows, Systems, Stages, Circulations

That brings us to the other crucial aspect of the sustainable materialism that is thoroughly reflected by our interviewees—the frequent use of systems language. We hear not only about food, but also food systems—not just energy, but energy systems. The focus is the flow from start to finish. One interviewee in sustainable fashion discussed the breadth of the scale of the fashion industry—and how much more complex materialist attention and management is in the industry:

> Farm to closet, farm to hanger, whatever. You know, it's different [with clothing], and in food it's a relatively straight line from farmer to supermarket or whatever. There may be a couple of people in between, but generally speaking, it doesn't circumvent the globe a bunch of times. Clothing does. You might be getting your fibre in one place and it might not even be spun or ginned or cleaned in that place. It might go somewhere else for that. Somewhere else for spinning or knitting, somewhere else for cutting and sewing, somewhere else for making. And then it might be consolidated in a single, global location before it's shipped all over the world. It can have circumvented the globe half a dozen times by the time it gets to a human being who is going to actually use it, wear it.        (Fashion activist, USA)

The breadth of knowledge of the flow of materials, and the issues at hand at each part of this process—from farm to table, field to hanger, sun or wind to appliance—is central to activists in these movements. This is not simply language or marketing stories, but an understanding about the meaning of a broad materialist endeavour, and what it takes to make such flows more attentive to sustainability and non-human relations. These broad articulations were quite common:

> [T]he whole ... piece is really about environment. I mean, there's people and place ... These things are completely intertwined and so what we're trying to cultivate is that system view of the world. The interconnection between all of these things. And once you see and honour that interconnection, hypothetically it's like you're smart enough to not damage any one of these stakeholders in your ecosystem ... [2]        (Food activist, UK)

---

[2] We love that this person went on to conclude with 'So I'm sorry, this is probably not what you wanted to talk about'.

For some, the premise is quite clear—and the focus is on the destructiveness of the current flow of materials: '[O]ur current industrial agricultural food system does such—our food comes to us by way of great violence to the planet, to the ecosystem, to the people who produce it, and then it does such violence to our bodies, right?'(Food activist, Australia). Likewise, there was much attention to the damage at various locales in the material flow or supply chain in standard fashion—again, recognition of the danger of the vital nature of some parts of the process, as environmental justice activists have identified:

> [Y]ou do a little bit of research and you find out the horrors of pesticides, not only on the environment, but also the farmers and also the workers who handle conventional cotton goods at every stage, you know, like not just the Cambodian factory workers fainting, but also I think it was even German women in an H&M packing and shipping department that were handling the clothes at almost their finished stages being affected by the chemicals in the clothing.                                    (Fashion activist, USA)

More positively, the response is also about circulations, but the building of more sustainable flows through systems, and the benefits that brings:

> Where are we looking at the system—and not just the system of human activity on top of a landscape that feeds us, but the living system that we're a part of…? And if we can take that step up and have the humility to see ourselves as participants in something that's larger, I think that's when we start to actually get to the place where we can be facilitators of moving this money thing that we made up into something that circulates and where we actually are all part of much healthier places.        (Food activist, USA)

Likewise, this shift to a more positive sustainable materialism is key to participants in sustainable fashion:

> [I]t's important to let people know or at least to have the possibility for people to know where this garment is coming from and how they made it and that's why I think the values of transparency, the values of traceability, the values of saving water are becoming more and more important. And we need to learn how to talk to the consumer about this because when sustainability issues come to the consumer, it's always a negative thing, like the world is ending, you're going to be poisoned. It's not something like enjoy this, because that is the best way for you to have a beautiful thing.
>                                    (Fashion activist, Australia)

Sustainable materialism in practice, in the reflections of the activists at the centre of new economic practices and an environmentalism of everyday life, is about understanding disconnection with the non-human—and reconnecting. It is about understanding the damage that comes from either ignorance or wilful neglect of material flows and systems, and the construction of more sustainable supply and material flows from origin to use.

Again, in addition to the recognition of agency or vitality in the non-human, and the ethics, politics, and economy that flow from that, we see two core ways of thinking about the reconstruction of sustainable materialist practice. First is the necessity of a rebuilt *connection* between human and non-human worlds; and second is understanding those connections not as simple two-way relations, but as systems, flows, and processes. In other words, what we are hearing from activists is a very political understanding of new materialism—a sustainable materialism, a practice of an environmentalism of everyday life. That practice challenges traditional environmentalism, some aspects of new materialist theory, and the mislaid criticisms of that theory that insist it is only post- or apolitical.

## Sustainable Materialism as Politics

We now turn to a central question of the academic critics of the approach of these materialist or vitalist movements—on the nature of their 'politics'. Both the practices of these kinds of movements, and their normative basis in a form of new materialism, are often attacked as post- or apolitical (Swyngedouw, 2009, 2010; Washick et al., 2015; Blühdorn, 2017). On the one hand, critics dismiss such action as individualist lifestyle acts or modes of psychologically coping with a post-liberal order; on the other, they are accused of an ontology that may not create a politics that matters.

Whereas it might be argued that some of the more theoretical proponents of the ideas of new materialism do not focus on its political implications, and other environmental practice movements have failed in their 'political' goals, our argument here is that this is not the case in either the discourse or practice of individuals and groups who think with, and attempt to practice, this new materialism. Here, we see movements actively working to understand and embrace the vitality and flow of material nature as they attempt to redesign systems that provide for basic human needs such as food, energy, and sustainable fashion. The critiques of a new and sustainable materialism simply misunderstand the motivations, goals, structures, and meaning of sustainable materialist action in the movements we explore.

## On the Post-Political

The post-political approach (Blühdorn, 2017) critically frames these movements and challenges their oppositional potential and impact. The idea of the post-political reflects a sense of a real loss of politics in practice. A historically engaging practice of 'the political'—that place of contestation, of argument, of agonism and antagonists—has been, from this perspective, increasingly replaced by a professionalized politics. Politics is now a realm of technocratic managerialism, both alienating and disempowering to citizens who are relegated to spectators and consumers, and condoning and enabling of the power of neo-liberalist discourse and practice. Many so-called political movements, ranging from individualist consumer boycotts up to global policy on carbon trading, are simply simulations of real politics—co-opted and complicit in this neo-liberal reality. They are performance or simulation, not an authentic expression of 'the political'.

Clearly, the world that post-political theorists describe is real, and many forms of social action deserve the critique. This approach, however, has often become a simple universalist blanket used to dismiss more nuanced movements—and the research surrounding them. Oddly, based in part on Rancière's (2004) notion of making visible, the post-political critique is often blind to movements attentive to such a sight-based politics and practice. As Larner has argued, the problem with the post-political approach is that it tends to see all action as complicit in governmentality, self-management, and self-discipline, and all movements as 'either co-opted or futile' (Larner, 2014, p.193). Put another way, much of this scholarship tends to construct the menu of options for movement actors as a choice between being 'for the system' or 'against the system', reinforcing the view that the poles of the dichotomy exhaust the possibilities. This creates a discursive vacuum in which it becomes difficult, if not impossible, to theorize the in-betweenness, contradiction and hybridity at the heart of this politics.

Swyngedouw's (2009, p.613) overview of post-political environmentalism serves as an example—he claims that all environmental groups see environmental problems as a side effect rather than an inherent aspect of neo-liberal capitalism; only address a singular universalist nature or people rather than the reality of particularities; only see a total global threat and an unnamed and disembodied enemy rather than core causal practices. These groups, he argues, all also agree that all such issues can be addressed through a depoliticized, diological, and non-confrontational politics. Granted, this analysis comes out of the focus on Copenhagen in 2009, and it clearly does apply to some of those groups officially engaging in the United Nations Framework Convention on Climate Change (UNFCCC) Conference of the Parties (COP) process. But opposition was also clearly in the streets and in the discourse (Kenis and Mathijs, 2014)—and the lack of any viable action coming out of the COP process rocked the movement and motivated even more radical actions and approaches. More importantly, as much as the analysis may accurately describe *some* environmental groups, it simply misses a good range of more authentically oppositional environmental activism. Swyngedouw universalizes his critique, and it is used by others as universal, without attention to the real plurality and diversity of environmentalisms and practices.

Blühdorn's critique of environmentalism—and environmental theorizing—is similarly limited, and limiting, in its universalizing tendency. He argues that 'in the wake of the post-ecologist turn' the 'profound unease with the alienation of scientific-technological-industrial modernity, and [a] belief in a better alternative, have largely evaporated' (Blühdorn, 2014, p.159). He insists that the localist, small-scale, ecologist ideals of the past 'retain little of their earlier appeal', and argues that the current politics of unsustainability is about management of, or resilience and adaptation to, increasing social injustice (Blühdorn, 2014). Worse, and more specifically in relation to the kinds of movements discussed here, Blühdorn insists that the kinds of practice we cover 'cannot plausibly be read as signalling a new eco-political departure' and or, instead, another example of sustaining the 'politics of unsustainability' (Blühdorn, 2017, p.43). Both the discourses and the practices, he claims, are better interpreted as 'the politics and governance of unsustainability' and as 'discourses of simulation'. They 'help to organise—quite contrary to their own self-perception and declared intentions—modern societies' journey towards ever more social inequality and ecological destruction' (Blühdorn, 2017, p.43).

In addition, Blühdorn sees these movements as individualizing, while working against 'fostering social solidarity, empowering the underprivileged and moving towards social equality' (2014, p.160). These new materialist movements, he insists, are simply *coping with* rather than *countering* unsustainable practices in their small and local niches. New materialism in practice, goes the argument, is a retreat from real politics.

We do not disagree with Blühdorn that parts of the environmental movement have lost their radical edge and become blunted by being mainstreamed. That is a long-standing critique of the major environmental groups, in particular in the US (see Dowie, 1995)—and this analysis was part of the justification for the unique nature of the environmental justice movement in its origins (Schlosberg, 1999b). This type of critique is certainly valid in the case of the mainstream discourse of sustainability, such as a watered-down notion of the Brundtland report for example, which clearly fits the conceptualization of a 'discourse of simulation' that has emboldened a technomanagerialist perspective and agenda. While these critiques are valid in some areas, new and sustainable materialist movements are not those movements; they often enthusiastically and authentically embody transformation and critique, at least in their discourse, and not the maintenance of the unsustainability that Blühdorn critiques.

That said, we also do not disagree that some of Blühdorn's critiques apply to some practices and aspects of contemporary environmental organizing, and even to some materialist groups. Blühdorn is right that there is an environmental consumerism that leads to material accumulation and lifestyle identities. We have addressed this trend in Chapter 2. Some of the new materialist practices do indeed favour the already privileged middle class—local food for those who can afford it, and especially sustainable fashion for the fashionista class. But our interviews reveal that these are constant stresses and concerns that activists and movements are mindful of, and address, in everyday practice. Importantly, many food justice movements are all about extending the meaning of healthy food to those currently denied it, and many efforts on community energy are targeted towards those who cannot put solar panels on their rented or inaccessible rooftops. And while sustainable fashion remains mainly unaffordable, actors in the movement are directly impacting various injustices across the full material cycle of clothing production—the conditions of workers and environments in growing, production, distribution, and waste. These are important, and impactful, political acts.

The problem is that Blühdorn refuses to engage with the reality that environmentalism has always been plural (Schlosberg, 1999b, p.3), and remains so in these materialist endeavours. Instead, and eschewing the diverse reality on the ground, he paints all materialist movements and actions with a single brush, and builds a unitary straw man—a singular ideology and practice out of a broad and complex set of theories, campaign themes, and actions. Blühdorn implies that these individual groups must take on every problem of modernity simultaneously, or they are complicit in every ailment we diagnose. So these movements, he says, fail 'to reverse the continuous rise of political inequality, growing concerns about the unsuitability of democratic processes for conditions of high differentiation and complexity, [and] the neoliberal instrumentalization of democracy and civil society' (Blühdorn, 2017, p.53). The obvious response here is that different movement groups address different of both human and ecological communities. Their articulated motivations a about actively working to separate people from the power flows of industrial ized food, destructive fossil fuels, and sweat-shopped disposable fashion—and just as actively work to create new and sustainable material practices attentive to human/non-human assemblages and agency.

Clearly, this is not simply a traditional politics, but one of transform-ational practice. As Haraway (2016, p.49) has suggested, the 'human social apparatus of the Anthropocene tends to be top-heavy and bureaucracy prone. Revolt needs other forms of action and other stories for solace, inspiration, and effectiveness.' Our interviewees oblige with a discourse and motivation to construct such innovative and power-challenging actions and systems. Most explicitly define these material acts as political acts; the very materialism is a new statement of environmental practice, a determined political strategy, in direct defiance of existing forms of political practice and power. These movements are about materialist, embodied, everyday prac-tices that are defined as political by the participants. Attentiveness to mater-ial practice, and the development, not just of ontologies but of alternative flows of materials through communities through new practice, is claimed as a political statement.

As such, these movements also illustrate a critical engagement with recon-structing political economy as part of this political action—they are economic as well as political. Coole and Frost (2010) insist that new materialism re-engages with geopolitical and socio-economic structures. Such critiques, explorations, and engagements, of course, if they are indeed the norm in practice, negate the critique of new and sustainable materialism as post-political. The discourses of these movements imagine and articulate the goal of new forms of economic, feminist, social, and environmental experimenta-tion—'utopian political–economic experiments' such as those celebrated by Gibson-Graham and Roelvink (2011), or Coles' 'visionary pragmatism' (2016). In her critique of the post-political dismissals of such movement-led experiments, Larner laments that 'we should draw attention to such alternative forms of living, working and expressing, and pause before dismissing them as always and inevitably coopted' (2014: 202).

In other words, the critiques of the *political* implications of new materialism often miss the broad political and economic implications of new and sustain-able materialist movements. These movements concerned with the flows of everyday life represent an important form of materialist politics. The desire for sustainability has spawned an interest in changing the very material relation-ship with the non-human realm in the satisfaction of everyday needs. This is

practices and problems—and the activists developing practices of sustainable materialism often report that they also act in other social movement groups that address a range of issues. Doing one thing prefiguratively does not preclude doing other political work—they are not mutually exclusive.

Blühdorn also argues that 'the prospects of these narratives and the related social practices developing any transformative potential are…even less favourable today than at earlier points in time' (2017, p.54). These stories of transformation, he argues 'are, sociologically speaking, rather implausible' (2017, p.57), and actually serve powerful interest groups. Unfortunately, Blühdorn offers no empirical evidence on which to base any of these claims; his critique seems to ignore the very attentiveness and diversity of the many transformative movements and activists that are responding directly and acutely to the traps he identifies. Without simply offering a rosy and celebra-tory picture of such activism, our point is that the heterogeneity of these movements, and their political approaches, motivations, and strategies, is illuminated by actual empirical work. The main point here is that it is not helpful to simply paint all such movements with a singular and universalizing brush. In the words of Andrée, Ballamingie, and Sinclair-Waters (2015, p.1468), we have allowed the critical heart of political analysis 'to create closures … concealing more progressive and potentially transformative ration-alities'. Edmund Harris (2009, p.55–6) makes a similar point about the performative nature of theorizing prefigurative politics when he notes 'it is important for scholars to consider how the choice of theoretical framing can limit the ability to recognise new political openings'.

Here we advocate, instead, that actual empirical work can help explore and expose the complexity of the discourses of these movements on new materi-alism, as well as their weaknesses and their potential for an authentic trans-formational politics. Aiken (2017) has made this argument for nuance against the simplistic post-political approach, and our own work reiterates the neces-sity of linking theorizing with such real-world examinations. Empirical study of the motivations and articulations of these movements illustrates the com-plexity, and informs a more nuanced analysis of their potential.

## On the Apolitical versus the Political

Approaching potential criticism of sustainable materialist movements from another direction, critics of both feminist new materialist and material vitalist theories offer another basis for the critique of the framing of these movements.

In particular, critics argue that new materialism focuses primarily on an *ontology* of the vitality of nature, and/either ignores more pressing political issues and/or encourages practices that are apolitical. Washick and Wingrove, for example, offer one of the more articulate critiques; they are critical of the idea that 'ethical insights fostered by the ontology of new materialism enable better, more compassionate politics and action' and that more 'knowing human [figures] will surface the stuff that can compel a new ethical orientation' (Washick et al., 2015, p.72). The critique is, in part, about the directionality of the relationship; they argue that the idea that adoption of this materialist ontology will then improve practice and ethics is 'fantasy'. 'That the new materialisms' ontology entails relationality is clear, but why relationality dictates a particular ethical position is not' (Washick et al., 2015, p.73). If the ethic is not there, they continue, neither is a productive politics. 'We can readily appreciate how new materialist figurations of the world might provide insight, delight, solace and joy, but our question remains: Do they offer imaginative, affective or strategic resources for political action?' (Washick et al. 2015, p.76). Washick et al. argue that there is very little in the approach that addresses 'systematically reproduced constraints', meaning that 'the scholarly imaginary sparked by new materialist ontologies runs the risk of producing a politics that does not really matter' (Washick et al., 2015, p.77).

Bennett (2010), who is the focus of this particular critique, has indeed offered an ontology about the vitality of the non-human—one that encourages us to enhance our own receptivity, based on the assumption that such a shift in ontology will lead to different everyday ethics and practice. But this is not the only possible understanding or approach to the political nature of new materialism. John Meyer, in contrast, argues that a politics that engages the everyday is one that 'begin[s] by engaging materiality as it is already manifest in practice' (Meyer, 2015, p.67). Meyer, in other words, illustrates that the directionality can go either way, and that a commitment to material change can then influence ontology (or not). Practice and ontology can clearly be co-produced (Barad, 2007). Mol (1999) argues that how we frame a problem not only identifies the problem in a particular way, but in doing so calls into being particular realities and their associated things, projects, problematics, and spatialities. Our practice and associated vocabulary shapes where the options for addressing the problem reside and what might be at stake in resolving the issue in that particular way.

Our empirical study of actual activists engaged in materialist movements shows that this directionality is less of an issue than the actual efficacy of the politics. We find actors articulating a new materialist ontology; they are also

quite dedicated to simultaneously practising ethical and impactful 'Seeing these issues as systems really does change the entire way you a your life, achieving political change, everything' (Fashion activist, UK) practice and ontology are mutually constitutive and interactive.

> So the project has allowed me to be able to talk about so many thing I find fascinating, and big, complex, global questions, but through a p solution. And that to me is what's really huge. I'm not really interest policy think tanks. I want action.                    (Food activist,

The point is that movements are already engaging with both ma practice and ontology simultaneously. The focus is on practices that the material flows of food, matter, energy from the natural world, thro production processes, into and through our bodies, and back into th human realm. Activists are building new institutions and systems in w. direct these material flows of everyday life in vitalizing, resilient, and s able ways, with specific attention to the relationship between the prov human needs and the environment in which those needs are met.

These new materialist movements illustrate exactly the kind of 'imag affective or strategic resources for political action' that respond to 'sy; ically reproduced constraints' (Washick et al., 2015, p.76–7); indeed, t self-consciously constructing a politics that 'matters'. Practices, move and institutions are being built in ways that explicitly direct the materia of everyday life in vitalizing, resilient, and sustainable ways. These sust materialist movements are actively trying to replace a politics of dist from the non-human with one of immersion, a politics of the domina nature with one that recognizes human beings as animals in emb material relationships with ecosystems and the non-human realm. 'Suc your animals are not now just bacon and eggs and T-bones. They're a co-labourers and fellow ministers in this great land-healing project', not of our interviewees (Food activist, USA).

There may very well be a fatigue with activism without output, w oppositionalism as a way of life *without* some sort of doing, living, p that *does* something, is *for* something and not just against. But this is not s about creating a simulated self that allows individuals to bridge an in dissonance between ideal and practice (Blühdorn, 2017). This is about n and building alternative practices, systems, flows—and transformations.

This is the core understanding of an environmentalism of everyda Activists insist that sustainable materialist movements act to replace pra and circulations that have had devastating consequences for the sustaina practices and problems—and the activists developing practices of sustainable materialism often report that they also act in other social movement groups that address a range of issues. Doing one thing prefiguratively does not preclude doing other political work—they are not mutually exclusive.

Blühdorn also argues that 'the prospects of these narratives and the related social practices developing any transformative potential are...even less favourable today than at earlier points in time' (2017, p.54). These stories of transformation, he argues 'are, sociologically speaking, rather implausible' (2017, p.57), and actually serve powerful interest groups. Unfortunately, Blühdorn offers no empirical evidence on which to base any of these claims; his critique seems to ignore the very attentiveness and diversity of the many transformative movements and activists that are responding directly and acutely to the traps he identifies. Without simply offering a rosy and celebratory picture of such activism, our point is that the heterogeneity of these movements, and their political approaches, motivations, and strategies, is illuminated by actual empirical work. The main point here is that it is not helpful to simply paint all such movements with a singular and universalizing brush. In the words of Andrée, Ballamingie, and Sinclair-Waters (2015, p.1468), we have allowed the critical heart of political analysis 'to create closures...concealing more progressive and potentially transformative rationalities'. Edmund Harris (2009, p.55–6) makes a similar point about the performative nature of theorizing prefigurative politics when he notes 'it is important for scholars to consider how the choice of theoretical framing can limit the ability to recognise new political openings'.

Here we advocate, instead, that actual empirical work can help explore and expose the complexity of the discourses of these movements on new materialism, as well as their weaknesses and their potential for an authentic transformational politics. Aiken (2017) has made this argument for nuance against the simplistic post-political approach, and our own work reiterates the necessity of linking theorizing with such real-world examinations. Empirical study of the motivations and articulations of these movements illustrates the complexity, and informs a more nuanced analysis of their potential.

## On the Apolitical versus the Political

Approaching potential criticism of sustainable materialist movements from another direction, critics of both feminist new materialist and material vitalist theories offer another basis for the critique of the framing of these movements.

In particular, critics argue that new materialism focuses primarily on an *ontology* of the vitality of nature, and/either ignores more pressing political issues and/or encourages practices that are apolitical. Washick and Wingrove, for example, offer one of the more articulate critiques; they are critical of the idea that 'ethical insights fostered by the ontology of new materialism enable better, more compassionate politics and action' and that more 'knowing human [figures] will surface the stuff that can compel a new ethical orientation' (Washick et al., 2015, p.72). The critique is, in part, about the directionality of the relationship; they argue that the idea that adoption of this materialist ontology will then improve practice and ethics is 'fantasy'. 'That the new materialisms' ontology entails relationality is clear, but why relationality dictates a particular ethical position is not' (Washick et al., 2015, p.73). If the ethic is not there, they continue, neither is a productive politics. 'We can readily appreciate how new materialist figurations of the world might provide insight, delight, solace and joy, but our question remains: Do they offer imaginative, affective or strategic resources for political action?' (Washick et al. 2015, p.76). Washick et al. argue that there is very little in the approach that addresses 'systematically reproduced constraints', meaning that 'the scholarly imaginary sparked by new materialist ontologies runs the risk of producing a politics that does not really matter' (Washick et al., 2015, p.77).

Bennett (2010), who is the focus of this particular critique, has indeed offered an ontology about the vitality of the non-human—one that encourages us to enhance our own receptivity, based on the assumption that such a shift in ontology will lead to different everyday ethics and practice. But this is not the only possible understanding or approach to the political nature of new materialism. John Meyer, in contrast, argues that a politics that engages the everyday is one that 'begin[s] by engaging materiality as it is already manifest in practice' (Meyer, 2015, p.67). Meyer, in other words, illustrates that the directionality can go either way, and that a commitment to material change can then influence ontology (or not). Practice and ontology can clearly be co-produced (Barad, 2007). Mol (1999) argues that how we frame a problem not only identifies the problem in a particular way, but in doing so calls into being particular realities and their associated things, projects, problematics, and spatialities. Our practice and associated vocabulary shapes where the options for addressing the problem reside and what might be at stake in resolving the issue in that particular way.

Our empirical study of actual activists engaged in materialist movements shows that this directionality is less of an issue than the actual efficacy of the politics. We find actors articulating a new materialist ontology; they are also quite dedicated to simultaneously practising ethical and impactful politics. 'Seeing these issues as systems really does change the entire way you approach your life, achieving political change, everything' (Fashion activist, UK). Again, practice and ontology are mutually constitutive and interactive.

> So the project has allowed me to be able to talk about so many things that I find fascinating, and big, complex, global questions, but through a path of solution. And that to me is what's really huge. I'm not really interested in policy think tanks. I want action. (Food activist, USA)

The point is that movements are already engaging with both materialist practice and ontology simultaneously. The focus is on practices that dictate the material flows of food, matter, energy from the natural world, through our production processes, into and through our bodies, and back into the non-human realm. Activists are building new institutions and systems in ways that direct these material flows of everyday life in vitalizing, resilient, and sustainable ways, with specific attention to the relationship between the provision of human needs and the environment in which those needs are met.

These new materialist movements illustrate exactly the kind of 'imaginative, affective or strategic resources for political action' that respond to 'systematically reproduced constraints' (Washick et al., 2015, p.76–7); indeed, they are self-consciously constructing a politics that 'matters'. Practices, movements, and institutions are being built in ways that explicitly direct the material flows of everyday life in vitalizing, resilient, and sustainable ways. These sustainable materialist movements are actively trying to replace a politics of distinction from the non-human with one of immersion, a politics of the domination of nature with one that recognizes human beings as animals in embedded material relationships with ecosystems and the non-human realm. 'Suddenly, your animals are not now just bacon and eggs and T-bones. They're actually co-labourers and fellow ministers in this great land-healing project', noted one of our interviewees (Food activist, USA).

There may very well be a fatigue with activism without output, with an oppositionalism as a way of life *without* some sort of doing, living, practice that *does* something, is *for* something and not just against. But this is not simply about creating a simulated self that allows individuals to bridge an internal dissonance between ideal and practice (Blühdorn, 2017). This is about making and building alternative practices, systems, flows—and transformations.

This is the core understanding of an environmentalism of everyday life. Activists insist that sustainable materialist movements act to replace practices and circulations that have had devastating consequences for the sustainability of both human and ecological communities. Their articulated motivations are about actively working to separate people from the power flows of industrialized food, destructive fossil fuels, and sweat-shopped disposable fashion—and just as actively work to create new and sustainable material practices attentive to human/non-human assemblages and agency.

Clearly, this is not simply a traditional politics, but one of transformational practice. As Haraway (2016, p.49) has suggested, the 'human social apparatus of the Anthropocene tends to be top-heavy and bureaucracy prone. Revolt needs other forms of action and other stories for solace, inspiration, and effectiveness.' Our interviewees oblige with a discourse and motivation to construct such innovative and power-challenging actions and systems. Most explicitly define these material acts as political acts; the very materialism is a new statement of environmental practice, a determined political strategy, in direct defiance of existing forms of political practice and power. These movements are about materialist, embodied, everyday practices that are defined as political by the participants. Attentiveness to material practice, and the development, not just of ontologies but of alternative flows of materials through communities through new practice, is claimed as a political statement.

As such, these movements also illustrate a critical engagement with reconstructing political economy as part of this political action—they are economic as well as political. Coole and Frost (2010) insist that new materialism re-engages with geopolitical and socio-economic structures. Such critiques, explorations, and engagements, of course, if they are indeed the norm in practice, negate the critique of new and sustainable materialism as post-political. The discourses of these movements imagine and articulate the goal of new forms of economic, feminist, social, and environmental experimentation—'utopian political–economic experiments' such as those celebrated by Gibson-Graham and Roelvink (2011), or Coles' 'visionary pragmatism' (2016). In her critique of the post-political dismissals of such movement-led experiments, Larner laments that 'we should draw attention to such alternative forms of living, working and expressing, and pause before dismissing them as always and inevitably coopted' (2014: 202).

In other words, the critiques of the *political* implications of new materialism often miss the broad political and economic implications of new and sustainable materialist movements. These movements concerned with the flows of everyday life represent an important form of materialist politics. The desire for sustainability has spawned an interest in changing the very material relationship with the non-human realm in the satisfaction of everyday needs. This is about the reconstruction of relationships in more sustainable practices of growing, distributing, eating, and recycling the material that we eat, enjoy, absorb, and pass through human practices.

Another key here is that the practice of sustainable materialism is a practice, in concert with others, in actively designed and lived relations and assemblages. As another of our interviewees puts it, 'we need to explore change as a collective practice...if we could harness our collective resources, we could really make something of it' (Energy activist, Australia). Mol argues that we should not settle simply for a new materialism, but instead develop a 'relational materialism', where the focus is more political than philosophical. Here, she argues, is where we can be sensitive to issues of ontology, materiality, and issues of good and bad at the same time (Mol, 2013, p.381). Likewise, Abrahamsson et al. (2015) note that the new materialism is not simply about actants impacting in a single direction: 'if matters act, they never act alone. *Relational* materialism is in order' (p.15). This kind of relational materialism is key to staying alive, argues Tsing. Every species 'requires liveable collaborations. Collaboration means working across difference... Without collaborations, we all die' (Tsing, 2015, p.28). Again, this is an active politics—'assemblages don't just gather lifeways; they make them' (Tsing, 2015, p.23). And it is not only the material realm that is an assemblage; it is the realm of motivations of these actors: power, justice, sustainability, community—an assemblage of reason and action, of political ontology and practice together.

In embodying new forms of practice, and being part of more sustainable flows of food, energy, and other everyday needs, sustainable materialist movements are examples of critique, resistance, and reconstruction. They represent what Hobson (2013) would call a counter-governmentality, or an environmental or sustainable governmentality. They are both affective and effective, a critical practice that actively counters both a blindness to ecological materiality, and a participation in the institutionalization of practice and power that benefits from that separation.

Larner (2014) has offered a solid and straightforward critique of this post-political rejection of environmental organizing, based on the kind of materialist movement groups discussed here—groups that are about building networks, seeking alternatives, being examples of new and best practice. They are groups that 'fundamentally question the status quo and actively seek political alternatives. In doing so, they illustrate how social movements may welcome, enact, and live radically different possibilities...' (Larner, 2014, p.191). These are environmentalisms that are highly critical of capitalism as currently practised, of colonialism and various other dominations, of the status quo relationship with the non-human. Agonism is clearly not lacking, even if militancy is represented or embodied in different ways. This is a combined sustainability, materialist, and political approach of the many groups and individuals we examined.

## Conclusion

This chapter has attempted to introduce, explore, and understand the unique aspects of the materialist understanding of sustainability articulated by environmental movements focused on flows of food, energy, and fashion. Overall, we find the discourse of new materialism embedded in the conceptions of sustainability that are articulated by activists focused on transforming material practices of everyday life. On the one hand, these actors and movements illustrate a concern with connectivity—with other human beings, and across various species boundaries. They take seriously the agentic nature of the non-human, and see such connections as absolutely crucial to an environmentalism of everyday life. Likewise, we see an understanding of material flows and systems, and of the role and impact of human intervention in those systems as we grow and make the food, energy, and clothing necessary to everyday life. New materialism—a sustainable materialism—is not simply an ontology, but a practice that is actively sought, promoted, celebrated, and lived by numerous movements. The claim here is not that all of environmentalism is headed in this direction, or even that such practices are the best, the only, or an adequate challenge to current practices in neo-liberal economic and political regimes. The point is simply that they understand, interpret, and practice a form of new and sustainable materialism.

Second, we have made an argument for the very political nature of these movements' understanding and practice of sustainability, and found that the critiques of its post-political or apolitical nature is inappropriate and misguided. The actors in the movements we interview understand their practice as collective political action. While not a traditional politics of movement groups—pressure and lobbying for values to be adopted into policy—neither is what we see and hear from activists a post-politics of individualist retreat or consumerism. They certainly offer 'imaginative, affective or strategic resources for political action' and address 'systematically reproduced constraints' (Washick et al., 2015) as they see them. But this is not about coping; it is about countering unsustainable practices and systems, and producing change from the material level up. Again, we may argue about the larger-scale effectiveness of such practices, and whether they will ever add up to disrupt and displace the practices they are designed to counter. But effectiveness is a different kind of question. What we have tried to demonstrate is that the actors in these movements certainly do not understand and articulate their actions as a retreat from politics; rather, they define their new and sustainable materialist acts as thoroughly political in nature.

Overall, what we see in the movement actors interviewed for this project is a simultaneous status of agonism with the status quo and the actors that produce, protect, and manipulate it and an intensive collaborative approach to the building of alternative and prefigurative networks of sustainable flows of materials and practice. This is not easy, and many social movement theorists have noted the difficulty of maintaining agonism when the idea is to spread, diffuse, and replicate one's practice. But these movements illustrate the possibility and potential of removing oneself and one's community from the replication of unsustainable flows, and of creating new and more sustainable material flows in collaborative and prefigurative practice. There is something here with which the post-politics critics of new materialism need to come to terms.

# PART III
# INNOVATIONS AND CONCLUSIONS

# 6

# New Directions and Virtues in Sustainable Materialist Movements

As we have examined and discussed the development and motivations of these sustainable materialist movements over the last few years, we have often been asked what makes these movements not only political, but unique. Why, our questioners have asked, should we focus on these particular movements of material action on food, energy, and sustainable fashion? Do they actually offer something *new*, or are they simply replicating other social movements or activist practices that we have seen before—even if current effects are on a larger scale? Our primary response to this classic 'so what?' question has been to note what we see as the unique and specific set of *political motivations* of the activists we interviewed, and their impressions of the political context, inspiration, and meaning of their work. We argue that sustainable materialism as a movement approach, while often misunderstood as a type of individualist value-based practice of sustainable consumption, is based in core concerns and motivations that differ from those at the centre of more individualist consumerist (or anti-consumerist) activists. As laid out in the previous chapters, these movements represent a unique politics that includes fatigue with traditional political and policy action, a dedication to a broad conception of social justice, an appreciation of (and resistance to) systems and flows of power, and a concern with the functioning and vitality of our entanglements with non-human systems.

But as we have engaged and spoken with the one hundred activists involved in food, energy, and sustainable fashion movements that are part of this project, a number of other unique elements, directions, and virtues of these movements and activists have become clear—both collective and individual. We address them here, in part to respond to the question of what is new and different, and in part to offer more depth, substance, and nuance to the discussion in Chapter 5 of the political nature of these movements. If the question we addressed there was *whether* the movements we examine are actually *political*, the issue here is about the strategies, structures, and virtues that make up and enable this particular approach to sustainable and materialist action. Sustainable materialism is a political strategy of developing collective, prefigurative, sustainable material systems.

On the one hand, we note three unique and core components of a sustainable materialist politics that set it apart—the new directions stemming from these movements. First, it is explicitly and inescapably *collective* and inexorably political, rather than individualist and consumerist. Second, this concern is *prefigurative*; it is a politics of purposefully embodied, constructed, and lived alternatives to the current and problematic material systems and flows in which they are embedded. Finally, and relatedly, it is concerned with *sustainability* of both human and non-human systems and relationships in those material flows. In all of these, collective value and action combine in the dedication and efforts to construct new and sustainable material systems.

And yet, as much as we focus on these collective concerns and characteristics of such movements, it is also clear that the activists we engaged also describe and inhabit key individual and prefigurative virtues—virtues key to the construction of the collective nature of sustainable materialism. Drawing on the experiences of the activists interviewed for this project, we suggest that at the core of prefigurative politics is a set of shared prefigurative virtues for engaging the messiness of the social world in the process of social transformation. Here, we describe this focus on collective action and material flows as being based on a *systems consciousness* on the part of individual activists. In addition, we argue that common to and key for activists are a commitment to a *prefigurative humility*, a deliberate *boldness* in the face of discomfort, and, crucially, a virtue of *care* to both one another and the larger ecological systems of which we are a part.

One key point here is that approaching prefigurative political action with a set of virtues like this enables an *affective* politics that can be leveraged for transformative social change. They are qualities of individuals, but they are key to the collective action of sustainable materialism as the focus of a movement. These virtues precede, enable, and constrain the choice of particular prefigurative strategies, so it is necessary that we incorporate them in our analysis of movement strategy, and examine the various ways in which they manifest in the individual lives and collective practices of the activists we interviewed.

After laying out both these movement characteristics and strategies on the one hand, and the prefigurative virtues on the other, we turn in Chapter 7 to ways of thinking about how these unique practices reflect recent theorizing about progressive activism more generally.

# The Practice of Sustainable Materialism—Three Core Aspects and Strategies

## Collective Action

Central to the whole endeavour of sustainable materialism, organized movement groups engaged in the movement are clearly and succinctly focused on collective action and the collective impact of their practices. Based on interviews, it is clear that movement action is not just about individual values and consumerist practices. Put simply, the post-individualist nature of sustainable materialist action is a key part of the political innovation and challenge of our interviewees.

On the one hand, such practice is easily distinguished from the liberal individualist focus of classic postmaterial actors or lifestyle politics, attentive to individual autonomy and self-expression. Activists do not explicitly belittle these aspects of contemporary liberal societies, but rather express the limits of such individualist liberal and political consumerist frameworks and insist on the necessity of the kind of collective and participatory action that forms sustainable materialist movements.

> We think of ourselves as people who have the capacity to purchase from the world, not people who have capacity to contribute to the world or to enjoy the world. We sort of see ourselves as kind of taking, not contributing. For me, that's the thing I'm interested in, is how you get people to feel more connected and less governed by the rules of business and more governed by the rules of humanity. But I think we need a bit of a political shot in the arm kind of thing to sort of start seeing ourselves as active citizens as opposed to consumers. (Fashion activist, UK)

In other words, sustainable materialist movements and actors do not simply perform individual consumer acts of choice; rather, the focus is on the participation in new collective institutions and material flows. Other studies concur. A special issue of *The International Journal of Consumer Studies* in 2015 laid out one of its key purposes as an attempt to 'move the discussion on lifestyles beyond hegemonic understandings of the individual consumer as market participant' (Wahlen and Laamanen, 2015, p.401). The idea was spurred by the understanding that many consumers 'do' politics, practice change, and live alternatives in ways that the individualist understanding of political consumerism cannot address. We find the same.

> I see social movements and collective action and working together as a community or a social movement is a vital thing—not getting your own

house sustainable, and there's been so much focus on that. So how do you bridge that idea of just doing it in your own home versus this huge political, a global issue—and you know people feel totally insignificant on whatever they do, whatever they do. So how do you construct it to make that link?

(Energy activist, Australia)

Of course, as discussed earlier in Chapter 2, some lifestyle movements do tie together individual action, including consumption, to a *perception* of collective action. As Haenfler, Johnson, and Jones note, 'as they act individually, participants subjectively understand their individual actions as having an impact beyond their personal lives, believing in both the power of their individual action and the power of non-coordinated collective action' (Haenfler, Johnson, and Jones, 2012, p.6; see also, Micheletti, 2003). While such a perspective illustrates why lifestyle movements are not necessarily only individualist action, such activists often act alone while seeing themselves as part of an Anderson-like 'imagined community'—a collective identity without real, direct connections (Anderson, 1983; see also Melucci, 1985).

However, sustainable materialist action, as embodied in the kinds of food, energy, and sustainable fashion movements we examined, is made up of more than individualist actions with imagined connections. Activists articulated clear collective action movements with specific and coordinated processes and goals. Stolle and Michelleti (2013, p.35) see the potential of political consumerism as having 'the power to potentially restructure society'. Such initiatives illustrate that 'the act of buying is not simply promoted individually, but socialised among a group of people, organised either formally or informally' (Forno and Graziano, 2014, p.142). Our argument, in contrast, is that those active in sustainable materialism are actually attempting to 'live into being' a restructured set of material processes. This active and participatory collective practice makes sustainable materialist political action qualitatively different than some other forms of individualized political consumerism.

The focus of many of our interviewees is similar to the collective action of that in intentional communities and ecovillages (Litfin, 2013; Schelly, 2017), but with an emphasis on those practices that are not physically removed or separated from the rest of everyday life—as unsustainable as they are. Sustainable materialism, as practised and understood by activists, is an engaged political project that collectivizes concern for the processes of consumption, and is attentive to the impacts and import of material flows from material to production to consumption to waste or reuse. And it is designed to exist alongside and as an alternative set of practices, institutions, and flows.

Sustainable materialist movements organize individual participation in a self-consciously collective project that combines consumption, citizenship, and responsibility, but that consciously moves beyond a singular focus on responsible consumption as an individual political action. Activists focus on relations with—and responsibility to—each other, the non-human realm, and the materials they use. The idea often referred to is of a relational, collective conception of political responsibility, bridging personal practice and the realization of alternative collective and entangled systems. Both the focus and structure of sustainable materialist movements, as articulated by participants, suggests that an individualist frame is inadequate to account for such activism.

## Prefigurative Materialism

Ultimately, the aim of sustainable materialist activism is to reconfigure a new relationship with, and institutionalization of, the material necessities of everyday life—and to set examples for others. It is, ultimately, a prefigurative materialism. As Foden (2012, p.151) describes, the central idea of prefigurative politics is in the practice, the doing, of alternatives. It is about proactive, practical, positive things that movements can do, and changes that can be constructed. Epstein long ago noted that prefigurative politics is based on participants 'act[ing] out a vision of a better world' (Epstein, 1991, p.122). For Yates (2015, p.18), there are three key elements to a prefigurative politics: it should be 'combined and balanced with processes of consolidation and diffusion', tied to ongoing micropolitics, and both imagine and actualize future goals in the present, and attempt to experiment and 'proliferate and perpetuate struggle'.

The focus, then, is on the activities of everyday life, and constructing them as consistent with a vision of a new politics, or way of interacting (see also Breines, 1989; Cornell, 2009). Prefigurative politics is submerged in everyday life, and this everyday practice reflects in the present the change being demanded (Melucci, 1985, p.801). The practice goes beyond simply a new place to shop, or particular products to buy, and instead becomes a broader living embodiment of a new set of values and practices. As Boggs long argued, the focus is on a consistency between everyday life and a political vision, embodying 'within the ongoing political practice of a movement...those forms of social relations, decision-making, culture, and human experience that are the ultimate goal' (Boggs, 1977, p.100). It is the lived practice of the 'politics of the possible' (Guthman, 2008). Or, as Foden has noted, 'instead of developing a theoretical destination, establishing it as orthodoxy and meticulously planning a strategy for arriving at that destination, the prefigurative approach lends itself especially to movements with multiple goals that are not (yet) fixed and are open to deliberation' (Foden, 2012, p.151).

This idea of a prefigurative material politics can be particularly related to food movements. Ostrom (2009, p.117), for example, sees the proponents of community-supported agriculture (CSA) eschewing conventional contentious politics and the usual political process, instead 'refashioning their daily eating, cooking, and shopping routines around the seasonal output of local agroecosystems... [and] reorienting their everyday habits and lifestyles in accordance with their values'. Activists are confident that such practice is a key way to bring about not only change to their own material lives, but also systemic change at a wider level. Others have argued that such CSAs, along with slow food movements, transition towns, ecovillages, and the like 'do not place at the centre of their repertoire predominantly contentious forms of actions but rather organised actions and networks aimed at supporting different forms of consumption' (Forno and Graziano, 2014, p.148). Further, it is not just about different *forms* of consumption, but different *systems* that provide for, manage, and engage the full flows of material life. For food and energy activists, the shift here is from individual or collective practices, such as ethical consumption, to collectively constructed alternative material systems: local, sustainable, just, and resilient food and energy systems.

Crucially, a prefigurative politics is not just reconstructive, but also illustrates a refusal to participate in unjust structures and practices (Haenfler, Johnson, and Jones, 2012, p.4). Sustainable materialist movements certainly act as if the existing structures exist, and the point is to both undermine and resist those, while constructing a workable alternative and replacement system for a particular commodity or set of commodities. It is clear that the movements see and share the critique that contemporary neo-liberal economic structures and processes, including conventional agricultural, energy, and fashion systems, are inherently damaging in both social and ecological terms. That critique is embedded in the insistence to step outside such systems and reorganize consumption and production in ways that both lessen that impact and stimulate new, sustainable, local economic processes (Forno and Graziano, 2014, p.148). While more individualized forms of political consumerism look to existing markets and structures to achieve political aims, a more prefigurative and sustainable materialism is about creating alternatives—new systems—in parallel to dominant institutions (Foden, 2012, p.152).

As Papadopoulos (2018, p.3) writes, experimental social movements are not simply about 'addressing existing institutions for redistributing justice but...the creation of alternative forms of existence that reclaim material justice from below'. Such movements are about experiments with the materiality of everyday life.

Such prefigurative politics is obviously collective, but our argument here is that they are also focused on the sustainable side of sustainable materialism. Dobernig and Stagl (2015) note that urban food movements in New York not only a focus on a prefigurative or 'counter-hegemonic strategy', but also on identities that exemplify 'shared ethos of re-engagement with nature, meaningful work, and authenticity' in an attempt to 'induce collective social change' (Dobernig and Stagl, 2015, p.452). While some argue that such movements illustrate that 'the self, rather than the streets, becomes the site of social change' (Haenfler, Johnson, and Jones, 2012, p.15), it is clear that such action is not just personal, but also prefigurative and collective—an intentional participation in a value-expressing alternative system of material flows, including flows across species.

## Sustainable Materialism and Material Flows

Of course, a crucial aspect of such a prefigurative sustainable materialism is the material—and a specific focus on changing the actual material processes and systems used to meet everyday needs such as food, energy, and clothing. The qualifier 'sustainable' is a key and integral part of this attention, as the materialist focus of these movement organizations is on the human place within, and impact on, flows of materials out of the non-human realm, into products, through the human community, and back out to the non-human realm through waste streams. The focus is on materials and flows alike; this is not just about supply chains, but rather the various impacts of those chains on human and non-human relations, communities, and functioning. Another important point here is that the discursive border of 'community' extends beyond the human to incorporate non-human actors and the material world—something integral to much of sustainable materialist activism.

Sustainable materialism can be understood as the political embodiment of new materialist ontology. As discussed in Chapter 5, the philosophical focus on new materialism (Bennett, 2010; Coole and Frost, 2010) examines the connections between human and non-human, the activity of those non-human actors, the vitality of the interconnections, and the embedded nature of human practices in a non-human material world. As Meyer writes on the new attention to both the material and the everyday, it is clear that there is a growing recognition 'that everyday life is the location for concern for material needs, but these are always fulfilled (or not) in a value-rich context' (Meyer, 2015, p.62). The insistence, he continues, is on reimagining materiality itself in a way that includes and pays attention to how 'the biological and the cultural, problems and values, the concrete and the abstract' invite our attention (Meyer, 2015, p.62). This attention to the materiality of practice is at the core of sustainable materialism movements.

Such movements embody practices that take the idea of a vibrant nature, and its values, as given. This illustrates, as discussed previously, the very political nature of new materialism—the reality that it embraces and represents both a different ontological vision of human/non-human relations, and in particular a vitality of all materials. In the movements around food, energy, and sustainable fashion systems, the point is that we see movements engaging with the reality of materiality and our immersion in and relation to elements that pass through our bodies due to a variety of everyday practices and experiences. Such attention does have its bonuses, as one of our interviewee's notes:

> A lot of people ask me, 'Why are you so happy all the time?' Well, one of the reasons is because, I say, 'How many people get to go out every morning on their back step and make this many beings happy?' You know, whether it's the microbes in the compost pile, the earthworms or the chickens being moved to a new salad bar or the cows dancing to a new salad bar. I mean, our life is wrapped up in making beings happy and that's not the life of a lot of people. (Food activist, USA)

A receptivity to the non-human and its part on material systems is imminent in the sustainable materialist practice and activism discussed here, and absolutely central to a vision of a different relationship with human and non-human alike.

The point here is not to develop, foster, and foist upon the public a singular new theoretical argument or valuation of the material. Rather, what we are seeing is a focus on the increasing recognition of the materiality, the vitality of matter that Bennett and others note, in the actual practices and strategies of new movements. Activists are bringing material practices—both the critique of problematic and environmentally unsustainable practice and the development of new, open, transparent, and sustainable practice—out into the open, and into the design and institutionalization of new material flows.

## Four Prefigurative Virtues

For members of these movements, personal and political authenticity and integrity is about matching and developing a sense of values with political and ethical collective action as they participate in reconfiguring and reconstructing systems that provide for the basic material practices of everyday life. Crucially, this idea of lived values is not presented in only an individualist 'ethical living' manner, but instead tied to an active, prefigurative, set of collective actions and new systems. But it is also clear that these collective, prefigurative, and sustainable political strategies are enabled by a set of more individual, but shared, virtues—what we are calling prefigurative virtues. They include a systems consciousness, prefigurative humility, boldness, and care.

## Systems Consciousness—Social and Environmental

For example, the quality that both enables and is fed by a sustainable materialist approach and strategy is that of a systems consciousness. Systems consciousness is the precursor to systems thinking (in its non-technical sense; see Senge, 1992; Jervis, 1997; Chapman, 2004) in that to *think* systems we must know that the world is composed of a web of systemic factors, actors, and social forces that themselves interact with and affect one another.

Systems consciousness is not the norm in liberal societies, due largely to the ontological and methodological individualism clearly built into the liberal political project. Ontopolitically, *neo*-liberalism reinforces not only highly individualized subjectivities but also limits our ways of seeing and enacting the social world *as a system*. Neo-liberalism is thus always both individualist and reductivist (Brown, 2015). To resist these neo-liberal subjectivities and their implications, a systems consciousness, as a number of our participants articulated, is therefore necessary. As one noted:

> [W]e live in a time where there's a kind of a segregated mentality, you know, that I can do my thing and it doesn't affect anything else. And we're realising that that's not really very accurate, that all that we do affects something. And so trying to connect those dots is a big deal.          (Food activist, USA)

Similarly, others clearly laid out the systematic approach:

> [We thought] what if we got all these ethical enterprises—it doesn't have to just be fashion—ethical enterprises together under this one building...

[Because] I can't do anything by myself, but here we all are together, and that's where the potential for larger change comes from.

(Fashion activist, Australia)

I think that people are understanding better and better that to organise in your own community can be effective, but it's also limited if you're not part of larger systemic change.                         (Energy activist, USA)

This concern often challenges some of the previously held basics of business:

Many large charitable organisations are working under models that we already know don't work. Unless we can transform their attitude towards how they're running themselves, we're doomed to recreate the system we have now, and the only way that that can happen is by offering something definite and based in community wealth creation. [The reality is] we can offer people the realisation that there are other ways to do this. That [conventional] business models don't work.            (Food activist, UK)

What's one little restaurant going to do if I don't actually change the system that supports us all? I need to go teach my competitors to do what I do. Without all of us doing it, nothing's going to change. And so it was *that* that we celebrate, really, that shift from competition and being the best, even competing in social responsibility, to actually recognising that we're all in this together.                           (Food activist, USA)

The core point here is simple: to change 'the system' activists must organize collectively. But, as is evident from the above quotes, the boundaries of the system are simultaneously a function of the activity of the system itself, and a product of the strategy of description involved. Systems consciousness, these interviewees suggest, goes beyond both the individual and even the 'local' of place-based community to embrace and understand the broader social, economic, and environmental processes that shape everyday lives, practices, limits, and possibilities.

In a similar vein, activists are aware that the way they frame particular systems can both open and close the possibilities for a transformative systems consciousness. For example, whether the trend towards calling food-based activism 'food systems activism' contributes to the level of systems consciousness amongst activists depends largely on whether the term is emphasized as *food* systems or food *systems*. The former bounds activism and inquiry into food alone, which can leave participants blind to how praxis can contribute to inequality in other parts of the system.[1] The latter is more conscious to the way

---

[1] This essential point is raised by many other scholars of progressive material movements, including Guthman (2006, 2011) and Agyeman (2013).

that food is but one lens (opening, window, opportunity) to engage more broadly in a set of political and material transformations that bind together the social, economic, and environmental.

Indeed, as interviewees express it, this grasp of interconnections is a necessary component of the systems consciousness required for their prefigurative political activism. As one noted, activists must be:

> [D]irected by a collective consciousness that [realizes] we're all interconnected. The things that I do only matter if they resonate with the things that you do. And that is why building community around this vision is so important.                                      (Food activist, USA)

Not only does this quote speak to how systems consciousness helps activists take these interconnections seriously, but it also shows that, in many ways, systems consciousness is closely connected to a prefigurative humility we will address shortly. That is, it recognizes the limits of individualized activity in being able to change the system, but also that a community of *knowers* is more able to understand the way that the system operates.

The commitment to *community* as system is vital as well. Part of the desire of prefigurative political projects, such as those of the activists we interviewed, is to rebuild different communities, based in and coupled to their systems consciousness. As neo-liberalism thrives on individualist norms, which are antithetical to the systems consciousness required for prefigurative projects, the neo-liberal project has resulted in the undermining of community, collective subjectivities and, as one participant put it, 'the ability of its citizens to join-the-dots'. Rebuilding community, then, becomes a necessary part of this oppositional and prefigurative politics. We see systems consciousness in community—and community in systems consciousness. This is possible, activists say,

> [i]f you cultivate this view of interconnectedness and interdependence and then create the space for lots of self-inquiry into values and meaning and what your connection is to the systems of the world and to your community.
> (Fashion activist, USA)

Many participants also expressed a sense of community and, therefore, a systems consciousness which included both human and non-human systems. The systems ethos includes and embraces the *sustainable* part of the sustainable materialist idea—an ethos that acknowledges human immersion and participation in non-human natural systems, and responds with a reflexive shift in the understanding of human engagement across species barriers in such entangled systems. That said, it would be a step too far to suggest that all activists in these movements fully embrace a posthuman ontology, or a clear decentring of the human subject (Papadopoulos, 2018); but a systems consciousness focused on both everyday materiality and sustainability certainly provides an avenue away from a destructive individualist humanism. As we noted in Chapter 5, we see the directionality of the relationship between a sustainable materialist ontology and practice go both ways—from ontology to engagement in practice, and from practice to the development of an understanding of broader ecological entanglements. This relationship can be co-constitutive.

The point here is that, however they frame their understanding of a given system, common to our participants is that understanding and engaging with *a* system is key. That is not to say that participants all have identical conceptions of the boundaries of such systems, but it is clear that they recognize the importance of *seeing* in systems and cultivating the systems consciousness that is necessary to do so. And, crucially, such a systems consciousness, as a prefigurative virtue, is related to and co-dependent on the development of collaborative, whole of system *strategies*, which many of the activists in food, energy, and sustainable fashion movements advocate for. It is the realization that 'in order to create change, we need to do systems work. In order to do systems work, we need to see the systems around us' (Food activist, Australia).

## Prefigurative Humility

Another common theme across participants is a humility with respect to their practice and its impact. This prefigurative humility, as we see it, is composed of a number of elements. First, prefigurative humility involves being aware of and acknowledging the limits of particular transformative projects. As one participant keenly noted:

> I think that might be possible to maybe turn the ship a little bit. I don't expect that we can turn it around, but it would be nice to think that we could perhaps, but I think that's why we all sort of labour away in our particular areas, is to try and move the ship a little bit towards the goals that we feel are represented by sustainability and environmentalism.
>
> (Food activist, Australia)

Indeed, views like this are common amongst participants who are often daunted by the prospect of how their particular movement, project, or practice can achieve what one participant referred to as 'an *admittedly* utopian vision'. The qualifier here is key. This 'admission' is an openness to the various challenges in actualizing transformative change in a messy, complex social system. But, crucially, it is expressed in a way—common to many of the activists we interviewed—that is ultimately reducible to a form of humility. In many ways, this humility is the cognitive strategy that activists employ to bridge the gap between a utopian dream and a pragmatic, feasible or *real* utopian *possibility* (which itself is a kind of cognitive dissonance). As one participant noted:

> I know that it is unlikely that we will achieve *real* change in my lifetime, but if I can, in my own way, see through tangible concrete changes in the way this community lives their lives, it will have been worth it.   (Energy activist, UK)

The second element of prefigurative humility is clearly illustrated in Transition Town leader Rob Hopkins' honest admission that 'I don't think that...we have all the answers'. That is, it is a humility with respect to what activists can possibly know about the transformative potential or their projects, or indeed of any possible negative, counterproductive, or system-reinforcing repercussions of their actions. Activists do not have all the answers, and they know that they do not.

> There is no nirvana yet. There is no perfection in terms of how do you do circular economy, non-polluting, 100 per cent endlessly recycled clothing that doesn't take advantage of people, doesn't pollute, doesn't use excessive water—it doesn't exist. So there is no perfection.   (Fashion activist, UK)

This epistemic humility is similar to the reflexivity noted by other movement scholars (for example, DuPuis and Goodman, 2005; Levkoe, 2011), but is at the same time both simpler and more expansive. At its core, it relates to the fact that, as one participant put it:

> None of us know what we're doing, or what will happen when we do what we're doing. There are going to be problems...and misunderstandings... and confusion, but, if we all start from that same playing field, we can figure it out along the way.   (Food activist, USA)

The kind of humility articulated here maps onto the impossibility of perfection both in the way that individual activists live their lives and in the way that prefigurative projects and social movements are enacted on a day-to-day basis. Activists articulate a reflexivity about their actions, but do so through practices that are ultimately humble and uncertain.

Additionally, it should be clear that prefigurative humility emerges from the interaction between its two core elements. To acknowledge the limits of individual and collective action (including the ways in which the knotty contradictions of the social world hamper attempts for people to authentically live their values) goes hand in hand with an acknowledgement of the epistemic limits within which we operate.

For activists caught in uncertain practices, or ones that highlight contradictory or different value positions, the humble reflexive response is something along the lines of 'I know it's not ideal'. Across the participants in this study there was a recognition that the way to work through these contradictions in knowledge, action, and possibility requires 'a lot of clumsiness'. One participant noted that such a position requires both 'an openness and willingness to be clumsy, but also an invit[ation] to others to be open in their clumsiness' (Food activist, USA). This feeling of clumsiness is what makes humility an affect. That is, it is what activists *feel* when they cannot make values meet, all the time, at all, or in ways that produce a positive effect (and affect).

This kind of humility has been both nascent and explicit in much of the writing on prefigurative politics. For example, renowned alter-globalization activist David Solnit (2003, p.xxviii) argued that activists must 'infuse our political work with ... humility and curiosity'. But, at least in academic scholarship, this argument about the virtue of movement humility has not been much engaged. It is a welcome virtue in the face of the radical certainty of many contemporary activists, some progressive, but mostly in the increasing number of authoritarian and populist movements. The argument here is that, in its various guises, humility is a key component of how sustainable materialist activists are currently going about their political projects of transformation.

## Boldness in the Face of Discomfort

In contrast, however, another prefigurative virtue that emerges from discussions with activists is that of being bold in the face of the discomfort that comes with transformative action. The dissonance that comes from the activity of clumsy non-attunement between differing and uncertain visions, activities, and practices is profoundly uncomfortable (as one participant noted, 'it sucks'). It requires activists that are patient, persistent, resilient—and bold. It is the recognition that, as one subject put it, 'this is a bumpy road, but we've all got to strap in to spite the system that made it bumpy in the first place'.

Activists approach this difficulty, the bumpy road, in different ways. As one noted, the process is a lot about:

> Cultivating that—not fearlessness, but recognising your fear, and also cultivating your deeper sense of values that allow you to say, 'Okay. I'm not going to perpetuate that system. That's wrong.' But the hard part about that, of course, is that to live and breath and put food on my children's table I have to perpetuate some elements of the system, and that does eat at me a little—but I keep moving.                    (Fashion activist, USA)

Whether fearlessness, 'boldness', courage, or 'a commitment to a different world meets sheer stupidity', common to participants is the experience of being 'torn'. Indeed, in many interviews, subjects were torn between utopian visions and practical realities (food localization meets a love of coffee, values-based business meets profit margin, anarchist sensibilities meet local zoning ordinances). As Beausoleil (2014, p.20) has noted: 'the possibilities and contours of perception are shaped by the textures, intensities, and resonances of the affective "sounding chambers" in which they occur'. The argument is that the affective experience of being out of tune is a way of staying attuned to those very same contradictions and tensions, keeping them in sight, within reach, in an active and ongoing process of revision.

The ability to abide, at least momentarily, the affective consequences of this dissonance, therefore, underpins what it means to do prefigurative politics. As Chatterton and Pickerill (2010, p.487, emphasis in original) put it, activists must be able to express an openness to a form of politics that is 'simultaneously *anti-*, *despite-* and *post-* capitalist' while, at the same time, acknowledging such a project is 'always going to be contradictory, interstitial and in the making'. They must be willing to be bold in the face of the discomfort of such action. And, indeed, many of the activists interviewed for this project recognize and act in spite of the discomfort that comes from not knowing how, if, or when harmony is possible. In a sense, this is where the virtues of humility and boldness engage and supplement one another. The experience of the activists engaged in this project makes clear that all sustainable materialist imaginations are ultimately fuelled by the affective labour of working through these contradictions.[2]

---

[2] Gibson-Graham make a similar, if slightly less empirically grounded point, in the introduction to their 2006 volume.

## Care

At the centre of a sustainable materialism as collective action, one key glue holding a systems ethic, humility, and boldness together in a collective and relational movement is the idea and practice of care. As one of our interviewees clearly put it, 'from what place are we innovating? From a place of caring. From a place of actually seeing something, from a place of love.' Clearly, care as a political or ethical consideration is both contested and complex. Puig de la Bellacasa's (2017) recent book on the subject starts by naming at least twenty different academic domains, each with multiple authors, where the idea of an ethic of care is addressed, from classics in political theory (Tronto, 1993) through to human–non-human relations (Haraway, 2008). That variety, she argues, illustrates the many understandings and meanings of care, and reveals 'how caring implicates different relationalities, issues, and practices in different settings'. Even in that diversity, however, Puig de la Bellacasa returns to Tronto's classic sense of care, that it includes all we do to maintain, continue, and repair the world—'our bodies, our selves, and our environment, all of which we seek to interweave in a complex, life-sustaining web' (Tronto, 1993, p.103).

We will not try to develop any singular theory of care, or pretend to apply the full breadth of this literature on the movements we examine. What we are suggesting, rather simply, is that there is a connection between ideas of care in feminist studies and the perspective and approach of activists in sustainable materialist movements. For example, Tronto laid out a distinction between care as an ethic of concern—'caring about' as an affective virtue—and care that happens in a material sense, or 'care giving'. As Puig de la Bellacasa notes, this 'distinction does not separate these modes of agency. What it allows us to emphasize is that a politics of care engages much more than a moral stance; it involves affective, ethical, and hands-on agencies of practical and material consequence' Puig de la Bellacasa (2017, p.4). The ethic and virtue of care is linked, in this sense, to the material practice of caring practice. Food systems activists note this affect of caring for the land, human bodies, and non-human systems, and realize it in more sustainable materialist food practices. Energy system activists do likewise, often focusing more broadly on care for broader ecological systems, climate change, and the provision of cheap and ethical energy. And sustainable fashion activists clearly bring a care for both landscapes and labourers into their supply chains, providing caring material practice—even when some of the outward focus can be seen as more aesthetic than virtuous.

For me, that's the thing I'm interested in, how you get people to feel more connected and less governed by the rules of business and more governed by the rules of humanity...I think commerce has a lot to answer for. I'm not even really that interested in conscious capitalism as a concept. I'm interested in actually empathetic activity.                    (Fashion activist, UK)

These approaches to care in sustainable materialist movements illustrate a move that encompasses the relationship between a virtue of care and its material realization in practice, but also a broader and more inclusive focus on care for community—attachment to and care for place, ecosystems, and human–non-human entanglements. Such care may begin very close to home:

So all of the people in our community believe in these kinds of values about what matters. One is that place does matter. That it is in a particular place that you can fall in love with a tree. It's hard to get your head around the Amazon, the loss and destruction of the rainforests today, but you can care very much about the gorgeous tree in your backyard and it's that relationship that allows for intimacy and love and caring.           (Food activist, USA)

That relationship to place—to preserving, to understanding, to caring for the physicality and the relationality of place—was an ongoing concern. The focus goes beyond the tree in the backyard, to the very development of thinking, of relating to others in systems, and innovating sustainable systems.

[Y]ou can actually do horrible things...if you're not actually operating from a place of caring. If you're not continuing to operate from some place of 'I love the pigs. I love the land. I love the people. I love all people.' And, in fact, everyone I know who has innovated these last 15 years, last 20 years, last 30 years...have originally started from some place of love. There's something they cared about, and that's where that's coming from and then they can keep innovating.                    (Food activist, USA)

For so long people have been excluded from having that warm glow in their heart that's solar ownership. For me, when I drive past panels, I look up at them and go 'oh that panel's mine' and know that I'm contributing to the future of this place...hopefully a sustainable one.   (Energy activist, Australia)

It is important to note one essential caveat here: while indisputably an issue of concern, and a posited virtue, there are clearly cautions and limits in the discussion—and, crucially, application—of care. While care is a recognized ethic, it would not be uncommon to find an ethic of care expressed, while the distribution of everyday 'caring' work at meetings, on farms, in collectives, and more, continues to be relegated to women. Further work should be done to explore this very gendered and power-based relegation of care work—the actual practice of everyday care, rather than care as an ideal virtue.

## Conclusions

The bulk of our study of movements of sustainable materialist practice—the concerns laid out in Chapters 2 through 5—is about the stated political, social, and environmental motivations of the activists in food system, community energy, and sustainable fashion movements. What we have tried to offer here is a discussion of the unique nature of these movements as movements.

On the one hand, we argue that the combination of a focus on collective action, prefigurative politics, and sustainability helps to differentiate the movement organizations we discuss from more individualist and consumerist movements aligned to ethical or sustainable consumption. Crucially, these strategies are differentiated in this discussion, but coexist and cogenerate in the eyes of activists we interviewed. A new form of environmental action must be thoroughly collective in nature, as individualist strategies cannot remake systems. Such materialist movements must set an example and be prefigurative, generating new systems, flows, and practices of the materials of everyday life. And they must be sustainable, focused on recognizing the reality of entangled human and non-human systems, and reconnecting and reconstructing them in mutually beneficial ways.

On the other hand, we see a set of virtues articulated across movement activists—of a systems consciousness, of both humility and boldness, and of care for beings, community, and place. Drawing these virtues together, the argument is that they, in total, speak to and enable an affective politics of transformation. That is, their affective nature opens up new ways of seeing and enacting the social and material world.[3] Such virtues, collectively embraced, can rupture existing social norms and fabrics to bring into focus new possibilities. For these activists, there is an advantage in feeling vexed, uncomfortable, clumsy, or unsure—but only if those feelings align with a humility about the prefigurative content of a vision for *systemic* transformation. As bell hooks (2000, p.4) noted, 'social change is neither safe nor comfortable'. There is an affective friction, awkwardness and irresolution to this political project, but

---

[3] This section draws significant inspiration from Ahmed (2004, 2014).

these disruptive characteristics are not simply a means to an end. Instead, they sustain prefigurative thought, collective activity, and sustainable materialist transformation. The point here is that the collective and prefigurative nature of movement strategies, and the affective nature of the prefigurative virtues, enables a creativity and community that leads to the envisioning and emplacement of alternatives—crucially, for our participants, *better* alternatives.

# 7

# Conclusion

## From Sustainable Materialism to System Change

This book would not be complete without a discussion of the political potential and limitations of sustainable materialist environmental movements. Our analysis throughout has shown that these recent developments in environmental activism—among movements focused on food systems, community energy, and sustainable fashion—have grown out of a combination of frustration with standard political tactics, concerns about political and corporate power, social justice, and ecological sustainability. These frustrations have spawned an interest in groups and actions that address a range of material systems and relationships, and create more vibrant local economies. In the previous chapter, our discussion moved beyond the stated motivations of activists to lay out what we see as the unique components of this sustainable materialist politics. In concluding, we examine what sets sustainable materialism apart from previous forms of environmental action, and what makes it a foundation for potential systemic transformation.

As laid out in Chapter 6, the experiences and perspectives of the hundred activists we spoke to over the course of this project emphasize that sustainable materialist politics is distinct in a number of key ways. First, sustainable materialism is explicitly and inescapably collective, rather than a form of individual action, political consumerism, or lifestyle politics. For these movements, the individual, the collective, the community, and the institutional are absolutely key and intertwined. Second, this politics is concerned with not just classical understandings of sustainability, but with material flows and practice, where value and action combine in the construction of new material systems. Activists see social change in not just doing good, but in being physically part of a redesigned ecosystem of material, institutional, and community processes and flows. This understanding of material collectivity is manifest in the alternatives that grow from the movements we have examined here—alternatives focused on the creation of new flows of material goods through and across the systems and networks that affect social and environmental flourishing. Finally, and relatedly, sustainable materialist politics is prefigurative politics.

It is about the construction and maintenance of embodied and constructed alternatives—a set of sustainable material practices that can serve as an example for replication, emulation, and expansion.

But all of this begs the question of whether not only the motivations, but also the long-term goals of sustainable materialist movements can be realized in practice. Can sustainable materialism act as a foundation for systemic transformation and, if so, how? In this chapter we suggest some answers to these questions, focusing on small-scale and local impacts on political engagement and environmental sustainability, on the way that movements' focus on local business helps to address economic insecurity, and on larger issues of systemic change in production and consumption systems. We then address the potential and real critiques and limitations of such action, and while we did not set out to do a comparative study, we turn to a short discussion of the key differences in sustainable materialism across the different domains and countries we examine. Finally, we conclude with suggestions for some key generative areas for future research and inquiry on sustainable materialism.

## Sustainable Materialists Against 'The System'

Extending from our discussion in Chapter 6, our argument is that, taken together, the ability of sustainable materialist movements to effectively wield prefigurative strategies and virtues enables both an effective and affective politics of transformation. Their coexistence opens up new ways of seeing and enacting the social and material world. Their use ruptures existing social norms and fabrics to bring into focus new possibilities. There is an advantage in feeling vexed, uncomfortable, clumsy, or unsure when that feeling overlaps with individual and collective humility about a vision for systemic transformation. As hooks (2000, p.4) noted, 'social change is neither safe nor comfortable'. There is undoubtedly an affective friction and sense of irresolution in the sustainable materialist political project, but its disruptive characteristics sustain prefigurative thought, activity, and transformation. The point here is that the affective nature of a sustainable materialist politics enables a creativity that leads to the envisioning of alternatives and, crucially, alternatives that deeply embody the sustainable materialist values embraced and expressed by the activists that we have featured throughout this book. In her discussion of democratic receptivity, Beausoleil (2014, p.20) argues that 'the possibilities and contours of perception are shaped by the textures, intensities, and resonances of the affective "sounding chambers" in which they occur'. We see this kind of affective experience of sustainable materialist politics, where activists recognize that being out of tune is really a way of staying attuned to contradictions and tensions that sit at the heart of system change, and keeping them in sight, within reach, in an active and ongoing process of revision. For sustainable materialists irresolution is inevitable, a way of life; but given what material practice entails and allows, this irresolution is also seen as part of a broader resolution and transformation. The experience of our participants makes clear that sustainable materialist imaginations are ultimately sustained by the affective labour of working through these contradictions, in everyday practice.

How, then, do the broad motivations, strategic approaches, prefigurative virtues, and their affective nature connect to various theories and perspectives on prefigurative strategies and approaches? What does the way people approach their political projects with these strategies and virtues mean for the way we conceptualize different strategies for the realization of transformational system change? We suggest that the sustainable materialist politics we see in practice resonate with the theoretical work being done on the conceptual structure of democratic and prefigurative strategies, including recent theoretical and strategic explorations of 'visionary pragmatism' (Coles, 2016), 'radical incrementalism' (Schram, 2015), 'optimal marginality' (McLaughlin, 2001), and 'alternative economies' (Gibson-Graham, 1996, 2006).

One core strategic approach that aligns with sustainable materialist activists is that of Coles' (2016) 'visionary pragmatism', which directly mirrors the sentiment of a number of participants who refer to their strategy as 'a contradiction in terms'. Indeed, as Coles (2016, p.26) notes 'visionary pragmatists seek the resonance and dissonance of this pairing'. While none of our participants actively referred to themselves as visionary pragmatists, it is clear that many would gravitate towards the idea—and it is easy to make the case for why. Visionary pragmatists, as Coles argues, recognize the ways in which utopian and pragmatic mindsets threaten and undermine each other, but use them in concert nonetheless in the knowledge that doing so opens up possibilities for escaping 'disabling dualisms' (McClintock, 2014, p.149). Many of our interviewees, when confronted with the realization that their activism is often fraught with tension and contradiction, would report that their focus was to 'just get on with it', transforming their food and energy systems by leveraging gaps and opportunities in the existing system—for example, by taking funding that only exists because the beneficiaries of capital and inequality are able to give to charity with their surplus profit, often to avoid or minimize tax obligations.

But these activists almost universally recognize that small steps are necessary and that means 'being pragmatic about what the existing system can offer, at least in the short-term' (Food activist, USA). In these ways, visionary pragmatism *as strategy* for system change is underpinned by prefigurative humility and boldness in the face of this discomfort and contradiction. Crucially, those food and energy systems activists who use this strategy as a framework to construct new mega-circulations of material goods do so not only with this humility, but also with the broader systems consciousness common to sustainable materialist activism. That is, visionary pragmatists seldom conceptualize prefigurative politics as an isolated act, and instead see it as necessarily bundled up in collaborations across different political spaces, geographic places, and temporalities. We are seeing this approach of a mix of humility, systems thinking, and a visionary mentality in the creation of localist alliances, food system collaboratives, sustainable fashion entrepreneurs, and networks of community-generated energy projects. Participants often expressed a sentiment that 'we must learn to walk before we can run, and that only happens when we work together' (Fashion activist, Australia). One, along similar lines, noted that:

> We can't usurp the power of multinational corporations overnight. But [their power] is not immutable, just as the divine right of kings was not immutable. Our strategy should be small steps: each focused on lessening the power available for them to wield against us—taking that power back [for ourselves] so we can use it to build a world we might value.
>
> (Food activist, USA)

It is this sentiment that relates to the second conceptualization of prefigurative strategy we see related to our work: that of 'radical incrementalism' as outlined by political scientist Sanford Schram. On Schram's (2015, p.184) terms, radical incrementalism is 'a process in which people push for change recognising it will not necessarily be as large as they might like but also in which small changes can do more than fine-tune the existing system'. In line with the analysis in the activist's quote above, it focuses its efforts on 'restructuring embedded power relations that prevent more ambitious changes from happening' (Schram, 2015, p.185) in order to lay the groundwork for future larger-scale change. In many ways, there are more similarities than differences between visionary pragmatism and radical incrementalism, which speaks both to the fact that they are underpinned by the same set of prefigurative virtues and that similar strategic approaches resonate across different types of prefigurative movements, visions, and practices. Indeed, radically incremental approaches are common across the progressive left, and include the more individualist practices of political consumerism discussed in Chapter 2—the boycotts and buycotts used by political consumers to pressure large corporations towards particular value positions. As one activist commenting on such actions put it:

> If they have to care about conditions for their workers [in China], then suddenly they have to reform a whole raft of their policies and procedures across the business. It's a feedback loop...and that is why it is so powerful.
>
> (Fashion activist, UK)

One key point here is that the activists we interviewed, if they were involved in such incremental and individualist action, only saw it as part of their larger focus on the development of new material systems.

A third, related conceptualization of prefigurative strategy deployed by activists is to 'see the margin as a site of radical openness...and possibility' (hooks, 1989, p.145) but do so in a way that embraces an *optimal* marginality (McLaughlin, 2001). Optimal marginality attempts to 'transfer ideas from the creative margins to the center...creating pressure for innovations' (McLaughlin, 2001, p.273). For McLaughlin, optimally marginal strategies attempt to utilize knowledge about the orthodoxy to simultaneously deconstruct and reassemble it from within. Put another way, optimal marginality seeks to move the centre, but to do so in strategic ways that engage its possibility-producing qualities. By way of illustration, one participant described market-based mechanisms as optimally marginal because:

> Being for profit I think is the only way to challenge [big corporates] because they're not feeling challenged by non-profits. They think they're invincible and that's their biggest weakness: they're big, they're bloated and they're out of touch and it's very hard to make a square into a circle. Like, you are a big fat square and for most of the world, that's fine and that's great, but there are a growing [number of] people that want circles and they can't do it. And they're trying so hard, you know. You'll see their little side boutiques that don't look like them and don't sound like them but is them and that's confusing, but the more I see that, I realise that these small guys must be giving them some anxiety, which I love and that's fantastic. Because the way they set up the game to play, people are not interested any more.
>
> (Fashion activist, USA)

This activist's point is that marginality can be used in strategic, *creative* ways to influence the rules of the game and the way they are reproduced by the dominant players. As a caveat, this is but one example of an optimally marginal strategy, and there are bound to be many others that take different forms across the prefigurative field, but this attitude was common across many interviews.

Again, this approach shares marked similarities with visionary pragmatism and radical incrementalism. Indeed, in many ways they are constituent parts of an overlapping strategy. What it adds, though, is a firm belief that we should focus our attention not on neo-liberalism's 'flanks of vulnerability' (Peck and Tickell, 2002, p.77), but on how it is possible to bring into being radical transmutations of its core. Activists and movements may offer broad critiques of neo-liberalism, for example, while at the same time working within the broader neo-liberal discourses and agendas in which they are inevitably embedded; such approaches and strategies are tools for prefigurative projects, at least in the short-term.[1]

Finally, we see creative similarities between our interviewees' political strategy and the kind of 'postcapitalism as an everyday politics' (Healy et al., 2018) that Gibson-Graham (1996, 2006), argued for in their now formative feminist economics texts *The End of Capitalism (As We Knew It)* and *A Postcapitalist Politics*. Gibson-Graham's work contained ground-breaking arguments for how we might rethink and reinvision alternative economies and, as noted in Chapter 2, Gibson continues this approach in recent col-laborations. Much of this work focuses on the proliferation of economic alternatives and practices that include the kinds of movements and practices we write about here, but Gibson-Graham also emphasizes a caring agency that involves deliberately motivated caring actions. These actions, and the everyday politics of alternatives that sustain them, aim to traverse the human–non-human nexus without blurring it into meaningless distinction. This is a similar approach to that of the Australian ecofeminist Val Plumwood (2002), who also wrote about the importance of embracing and caring for the marginalized, including the non-human. This combination of care as a virtue in the development of prefigurative economic alternatives is undoubtedly strategic. Indeed, drawing on feminist geographies and political ecology, Graddy-Lovelace (2018) insists, a broad landscape of care frame-work discloses the matrix of human and beyond-human care. Put simply, the work of care involves an active focus virtue, as much as how that virtue informs the choice of strategy action, and the prefigurative vision of 'a post

---

[1] See also McCarthy (2006) for a great analysis of this point by way of community forestry in British Columbia and the United States.

capitalism of everyday politics'. In many ways this should be unsurprising. Feminist theory and practice has always been focused on problematizing false or arbitrary boundaries, even while emphasizing care as a virtue (see Puig de la Bellacasa, 2017).

This relationship between care as a virtue and as a strategy is crucial. Recognizing care as a distinct prefigurative strategy does not mean that we dismiss the analytic boundary between virtue and strategy. It does, however, emphasize the need to recognize the ways in which the boundary is porous—and useful—in practice. At the same time, to conflate virtue and strategy—as the bulk of academic scholarship tends to do—creates problems both analytically and for practice. It makes invisible the possibilities for reformulating what it means to do prefigurative politics that are enabled only by engaging with the resonance and dissonance between them. Even though they are necessarily wielded relationally, they are analytically inequivalent and irreconcilable. Prefigurative scholarship that equates virtue and strategy and, therefore—as history shows—will likely focus its attention on strategy to the analytic exclusion of virtue, will lead to normative arguments for particular strategies and approaches that are ultimately suboptimal when used in practice. This focus on the caring strategies inherent in a 'postcapitalism as everyday politics' makes clear that for prefigurative scholarship to contribute to a vision of transformative social change, prefigurative virtues and prefigurative strategies must be seen as coexistent, co-dependent and mutually reinforcing. And, crucially, doing so acknowledges the *whole* everyday experience of the ongoing struggle that is prefigurative practice, as we have learned from the activists we have interviewed.

## Strategy, Experimentation, and Scale

At the core of each of these different prefigurative approaches is an important commitment to experimentation *as strategy*. Indeed, many others—including Yates (2015), Dixon (2014), Maeckelbergh (2011), and Wright (2010)—have argued that experimentation is a key component of prefiguration. In many ways a measure of experimentation is inescapable due to the messy and heavily context-dependent nature of the socio-economic system. Strategies that *embrace* experimentation, in contrast, are born both from a deliberate humility and boldness in the face of discomfort. They recognize that, as one activist put it:

> There's real insight in those Chumbawamba lyrics 'I get knocked down, but I get up again, you're never gonna keep me down'...that's what our reality

is. In truth, most of the time getting knocked down is probably my own
fault, ... for not thinking things through, but that's fine, you're still not gonna
keep me down.                                              (Energy activist, UK)

Crucially, then, prefigurative experimentation is a necessity for strategies that
are iterative, incremental, and pragmatic, constantly searching for opportuni-
ities to transform the system in the ever-fluid present. Put simply, prefigurative
politics is inescapably experimental. Or, as Wright (2010, p.373) notes, 'the
struggle ... forward ... is an experimental process in which we continually test
and retest the limits of possibility and try, as best we can, to create new
institutions that will expand those limits themselves'. The key point here is
that how a particular collectivity of sustainable materialist activists approach
system change depends entirely on context; indeed, Wright argues that different transformative strategies must be used with a 'flexible strategic pluralism' (Wright, 2010, p.371). We see such flexibility and pluralism across the
countries and sectors of this study.

One of our observations here is that inherent to a politics that is both
alienated from traditional political action and engaged in incremental and
iterative experimentation is a redefinition of the scale or focus of the problems
it addresses downward towards the everyday and the material. This focus has
allowed for more engaged and effective experimentation in both a macro and
micro sense. As Weick (1984, p.40) notes, the 'reformulation of social issues as
mere problems allows for a strategy of small wins wherein a series of concrete,
complete outcomes of moderate importance build a pattern that attracts allies
and deters opponents'. So, at the micro level, activists *affectively* like small
wins and an everyday living of values: such practices and victories 'feel nice',
as one participant noted. And, crucially, they offer a counterbalance to the
discomfort inherent in prefigurativism, providing a safety valve for activists
so that they can, in at least one sense, feel satisfaction in the success of a
given project. This safety valve, the occasional feeling of success or victory, is
crucial to maintaining momentum for the movements we have examined,
enabling experimentation and more effective interventions. The rescaling
and materializing of concerns about broad social problems resonates with a
systems consciousness while simultaneously giving people ways to act that
have practical purchase and impact. This combination of focus, engagement,
success—and connection—is empowering. As one activist noted:

small wins don't have to be isolated wins. The value of [this network] to me is
that I am connected to others doing similar work, chipping away at their own
individual projects. But, if I couldn't see what they were doing I would be

lost...lost and I would feel that I had to do it all myself...which is endlessly daunting.                                                                (Food activist, Australia)

At the macro level, redefining the scale of a specific prefigurative project resonates with the core ally-winning *pragmatic* objective espoused by our participants. As Hopkins (2014) notes, a key strategy of the transition movement is to reach beyond the bubble of immediate issues and networks to engage with others—that is the link between local action, transition, and system transformation. Experimentation, and local projects in a networked context, can achieve this end, and become a kind of 'gateway drug'. In this strategic, iterative process, small wins, within a broader systems framework, bring activists to embrace and develop the capacity to 'think big' and extend networks, impacts, replication, and scale.

Ultimately, sustainable materialism is like many other prefigurative struggles. As Wright suggests, prefigurative strategies present 'a rough map' (2010, p.371)—of *systemic* transformation that will not be without its constant challenges and inevitable mistakes. But he thinks it unlikely—as do we and most, if not all, of our participants—that 'a system without contradictions, without destructive unintended consequences of individual and collective action, [in short] a system in self-sustaining emancipatory equilibrium' is possible (Wright, 2010, p.370). In many ways irresolution is *the* resolution. The work that sustainable materialist activists do to achieve systems change will always be iterative, incremental, and pragmatic, constantly searching for opportunities in the ever-fluid present, constantly responding to forces of power that seek to subvert the new alternatives it produces. As a reflexive mode of political action, these contradictions and unintended consequences are a fecund nexus for developing effective and ethical strategies to reformulate the way that social systems are organized to deliver the basic goods of life.

Most importantly, the argument presented in this book has aimed to emphasize that examining and engaging the perspectives of movement actors *themselves* enables us to more accurately theorize the space between 'actually existing neoliberalism' (Brenner and Theodore, 2002) and 'actually existing radicalism' (Sbicca, 2014) as a site of transformative possibility, nonetheless grounded in the unavoidable incrementalism of social change. Again, the key point here is that activists regularly and self-reflexively acknowledge the contradictions and tensions at the heart of their practice, as is clearly seen in the primary data presented throughout this book. We cannot therefore accept broad theoretical arguments that are blind to the many shades of prefigurative practice being attempted, and to those reflections on such experiments. As Levkoe (2011, p.700) aptly notes 'the struggle is not all or nothing', so our theories must adapt to this reality of experimentation around alternative material systems and relationships in various sectors. And, crucially, engaging with activist perspectives themselves is a necessary part of this undertaking.

## Differences in Sustainable Materialism Across Countries and Movements

As we stated at the outset, while this study engaged with activists across three countries and three sectors, it was not meant to be a *comparative* study. Rather, the goal has always been to explore the similarities in political motivations and frameworks for activists and movements focused on new and sustainable material flows in the US, the UK, and Australia; the point has been to develop an initial theoretical framework with which to understand such collective action. Across food, energy, and fashion, we actively sought out participants who were pressing forward with these new forms of material action, often having made connections with them through classic snowball sampling of scholar activist colleagues, and then the initial interviewees, knowing in advance that our participants embodied many of the developments we were interested to explore. We fully acknowledge, of course, that this presents a certain selection bias, though the point was to understand, in particular, this kind of activism distinct from other forms. Still, we have gone to significant lengths to ameliorate any particular selection bias in the broader analysis and presentation of our findings.

Perhaps unsurprisingly, given the countries we examined, the findings of this study were largely geographically homogeneous. Across the US, the UK, and Australia we found that sustainable materialist activists were uniformly motivated by theoretical frames that we have presented in this text. There is, of course, a range of economic, cultural and social similarities that helps explain this homogeneity. All three countries are Western liberal democracies with Anglo-Saxon roots; two of the three are settler colonial countries—and the third a major colonizer. More specifically, as Dryzek et al. (2003) have previously shown, the environmental movements in these countries share similar roots and have similar trajectories. In particular, they emphasized that the shape and fortunes of environmentalism are heavily influenced by the state's orientation to political participation by civil society, which can feature inclusion or exclusion, and be more or less passive or active. While we have not explored the role of the state actively here, Dryzek et al.'s (2003) framework helps to explain some of the political similarities we find.

While we have laid out the clear similarities in the motivations, virtues, and strategies across the hundred activists we interviewed as part of this project, it is also worth considering, in closing, some of the key differences across both the geographic contexts and the different movements we examined—in food, energy, and fashion. We have outlined, from a particular sample of activists, a new framework to explore the concept of sustainable materialism in both theory and practice. The framework is an invitation to empirical researchers to test and retest our findings, to pull and twist at the edges of what we have outlined, and to suggest amendments and additions that help explain these forms of material activism in different places, spaces, and temporalities. For example, and as noted in Chapter 2, we expect that if we had included participants from southern Europe we would have likely seen more focus on austerity which could have added an additional theoretical motivation around economic justice and self-determination, a point which has empirical grounding in work that has focused on similar movements in that region (D'Alisa et al., 2015; Giugni and Grasso, 2016; Kousis and Paschou, 2017).

In our own reflections as well, there are some particular variations across place and sector worth emphasizing. First, given the rampant monopolization of the food and energy industries in Australia, which is highly politicized and receives significant media attention, our Australian participants undoubtedly mentioned the economic concentration of power more than their counterparts in the UK and the USA. This manifested in an awareness of power relationships, their connection to rising inequality and reducing levels of meaningful political control and participation. Second, while the concern for justice, broadly and pluralistically defined, was universal across those we spoke to, we found a greater attentiveness to issues of environmental justice among our USA participants, particularly as it related to issues of race and class. Again, this is perhaps unsurprising, given the roots of the environmental justice movement in the USA (Agyeman et al., 2016) but, as is clear from the quotes we presented in Chapter 3, is borne out in the way that US-based sustainable materialists use environmental justice as a connective tissue to bind their other motivations and concerns. Third, while we mention differences between countries, it is also crucial to note, and to further explore, the differences within each as well. For example, there is a split between urbanites and rural folk that deserves more empirical investigation, particularly around food, and around how different conceptualizations of place within movements shape how they are motivated by a vibrant conceptualization of sustainability.

In terms of the differences between different domains—food, energy, and fashion—we identified a number of key distinctions. First, unlike the food and fashion domains, there is limited discussion of the role of the *body* in the critique of existing material flows and the creation of new ones by those involved in sustainable energy activism. We suggest, as did many activists to whom we posed the question, that this may be due to the physical distance between the material product that is energy and the body—itself an indication of the relatively privileged status of community energy activists in the US, the UK, and Australia, distinct from the people who bear the brunt of the physical impacts of fossil fuel mining, transport, refining, and burning. Of course, the entanglement with activist bodies still exists, but for the energy activists we interviewed, this physicality is relatively further removed or disembodied than it is in the food or fashion sectors.

A second difference we found is that those activists in sustainable fashion were, in general, most hyper-aware of the systemic nature of their practice and activism. They understood, and routinely articulated, how individual practices of primary production, design, manufacture, transport, and distribution contribute to unsustainable fashion *systems* just as much as they believed their own work—only ever a small piece of the puzzle—contributed to building new material mega-circulatory structures to displace the mainstream fashion industry. Tracing the history of this systems consciousness, it would be remiss not to reflect on the Rana Plaza disaster, which has enduring affect and was mentioned spontaneously by all but one of our fashion interviewees. Rana is referenced most often as a focal point for understanding how different pieces of the supply chain—'the system'—come together, but also as a case in point as to why social and environmental justice concerns should be inseparable in the sustainable fashion movement.

The third interesting distinction between the three sectors is that we found food activists to be the most actively concerned with the idea and practice of community. On the one hand, this is likely because eating is a communal act; but we also had numerous conversations about the social nature of farmers markets, local stores and cafés, food sharing, and social enterprise. While sustainable fashion and community energy advocates often expressed a concern with community, there were groups where community was less about being involved in projects as participants, and more about community as the result or beneficiary of the public good it produced.

In all of this, we simply point out some of the ongoing work to be done in the broader examination of sustainable materialism and its associated movements. In addition to these initial limitations with regard to geographic location, and to sectoral differences around issues of bodies, systems, and communities, more work needs to be done around the intersectoral overlaps and engagements. Many activists we interviewed clearly recognize that there are links between the domains in which they work and the larger systems and flows through communities; this was particularly the case among food and sustainable fashion activists. We also found almost uniformly in these two domains that activists engaged in cross-domain participation and learning about what worked, and often mirrored slogans such as 'you are what you eat' and 'you are what you wear', as well as 'farm to table' and 'field to hanger'. Coming back to our earlier discussion of system change, more can be done here on the entanglements and coordination issues surrounding various sustainable materialist sectors and efforts.

## Limitations, Critiques, and Challenges

All of that assumes a value to this kind of approach, and to such movements' ability to engage with real and sustained change. Not all of our associates in the academy agree. At various points in this project, both at conferences and in conversations with colleagues, we have been accused of romanticizing the potential of sustainable materialism to achieve its stated aims and objectives. Plainly, while admitting the core challenges and the power of the status quo, we disagree with this kneejerk rejection, and suggest that our discussion of the prefigurative virtues and strategies that underpin this politics shows without question that sustainable materialists are self-aware, self-reflexive, and deeply committed to a pragmatism that tackles head on the realities of a complex, messy, and often-violent world. That said, it would be remiss of us not to discuss some of the key limitations of this approach here.

First, there is a significant risk that, as sustainable materialist solutions take root, become financially self-sustaining, and expand across or beyond particular places, they are co-opted or acquired by more powerful—likely capitalist—interests. This trajectory is not purely hypothetical. There are numerous examples of where niche innovations in environmental sustainability have been co-opted by powerful interests (Smith, 2006; Bergman et al., 2010). The history of the 'organic' food label is a case in point. What began as a grassroots movement, became a business as the discursive power of the organic label grew. Similarly, the US food retailer Whole Foods Market, once a niche food business focused on organics, was recently acquired by Amazon, a company deeply enmeshed in systems of injustice and oppression, in particular around labour practices, that the sustainable materialist movement seeks to subvert.

The reality of the modern economic system is that dominant interests seek to acquire challengers as they grow and scale, and sustainable materialist activists will need to plan for this reality as they embed alternatives in the mainstream. Again, though, this risk of co-optation is in many ways driven by a relentless focus on scaling-up as a goal for the movement. We suggest this focus is displaced. Just as Young (1990) famously suggested that merit is an ideology that serves those in power, the focus on scaling alternatives has become its own ideology that does little to actually serve the interests of those attempting to change the system. As we argued in Chapter 4, many sustainable materialist activists see replication, rather than scale, as the ultimate goal of their political project; such a focus on scaling-out rather than scaling-up is also becoming a strategy of other progressive movements, including radical municipalism (Roth and Russell, 2018). Energy is a particularly generative example here: our interviewees in this domain almost uniformly emphasized the importance of distributed, community-owned, and *replicable* models of sustainable energy production and distribution. These alternatives are real and are taking root, and while we should be aware of their challenges in the face of immense power, it is deeply disingenuous and disempowering to simply write them off as romantic and inconsequential projects with little chance of success, based on a problematic assumption of scaling-up.

Second, we have been regularly challenged on whether the stated values and motivations of sustainable materialist activists that we discuss here actually align with their everyday practices. Are they as committed to social and environmental justice as they say they are? Do they really pay attention to all aspects of a supply chain? While activists say they are motivated by more inclusive participation in the political sphere, do their internal governance structures live up to this ideal? Does attention to the vitality of the non-human really come into everyday practices and processes? Where is the proof? These are of course important questions, and the gap between stated motivations and practices is well established in the environmental behaviours literature (Kollmuss and Agyeman, 2002). We recognize that a disconnect between ideal and practice is a reality, and that individual activists have complex lives—as do movement organizations—but critics often set an insurmountably high bar with this sort of challenge. Motivations matter, as does the work that activists do, reflexively, to see those motivations made real in their organizations and their own lives. On the one hand, our focus is on the stated motivations and ideals of these sustainable materialist activists; the point is to understand those motivations and ideals, as reported by our interviewees. Admittedly, we are not examining the actual practices and outcomes of these movements, and so cannot report on the consistency, or inconsistency, between what we were told and how organizations actually act. At the same time though, perfection is not possible, and we have to be careful about the standards by which we judge political practice. Explicit hypocrisy is one thing; authentic, if incomplete, efforts are quite another. Both of us, for example, seek to practice everyday lives and consumptive practices that align with the sustainable materialist values we have learned over the course of this project. As academics living in Australia, however, we also occasionally fly to conferences, a practice that undoubtedly results in significant environmental harms. Our participants live similarly mixed and non-ideal lives.

The point is that this activism has not failed when it is unable to meet the incredibly high bar of fully sustainable materialist lives. Instead, reflexivity is key, as is being able to think strategically about how best to bring about mega-circulatory systems change, both of which are characteristics we have shown to be common across our participants. More simply, though, it does not take much work to look beyond the motivations we cite here to see the practical work that sustainable materialists are doing across the world—from new urban agriculture systems in Detroit, to community energy generation in Hepburn, Australia that serves 8,000 homes, to small fashion designers in the UK banding together to support the production of sustainable cotton and sustainable livelihoods in India. At a certain point, even academics have to accept the positive impact of such real experiments. It is not that pessimism does not have its place, but that it should be subsumed within the pragmatic valence necessary to bring about visionary change. The reality of these alternatives speaks volumes—only one of which we have written here.

Third, while we have argued throughout this book that the power and possibility of sustainable materialism is underpinned by its commitment to system change, institutional, governance and funding concerns often necessitate that groups shy away from collaboration. The risk here is the production of a siloed mentality that is antithetical to the broader sustainable materialist cause. There is truth in the well-worn saying 'divide and conquer'. While different parts of an alternative system are barricaded away from the others, they will never replace the existing one. Existing systems are resilient and antifragile (Taleb, 2012), they require substantial perturbation to shift their dynamics towards more just and sustainable futures. The challenge here is that, while siloes are bad for systems change, they are, at times, necessary due to a range of structural considerations that sustainable materialists must attend to if they are to remain viable in the current system. Activists we spoke to realize this tension, and we suggest that this awareness is a key part of mitigating the risks associated with a siloed mentality. As we argued in Chapter 6, sustainable materialists' commitment to systems consciousness is necessary to maintain the focus on mega-circulatory change. This must be an active disposition; while many people think they are good systems thinkers, many simply are not. Most members of the public have a perceptive bias towards linear causality (Sterman, 1994), which presents a problem for theorizing, let alone changing, the social world in and for systems.

Finally, collaboration with local government is often necessary to achieve place-based systems change and to help movements grow and replicate (Ornetzeder and Rohracher, 2013; Feola and Nunes, 2014). We spoke to many activists who were initially drawn to sustainable materialist work, in part through the kind of fatigue with traditional politics we laid out in Chapter 2, and yet they soon realized that they needed to engage in political processes at the local level to re-zone lots for farmers markets, or get access to rooftops for community solar. This kind of work presents a number of risks and challenges. Local government is complex, and regulatory structures differ widely across contexts. On the one hand, activists risk losing their activist streak as they are forced to work within structures that have worked—or been used—to bring about the unsustainable present. On the other, local government is often spoken about as a key ally in bringing about place-based change; many of the activists we interviewed talk about the important support they get from their city governments. This kind of help is important, and we must be realistic about the fact that groups and individuals that cannot achieve sustained change often face burnout and/or failure. Again, the activists we spoke to about these risks were acutely aware of them. The decision to collaborate with government actors is not made without careful consideration and, more often than not, groups see these kinds of collaborations as a form of visionary pragmatism that carefully uses the tools of the state to recreate it from within. Indeed, it would be a worthwhile project to combine the efforts towards institutionalizing the sustainable materialism we address here with concurrent endeavours towards more radical and inclusive urbanism or municipalism, as we suggest below.

## Future Areas of Inquiry

Finally, and with not a hint of irony, this is just the beginning. From inception to point of publication, this project has taken about seven years—years spent thinking, cajoling, conversing and debating about the shape and contours of this growing materialist form of environmental politics. There is, however, much more work to be done. Our focus in this book has been to outline a new theory and practice of sustainable materialism; we have also, where possible, sought to link this work to that of others working in similar spaces. A lot can happen in seven years, though, and in that time there has been a clear explosion in the popularity and application of a wide range of sustainable materialist practices. In academic inquiry as well, there have been wide ranging efforts to interrogate these developments from different perspectives, in different disciplines, and to different ends. Sustainable materialism is now a broad and pluralistic field of practice and evaluation, and there remains significant scope for future academic exploration that tackles different empirical questions, and connects the theoretical framework outlined here to other areas of inquiry. In particular, we see a number of particularly generative areas for future work.

First, there is scope to explore how sustainable materialism is connected to the emergence of nature-based solutions to the inevitable experience of climate change in the world's cities. Nature-based solutions use the natural properties of ecosystems to achieve positive system change. They have the potential to limit impacts of climate change, enhance biodiversity and improve environmental quality while contributing to economic activities and social well-being. Examples are green roofs and city parks that limit heat stress, city lagoons that store water, and permeable surfaces, vegetation and rain gardens to intercept storm water. Yet despite their significant potential, the use of such nature-based solutions for adaptation and resilience remains marginal, fragmented, and highly uneven within and between cities (Edwards and Bulkeley, 2018; Romero-Lankao et al., 2018). This is a growing area in studies of urbanization and sustainability, but, to date, its proponents tend to leave out the intersections of such environmental solutions and the experiences of everyday life. There are a number of connections between nature-based solutions and sustainable materialism that could be explored: How might sustainable materialist practices embrace or contribute to nature-based solutions? How could nature-based solutions be incorporated as part of different alternative material flows levied by sustainable materialist activists and processes? As noted above, these questions are particularly pertinent given the rise in interest in new municipalism, with cities being heralded as the new hope in driving social and economic transformation. A sustainable materialist approach to nature-based solutions could be based in new and radical municipal models of public participation and inclusion.

Second, following from activists' concern with the sustainability and ecological flows of their local environments, there is value in a further explanation of the lines between sustainable materialism and attachment to place. Place attachment is understood as the bond between people and the places they live, prompting examinations of the role of physical places in individual and community identity (Manzo and Devine-Wright, 2013). This bond is emotionally constituted through place-based experiences, and its basis in subjective memories and understandings means that place attachment can be highly complex (Manzo and Devine-Wright, 2013). It is perhaps this complexity that has resulted in an abundance of research that focuses primarily on physical disruptions to place, neglecting the 'psychological, symbolic, and particularly emotional aspects of healthy human habitats' (Agyeman et al., 2009, p.509). This focus on place attachment could be a clear and important response to environmental injustice; there, community concerns are often about the damage being done to place, and so to identity, health, and community. On the contrary, sustainable materialism can help build a more positive and constructive relationship with place, rewriting the meaning of living in a particular place (Schlosberg, Rickards, and Byrne, 2017). We see this, for example, in the way that attention to food systems has been revitalizing neighbourhoods, environments, and economies in Detroit—long a victim of both social and environmental injustices. All sustainable materialist practices occur, and are rooted, in a particular place. How they sustain or forge new connections to and between individuals, collectives, and the places they inhabit is a potentially fertile area of inquiry.

Third, there is much more work to be done to explore the theoretical and empirical links between sustainable materialism and just sustainabilities (Agyeman, 2013). Just sustainabilities can be thought of as an infusion of ideas of equity and justice into a discourse whose sole focus at that time was on environmental sustainability. The argument, put simply, was 'sustainability cannot be simply a "green", or "environmental" concern, important though "environmental" aspects of sustainability are. A truly sustainable society is one where wider questions of social needs and welfare, and economic opportunity are integrally related to environmental limits imposed by supporting ecosystems' (Agyeman et al., 2016, p.326). There are obvious overlaps here with the theoretical argument that we have advanced and, in many ways, just sustainabilities could operate an alternative frame for theorizing the discourses arising from many of these movements. More theoretical work could be done to understand how sustainable materialism itself is a pluralistic moniker and theoretical corpus, similar to Schlosberg's (1999b) evaluation of environmentalism. We have provided one explanation of this intersection, but there are, of course, many other ways of understanding this relationship between sustainability, justice, and material practice that are possible and indeed likely.

Fourth, while it has not been our focus here, there is more empirical work needed on the emergence, shape, form, and structure of sustainable materialist practices and collectives outside of the wealthy and (over)industrialized countries we have explored here. We know from the work of scholars like Shiva (2007, 2008) and Esteva and Prakash (2013) that there are many such movements long established in the global South. Sustainable materialism is, for many, simply a way of life. Are there differences in motivations, strategies, values, and virtues from what we have described here? And, if so, what are they? How can they be explained? We think it reasonable to assume that the contours of the sustainable materialism we have explored here will not perfectly intersect with the experience of activists everywhere. However, there will clearly be overlaps in both conceptions of resistance and practices of reconstruction, and we would advise against forcing a false distinction where one may not exist. The experience of Guha and Martinez-Alier (1997) should be front of mind in this endeavour: while many assumed that those in poor countries could not have postmaterial environmental values, Guha and Martinez-Alier made clear that the singular distinction between the 'environmentalism of the rich' and an 'environmentalism of the poor' is quite complex, and the reality of the latter illustrated a mistaken assumption at the heart of postmaterialism. How a sustainable materialist approach fits with various environmentalisms of the poor, and environmentalisms in the global South, is, of course, an open question, but one that deserves further examination.

Next, we have limited our work here to three key sectors, but there is much work to be done exploring sustainable materialism—theoretically, empirically, comparatively—in other domains and industries. We see across a whole range of areas beyond food, energy, and fashion, the growing recognition of, and immersion in, the material relationships we have with the resources we use, and the transformation of means of production that have been both alienating and unsustainable. There is a range of possibilities here, from alternative currencies, financing and slow money, to transport, to greening cities, to crafting and maker movements. Crafting and making is a growing, and particularly generative, case. There are growing craft/arts markets in many cities, from long-standing ones in the Pacific Northwest of the US, to newer mobile markets like Finders Keepers in Australia. Crafters have also created broad online communities and markets, such as the niche and ecologically oriented group on the larger online marketplace Etsy, or alternatives like ArtFire or Zibbet. Here, becoming or supporting crafters using local labour and sustainable materials, or bringing the handmade back into everyday life, are simultaneously acts of individual resistance and institutional reconstruction (see, for example, Payne, 2011; Anderson, 2012; Matchar, 2013). Similarly, this focus on re-engaging material relationships in the provision of everyday life is complemented by the evolution of a movement of open source programmers, tech modders, and makers focused on DIY technologies and communities—illustrated, for example at Maker Faires that began in the San Francisco Bay Area. Here, the focus is on the alienation of technology, and yet it shares sustainable materialism's interest in unplugging from the mega-circulations of global capitalism, and the importance of creating alternative flows that keep materials, making, and repairing at the personal and community level.

Finally, we suggest that our discussion begs an unanswered normative question: what are the implications of sustainable materialist thought and practice for how we ought to remedy material injustices in the era of the Anthropocene, one of complex global economic and environmental disaster? In complex, entangled, and interconnected times, modern understandings of responsibility are insufficient. It is no longer possible to assign responsibility to redressing a singular injustice to the actor that brought it about. Not only are injustices multiple and interconnected, so to are the actions that give rise to them. Individual notions of attribution and blame that are so deeply enmeshed in liberal political thought will simply not work for an increasingly entangled world.

Instead, we need to move to a post-liberal playing field, one that instils a belief that we are capable of responding to material injustices without presuming to be sovereign over them (Lavin, 2008). Lavin makes clear in his grounding-breaking work *The Politics of Responsibility* that it is possible to champion the practical benefits of linear causality and individual responsibility (for politics and everyday life) while challenging its ontological commitments. A post-liberal ethic humbles us in forcing us to recognize our own situated, entangled existence, while simultaneously demanding a responsibility to, and for, that existence.[2] We suggest that the practices of sustainable

---

[2] Young (2006) makes a similar point about global justice and sweatshops, a body of work she was sadly unable to take to the point of conclusion.

materialism help to conceptualize a collective, shared, and post-liberal conceptualization of responsibility, justice, and the political. Many of our participants made passing comments that gestured in this direction, and while more work is needed to flesh out these contours, this project and the methodology we have used throughout presents a real opportunity to work *with* sustainable materialist activists to co-produce a normative theory of responsibility for the Anthropocene.

## On Possibility

Here at the end, the core point returns to where we started, with the claim that this book is about possibilities. For the activists we interviewed, more just and sustainable futures are possible, and it is those possibilities we return to as we conclude this book. These potential futures, alternative flows, and reconstructions of systems are real, flourishing, and multiple—and they are also embodied. To finish, we thought it fitting to return to the experiences of three women who were involved in this project as participants, but have since become our good friends; three women who deeply embody sustainable materialist thought and practice in their own lives, and who lead organizations that are at the forefront of breaking down systems of oppression and marginalization to bring about different futures. Each in their own way, as much as the organizations they lead, is proof that a different way is possible—an illustration of the reality and embeddedness of alternative and sustainable flows of material goods. First, Devita Davison, the Executive Director of FoodLab Detroit, an organization at the heart of the one of the world's largest alternative food economies, who loves to tell us that her work is not about food, it is about movement-building—building a movement that, with authority, can give shape to a future that sees power held in and for communities. Next, Kath Delmeny of Sustain, an alliance in the UK of 100 organizations at the national level and hundreds more at the local level, working towards a healthy, fair, and sustainable system for food, farming, and fishing, who said simply that the work of change is like climbing a mountain, though the view from the top will be clear and beautiful. And, finally, Leslie Lindo from the Business Alliance for Local Living Economies (BALLE), an American organization that represents thousands of communities and conveners, entrepreneurs, investors, and funders who are defying business as usual, who told us that none of this is going to be easy, but with 'just enough hurt and enough hope and enough unity and enough struggle' something else is possible. It *is* possible, and these women represent the kind of intrusion and cataclysmic touch necessary to make new, empowered, sustainable material systems.

Our choice to reference a novelist in the introduction to this work was a deliberate one. Both of us, and perhaps many of you, gravitate towards fiction, speculative fiction, or science fiction as a way of practicing the future together. The same is true of our participants, who are practicing a future economy, building and practicing social, environmental, economic justice, living into being new stories and ways of life. Sustainable materialists, across the world, have embraced not only the possibility, but also the responsibility—ethical, political, material—of building a new world, paying attention to what emerges from the cataclysmic overlap between the old and the new. Again, none of this is easy, but the work of sustainable materialism is creating alternatives that focus on critical connections instead of critical mass. It is about focusing on alternatives that spur on creative and compassionate systems that cannot be ignored—that make, as one of our participants put it, 'the alternative irresistible'.

The alternatives that we have discussed throughout this book are real, and they are happening right now. But the prefigurative politics of sustainable materialism is also about illuminating other possible futures, just as the work of some of our favourite speculative novelists is to spark the imagination of readers to help them envision alternatives to our own broken world (see, for example, the Octavia Butler Legacy Network). The sustainable materialists we have referenced throughout this work illustrate in a very real way that alternative practices, counterflows, and new and completely different material relationships with each other and the non-human realm are imaginable and possible—just as possible as our current reality. Their collective practice is an anthology of compelling and irresistible stories that show the power of a material vision for building more sustainable futures. They invite us all to write ourselves into that future, naming the principles of inclusion, justice, and sustainability, and building an economy in which power is empowering—a future in which we can practice, in all the ways that are possible, the world we want to see and be.

# About the Authors

**David Schlosberg** is Professor of Environmental Politics in the Department of Government and International Relations, Payne-Scott Professor, and Director of the Sydney Environment Institute at the University of Sydney. His main research interests are in environmental and climate justice, food justice, climate adaptation and resilience, and environmental movements and the practices of everyday life. His authored, co-authored, or co-edited books include *Environmental Justice and the New Pluralism, New States and Social Movements, Defining Environmental Justice, The Oxford Handbook of Climate Change and Society, The Climate-Challenged Society,* and *The Oxford Handbook of Environmental Political Theory*—all with Oxford University Press. His work has been funded by the US National Science Foundation and the Australian Research Council. He has been a visiting scholar at the London School of Economics, Australian National University, Princeton University, University of Washington, and UC Santa Cruz, amongst others.

**Luke Craven** is a Research Fellow in the Public Service Research Group at the University of New South Wales, Canberra. His research focuses on developing new tools to understand and address complex policy challenges. He works with a range of public sector organizations to adapt and apply systems frameworks to support policy design, implementation, and evaluation. He is known for developing the System Effects methodology, which is widely used to analyse complex causal relationships in participatory and qualitative data. He is also involved in a number of collaborative projects that are developing innovative solutions to complex policy challenges, which includes work focused on food insecurity, health inequality, and climate resilience. He holds a PhD in Political Science at the University of Sydney, where he remains affiliated with the Sydney Environment Institute and the Charles Perkins Centre.

# Bibliography

Abrahamsson, S., Bertoni, F., Mol, A., and Martin, R. I. 2015. 'Living with Omega-3: New Materialism and Enduring Concerns', *Environment and Planning D: Society and Space*, 33, 4–19.

Abramsky, K. 2010. *Sparking a Worldwide Energy Revolution: Social Struggles in the Transition to a Post-Petrol World*. Oakland, CA: AK Press.

Agyeman, J. 2013. *Introducing Just Sustainability: Policy, Planning, and Practice*. London: Zed Books.

Agyeman, J., Bullard, R. D., and Evans, B. (eds.) 2003. *Just Sustainabilities: Development in an Unequal World*. Cambridge, MA: MIT Press.

Agyeman, J., Devine-Wright, P., and Prange, J. 2009. 'Close to the Edge, Down by the River? Joining up Managed Retreat and Place Attachment in a Climate Changed World', *Environment and Planning A*, 41: 509–513.

Agyeman, J., Schlosberg, D., Craven, L., and Matthews, C. 2016. 'Trends and Directions in Environmental Justice: From Inequity to Everyday Life, Community, and Just Sustainabilities', *The Annual Review of Environment and Resources*, 41, 321–340.

Ahmed, S. 2004. *The Cultural Politics of Emotion*. New York: Routledge.

Ahmed, S. 2014. *Willful Subjects*. Raleigh, NC: Duke University Press.

Aiken, J. T. 2017. 'The Politics of Community: Togetherness, Transition and Post-Politics', *Environment and Planning A*, 49, 2383–401.

Alaimo, S., and Hekman, S. 2008. *Material Feminisms*. Bloomington, IN: Indiana University Press.

Alkon, A. H. 2014. 'Food Justice and the Challenge to Neoliberalism', *Gastronomica: The Journal of Critical Food Studies*, 14, 27–40.

Alkon, A. H. and Agyeman, J. (eds.) 2011. *Cultivating Food Justice: Race, Class, and Sustainability*. Cambridge, MA: MIT Press.

Alkon, A. H. and Guthman, J. 2017. *The New Food Activism: Opposition, Cooperation, and Collective Action*. Oakland, CA: University of California Press.

Anderson, B. 1983. *Imagined Communities*. London: Verso.

Anderson, C. 2012. *Makers: The New Industrial Revolution*. New York: Crown Business.

Andrée, P., Ayres, J., Bosia, M. J., and Massicotte, M. J. (eds.) 2014. *Globalization and Food Sovereignty: Global and Local Change in the New Politics of Food*. Toronto: University of Toronto Press.

Andrée, P., Ballamingie, P., and Sinclair-Waters, B. 2015. 'Neoliberalism and the Making of Food Politics in Eastern Ontario', *Local Environment*, 20, 1452–72.

Australian Bureau of Statistics. 2016. Australian Demographic Statistics. http://www.abs.gov.au/Population (accessed 28 September 2018).

Barad, K. 2007. *Meeting the Universe Halfway: Quantum Physics and the Entanglement of Matter and Meaning*. Durham, NC: Duke University Press.

Barry, J. 2012. *The Politics of Actually Existing Unsustainably: Human Flourishing in a Climate-Changed, Carbon-Constrained World*. Oxford: Oxford University Press.

Beausoleil, E. 2014. 'The Politics, Science, and Art of Receptivity', *Ethics & Global Politics*, 7, 19–40.

Beck, U. 1997. *The Reinvention of Politics: Rethinking Modernity in the Global Social Order*. Oxford: Polity.

Bennett, J. 2010. *Vibrant Matter: A Political Ecology of Things*. Raleigh, NC: Duke University Press.

Bergman, N., Markusson, N., Connor, P., Middlemiss, L., and Ricci, M. 2010. 'Bottom-up, Social Innovation For Addressing Climate Change', Sussex Energy Group Conference— ECEEE, 25–26 February. Brighton, Sussex, UK.

Berry, W. 2010. *What Are People For?* Berkeley, CA: Counterpoint Press.

Bevington, D. and Dixon, C. 2005. 'Movement-Relevant Theory: Rethinking Social Movement Scholarship And Activism', *Social Movement Studies*, 4, 185–208.

Bickford, S. 1996. *The Dissonance of Democracy: Listening, Conflict, and Citizenship*. Ithaca, NY: Cornell University Press.

Blühdorn, I. 2013. 'The Governance of Unsustainability: Ecology and Democracy after the Post-Democratic Turn', *Environmental Politics*, 22, 16–36.

Blühdorn, I. 2014. 'Post-ecologist Governmentality: Post-democracy, Post-politics and the Politics of Unsustainability', in Wilson, J. (ed.) *Post-Political and its Discontents: Spaces of Depoliticisation, Spectres of Radical Politics*. Edinburgh: Edinburgh University Press.

Blühdorn, I. 2017. 'Post-Capitalism, Post-Growth, Post-Consumerism? Eco-Political Hopes Beyond Sustainability', *Global Discourse*, 7, 42–61.

Boggs, G. L. 1977. *Women and the Movement to Build a New America*. Detroit, MI: National Organization for an American Revolution.

Bomberg, E. and McEwan, N. 2012. 'Mobilizing Community Energy', *Energy Policy*, 51, 435–44.

Bonfiglio, O. 2012. 'Big Government and Big Corporations Befriend the Local Food Movement', *Energy Bulletin*. olgabonfiglio.blogspot.com/2012/02/big-government-and-big-corporations.html (accessed 17 May 2013).

Bosi, L. and Zamponi, L. 2015. 'Direct Social Actions and Economic Crises: The Relationship between Forms of Action and Socio-Economic Context in Italy', *Partecipazione e Conflitto*, 8, 367–91.

Botsman, R. and Rogers, R. 2010. *What's Mine Is Yours: The Rise of Collaborative Consumption*. New York: Harper Business.

Brafman, O. and Beckstrom, R. A. 2007. *The Starfish and the Spider: The Unstoppable Power of Leaderless Organization*. London: Penguin Books.

Breines, W. 1989. *Community and Organization in the New Left, 1962–1968: The Great Refusal*. New Brunswick, NJ: Rutgers University Press.

Brenner, N. and Theodore, N. 2002. 'Cities and the Geographies of "Actually Existing Neoliberalism"', *Antipode*, 34(3), 349–79.

Broad, G. M. 2016. *More Than Just Food: Food Justice and Community Change*. Oakland, CA: University of California Press.

Brown, W. 2015. *Undoing the Demos: Neoliberalism's Stealth Revolution*. Cambridge, MA: MIT Press.

Brundtland, G. 1987. *Our Common Future: Report of the 1987 World Commission on Environment and Development*. Oslo, Norway: United Nations.

Bullard, R. 1990. *Dumping in Dixie: Race, Class, and Environmental Quality*. Boulder, CO: Westview Press.

Bullard, R. (ed.) 1993. *Confronting Environmental Racism: Voices from the Grassroots*. Boston, MA: South End Press.

Carr, A. 2010. 'Detroit: The Business Of Urban Agriculture', The Boggs Blog [Online]. conversationsthatyouwillneverfinish.wordpress.com/2010/08/11/detroit-the-business-of-urban-agriculture.

Casey, E. 1993. *Getting Back into Place: Toward a Renewed Understanding of the Place World*. Bloomington, IN: Indiana University Press.

Casey, E. 1997. *The Fate of Place: A Philosophical History*. Berkeley, CA: University of California Press.

Chapman, J. 2004. *System Failure: Why Governments Must Learn to Think Differently*. London: Demos.

Chatterton, P. and Pickerill, J. 2010. 'Everyday Activism and Transitions Towards Post-Capitalist Worlds', *Transactions of the Institute of British Geographers*, 35, 475–90.

Chesters, G. 2012. 'Social Movements and the Ethics of Knowledge Production', *Social Movement Studies*, 11, 145–60.

Cohen, M. J., Brown, H. S., and Vergragt, P. 2013. *Innovations in Sustainable Consumption: New Economics, Socio-technical Transitions and Social Practices*. Cheltenham: Edward Elgar Publishing.

Coles, R. 2012. 'The Promise of Democratic Populism in the Face of Contemporary Power', *The Good Society*, 21, 177–93.

Coles, R. 2016. *Visionary Pragmatism: Radical and Ecological Democracy in Neoliberal Times*. Raleigh, NC: Duke University Press.

Coole, D. and Frost, S. 2010. *New Materialisms: Ontology, Agency, and Politics*. Durham, NC: Duke University Press.

Cornell, A. 2009. 'Anarchism and the Movement for a New Society: Direct Action and Prefigurative Community in the 1970s and 80s', *Perspectives on Anarchist Theory*, 12, 36–69.

Creamer, E., Eadson, W., van Veelen, B., Pinker, A., Tingey, M., Braunholtz-Speight, T., Markantoni, M., Foden, M., and Lacey-Barnacle, M. 2018. 'Community Energy: Entanglements of Community, State, and Private Sector', *Geography Compass*, 12, 1–16.

Crouch, C. 2004. *Post-democracy*. Cambridge: Polity Press.

Crouch, C. 2016. *Society and Social Change in 21st Century Europe*. London: Palgrave Macmillan.

D'Alisa, G., Forno, F., and Maurano, S. 2015. 'Grassroots (Economic) Activism in Times of Crisis: Mapping the Redundancy of Collective Actions', *Partecipazione e Conflitto* 8(2), 328–42.

de Moor, J. 2016. The Two-Dimensional Structure of Political Opportunities: A Quantitative and Mixed-Methods Analysis of the Effect of Political Opportunity Structures on Nonelectoral Participation. PhD Thesis, University of Antwerp.

Di Chiro, G. 2008. 'Living Environmentalisms: Coalition Politics, Social Reproduction, and Environmental Justice', *Environmental Politics*, 17, 276–98.

Di Chiro, G. 2010. 'Polluted Politics? Confronting Toxic Discourse, Sex Panic, and Eco-Normativity', in Mortimer-Sandilands, C. and Erickson, B. (eds.) *Queer Ecologies: Sex, Nature, Politics, Desire*. Bloomington, IN: Indiana University Press.

Delanty, G. 2003. *Community*. London: Routledge.

Della Porta, D. 2013. *Can Democracy Be Saved?: Participation, Deliberation and Social Movements*. Cambridge: Polity Press.

Dirlik, A. 1999. 'Place-based Imagination: Globalism and the Politics of Place', *Review*, 22, 151–87.

Dirlik, A. 2000. 'Place-based Imagination: Globalism and the Politics of Place', in Dirlik, A. (ed.) *Places and Politics in the Age of Globalization*. New York: Rowman and Littlefield.

Dixon, C. 2014. *Another Politics: Talking Across Today's Transformative Movements*. Berkeley, CA: University of California Press.

Dobernig, K. and Stagl, S. 2015. 'Growing a Lifestyle Movement? Exploring Identity-Work and Lifestyle Politics in Urban Food Cultivation', *International Journal of Consumer Studies*, 39, 452–8.

Dowie, M. 1995. *Losing Ground: American Environmentalism at the Close of the Twentieth Century*. Cambridge, MA: MIT Press.

Dryzek, J., and Pickering, J. 2019. *Politics of the Anthropocene*. Oxford: Oxford University Press.

Dryzek, J., Downes, D., Hunold, C., and Schlosberg, D. 2003. *Green States and Social Movements: Environmentalism in the United States, Britain, Germany, and Norway*. Oxford: Oxford University Press.

Dubuisson-Quellier, S. 2015. 'From Targets to Recruits: The Status of Consumers within the Political Consumption Movement', *International Journal of Consumer Studies*, 39, 404–12.

Dunlap, R. E. and York, R. 2008. 'The Globalization of Environmental Concern and the Limits of the Postmaterialist Values Explanation: Evidence from Four Multinational Surveys', *The Sociological Quarterly*, 49, 529–63.

DuPuis, E. M. and Goodman, D. 2005. 'Should We Go "Home" To Eat? Toward a Reflexive Politics of Localism', *Journal of Rural Studies*, 21, 359–71.

Edwards, G. A. S. and Bulkeley, H. 2018. 'Heterotopia and the Urban Politics of Climate Change Experimentation', *Environment and Planning D*: Society and Space, 36 (2), 350–69.

Edwards, G. A. S., Reid, L., and Hunter, C. 2016. 'Environmental Justice, Capabilities, and the Theorization of Well-Being', *Progress in Human Geography*, 40(6), 754–69.

Epstein, B. 1991. *Political Protest and Cultural Revolution*. Berkeley, CA: University of California Press.

Esteva, G. and Prakash, M. S. 2013. *Grassroots Post-Modernism: Remaking the Soil of Cultures*. London: Zed Books.

Eversberg, D. and Schmelzer, M. 2016. 'Critical Self-Reflection as a Path to Anti-Capitalism: The Degrowth-Movement', *Resilience*. https://www.resilience.org/stories/2016-02-24/critical-self-reflection-as-a-path-to-anti-capitalism-the-degrowth-movement/ (accessed 4 March 2019).

Feola, G. and Nunes, R. 2014. 'Success and Failure of Grassroots Innovations for Addressing Climate Change: The Case of the Transition Movement', *Global Environmental Change*, 24, 232–50.

Figueroa, R. M. 2003. 'Bivalent Environmental Justice and the Culture of Poverty', *Rutgers University Journal of Law and Urban Policy*, 1, 27–42.

Foden, M. 2012. 'Everyday Consumption Practices as a Site for Activism: Exploring the Motivations of Grassroots Reuse Groups', *People, Place and Policy Online*, 6, 148–63.

Forno, F. and Graziano, P. R. 2014. 'Sustainable Community Movement Organisations', *Journal of Consumer Culture*, 14, 139–57.

Foucault, M. 1980. *Power/Knowledge*. New York: Vintage.

Foucault, M. 2009. *Security, Territory, Population: Lectures at the College de France 1977–78*. New York: Picador.

Fraser, N. 1997. *Justice Interruptus: Critical Reflections on the 'Postsocialist' Condition*. New York: Routledge.

Fridell, G. 2007. *Fair Trade Coffee: The Prospects and Pitfalls of Market-Driven Social Justice*. Toronto: University of Toronto Press.

Frost, S. 2018. 'The Biocultural is a Pluripotent Concept for Theory: A Response to Six Provocations', *Theory & Event*, 21, 549–61.

Gabrielson, T. and Parady, K. 2010. 'Corporeal Citizenship: Rethinking Green Citizenship through the Body', *Environmental Politics*, 19, 374–91.

Geels, F. W. 2011. 'The Multi-Level Perspective on Sustainability Transitions: Responses to Seven Criticisms', *Environmental Innovation and Societal Transitions*, 1, 24–40.

Gharajedaghi, J. 1999. *Systems Thinking: Managing Chaos and Complexity: A Platform for Designing Business Architecture*. Burlington, MA: Elsevier.

Gibson Graham, J.-K. 1996. 'Querying Globalization', *Rethinking Marxism*, 9, 1–27.

Gibson-Graham, J.-K. 2006. *A Postcapitalist Politics*. Minneapolis, MN: University of Minnesota Press.

Gibson-Graham, J.-K. and Roelvink, G. 2011. 'The Nitty Gritty of Creating Alternative Economies', *Social Alternatives*, 30, 29–33.

Giugni, M. and Grasso, M. T. 2016. *Austerity and Protest: Popular Contention in Times of Economic Crisis*. London: Routledge.

Gordon, J. A. and Hill, C. 2015. *Sustainable Fashion: Past, Present, and Future*. New York: Bloomsbury.

Gordon, M. 2011. 'Listening as Embracing The Other: Martin Buber's Philosophy of Dialogue', *Educational Theory*, 61, 207–19.

Gottlieb, R. 2005. *Forcing the Spring: The Transformation of the American Environmental Movement*. Washington, DC: Island Press.

Gottlieb, R. and Joshi, A. 2010. *Food Justice*. Cambridge, MA: MIT Press.

Graddy-Lovelace, G. 2018. 'Plants: Crop Diversity Pre-Breeding Technologies as Agrarian Care Co-Opted?', *Area*. https://doi.org/10.1111/area.12499.

Graham, J. G. and Roelvink, G. 2009. 'An Economic Ethics for the Anthropocene', *Antipode*, 41, 320–46.

Groves, C. 2015. 'The Bomb in My Backyard, the Serpent in My House: Environmental Justice, Risk, and the Colonisation of Attachment', *Environmental Politics*, 24, 853–73.

Guha, R. 1989. 'Radical American Environmentalism and Wilderness Preservation: A Third-World Critique', *Environmental Ethics*, 11, 71–83.

Guha, R. and Martinez-Alier, J. (eds.) 1997. *Varieties of Environmentalism*. London: Earthscan.

Guidi, R. and Andretta, M. 2015. 'Between Resistance and Resilience: How do Italian Solidarity Purchase Groups Change in Times of Crisis and Austerity?' *Partecipazione e Conflitto*, 8, 443–77.

Guthman, J. 2006. 'Neoliberalism and the Making of Food Politics in California', Geoforum, 39(3), 1171–83.

Guthman, J. 2008. 'Bringing Good Food to Others: Investigating the Subjects of Alternative Food Practice', *Cultural Geographies*, 15, 431–47.

Guthman, J. 2011. *Weighing In: Obesity, Food Justice, and the Limits of Capitalism*. Oakland, CA: University of California Press.

Gwilt, A. 2014. *A Practical Guide to Sustainable Fashion*. New York: Fairchild Books.

Haenfler, R., Johnson, B., and Jones, E. 2012. 'Lifestyle Movements: Exploring the Intersection of Lifestyle and Social Movements', *Social Movement Studies*, 11, 1–20.

Haraway, D. 2008. *When Species Meet*. Minneapolis, MN: University of Minnesota Press.

Haraway, D. 2016. *Staying with the Trouble*. Durham, NC: Duke University Press.

Hargreaves, T., Longhurst, N., and Seyfang, G. 2013. 'Up, Down, Round and Round: Connecting Regimes And Practices In Innovation For Sustainability', *Environment and Planning A*, 45, 402–20.

Haroutunian-Gordon, S. and Laverty, M. J. 2011. 'Listening: An Exploration of Philosophical Traditions', *Educational Theory*, 61, 117–24.

Harris, E. 2009. 'Neoliberal Subjectivities or a Politics of the Possible? Reading for Difference in Alternative Food Networks', *Area*, 41, 55–63.

Healy, S., McNeill, J., Cameron, J., and Gibson, K. 2018. 'Pre-empting Apocalypse? Post-capitalism as an Everyday Politics', *Australian Quarterly*, 89, 28–33.

Heinze, L. 2017. 'Fashioning Sustainability: Understanding the Dynamic Practices of Sustainable Fashion', PhD thesis, Department of Gender and Cultural Studies, University of Sydney.

Heise, U. K. 2016. *Imagining Extinction: The Cultural Meanings of Endangered Species*. Chicago, IL: University of Chicago Press.

Hess, D. J. 2009. *Localist Movements in a Global Economy: Sustainability, Justice, and Urban Development in the United States*. Cambridge, MA: MIT Press.

Hobson, K. 2013. 'On the Making of the Environmental Citizen', *Environmental Politics*, 22, 56–72.

Holifield, R., Porter, M., and Walker, G. (eds.) 2010. *Spaces of Environmental Justice*. Hoboken, NJ: Wiley.

Holland, B. 2008. 'Justice and the Environment in Nussbaum's "Capabilities Approach": Why Sustainable Ecological Capacity is a Meta-Capability', *Political Research Quarterly*, 62, 319–22.

Holland, B. 2014. *Allocating the Earth: A Distributional Framework for Protecting Capabilities in Environmental Law and Policy*. Oxford: Oxford University Press.

Honig, B. 2017. *Public Things: Democracy in Disrepair*. New York: Fordham University Press.

hooks, b. 1989. *Yearning: Race, Gender, and Cultural Politics*. Boston, MA: South End Press.

hooks, b. 2000. *Feminist Theory: From Margin to Center*. London: Pluto Press.

Hopkins, R. 2008. *The Transition Handbook: From Oil Dependency to Local Resilience*. White River Junction, VT: Chelsea Green.

Hopkins, R. 2011. *The Transition Companion: Making Your Community More Resilient In Uncertain Times*. White River Junction, VT: Chelsea Green.

Hopkins, R. 2014. 'Responding to Ted Trainer: There's a Lot More to Transition than Community Gardens'. https://www.transitionnetwork.org/blogs/rob-hopkins/2014-09/respondingted-trainer-theres-lot-more-transition-community-gardens.

Inglehart, R. 1977. *The Silent Revolution: Changing Values and Political Styles Among Western Publics*. Princeton, NJ: Princeton University Press.

Inglehart, R. 1989. *Culture Shift In Advanced Industrial Society*. Princeton, NJ: Princeton University Press.

Inglehart, R. 1995. 'Public Support For Environmental Protection: Objective Problems And Subjective Values In 43 Societies', *PS: Political Science & Politics*, 28, 57–72.

Inglehart, R. 1997. *Modernization and Postmodernization*. Princeton, NJ: Princeton University Press.

Inglehart, R. and Welzel, C. 2005. *Modernization, Cultural Change, and Democracy: The Human Development Sequence*. Cambridge: Cambridge University Press.

Jervis, R. 1997. *System Effects: Complexity in Political and Social Life*. Princeton, NJ: Princeton University Press.

Kenis, A. 2016. 'Ecological Citizenship and Democracy: Communitarian Versus Agonistic Perspectives', *Environmental Politics*, 25, 949–70.

Kenis, A., and Mathijs, E. 2014. 'Climate Change and Post-Politics: Repoliticizing the Present by Imagining the Future?', *Geoforum*, 52, 148–56.

Khan, G. A. 2012. 'Vital Materiality and Non-Human Agency: An Interview with Jane Bennett', in Browning, G., Prokhovnik, R., and Dimova-Cookson, M. (eds.) *Dialogues with Contemporary Political Theorists*. International Political Theory Series. London: Palgrave Macmillan.

Kim, C. J. 2015. *Dangerous Crossings: Race, Species, and Nature in a Multicultural Age*. Cambridge: Cambridge University Press.

Knox, H. and Huse, T. 2015. 'Political Materials: Rethinking Environment, Remaking Theory', *Distinktion: Scandinavian Journal of Social Theory*, 16, 1–16.

Kollmuss, A. and Agyeman, J. 2002. 'Mind the Gap: Why do People Act Environmentally and what are the Barriers to Pro-Environmental Behavior?', *Environmental Education Research*, 8(3), 239–60.

Kompridis, N. 2006. *Critique and Disclosure. Critical Theory between Past and Future*. Cambridge, MA: MIT Press.

Kousis, M. and Paschou, M. 2017. 'Alternative Forms of Resilience: A Typology of approaches for the study of Citizen Collective Responses in Hard Economic Times', in special section, *Alternative Forms of Resilience Confronting Hard Economic Times. A South European Perspective*, PArtecipazione e COnflitto, 10(1), 136–68.

Kurtz, H. E. 2015. 'Scaling Food Sovereignty: Biopolitics and the Struggle for Local Control of Farm Food in Rural Maine', *Annals of the American Association of Geographers*, 105, 859–73.

Larner, W. 2014. 'The Limits of Post-Politics: Rethinking Radical Social Enterprise', in Wilson, J. (ed.) *The Post-Political and its Discontents: Spaces of Depoliticisation, Spectres of Radical Politics*. Edinburgh: Edinburgh University Press.

Latour, B. 2011. 'Love Your Monsters', in Shellenberger, M. and Nordhaus, T. (eds.) *Love Your Monsters: Postenvironmentalism and the Anthropocene*, Oakland, CA: Breakthrough Institute.

Lavin, C. 2008. *The Politics of Responsibility*. Champaign, IL: University of Illinois Press.

Levkoe, C. Z. 2011. 'Towards a Transformative Food Politics', *Local Environment*, 16, 687–705.

Litfin, K. 2013. *Ecovillages: Lessons for Sustainability*. Cambridge: Polity Press.

Loftus, A. 2012. *Everyday Environmentalism: Creating an Urban Political Ecology*. Minneapolis, MN: University of Minnesota Press.

Macedo, S., Alex-Assensoh, Y. M., Berry, J. M., Brintnall, M., Campbell, D. E., Fraga, L. R., Fung, A., Galston, W. A., Karpowitz, C. F., and Levi, M. (eds.) 2005. *Democracy at Risk: How Political Choices Have Undermined Citizenship and What We Can Do About It*. Washington, DC: Brookings Institution Press.

MacGregor, S. 2006. *Beyond Mothering Earth: Ecological Citizenship and the Politics of Care*. Vancouver: University of British Columbia Press.

Maeckelbergh, M. 2011. 'Doing is Believing: Prefiguration as Strategic Practice in the Alterglobalization Movement', *Social Movement Studies*, 10, 1–20.

Mair, P. 2013. *Ruling the Void: The Hollowing of Western Democracy*. London: Verso Books.

Maniates, M., Conca, K., and Princen, T. 2002. *Confronting Consumption*. Cambridge, MA: MIT Press.

Mansfield, B. and Doyle, M. 2017. 'Nature: A Conversation in Three Parts', *Annals of the American Association of Geographers*, 107, 22–7.

Manzo, L. C. and Devine-Wright, P. (eds.) 2013. *Place Attachment: Advances in Theory, Methods, and Applications*. London: Routledge.

Marres, N. 2012. *Material Participation: Technology, the Environment and Everyday Publics*. New York: Palgrave Macmillan.

Martindale, L. 2015. 'Understanding Humans in the Anthropocene: Finding Answers in Geoengineering and Transition Towns', *Environment and Planning D: Society and Space*, 33, 907–24.

Martineau, W. and Squires, J. 2012. 'Addressing the 'Dismal Disconnection': Normative Theory, Empirical Inquiry and Dialogic Research', *Political Studies*, 60, 523–38.

Martinez-Alier, J. 1995. 'The environment as a luxury good or "too poor to be green"?', *Ecological Economics*, 13, 1–10.

Martinez-Alier, J. 2012. 'Environmental Justice and Economic Degrowth: An Alliance Between Two Movements', *Capitalism Nature Socialism*, 23, 51–73.

Matchar, E. 2013. *Homeward Bound: Why Women are Embracing the New Domesticity*. New York: Simon and Shuster.

McCarthy, J. 2006. 'Neoliberalism and the Politics of Alternatives: Community Forestry in British Columbia and the United States', *Annals of the Association of American Geographers*, 96(1), 84–104.

McClintock, N. 2014. 'Radical, Reformist, and Garden-Variety Neoliberal: Coming to Terms with Urban Agriculture's Contradictions', *Local Environment*, 19, 147–71.

McLaughlin, N. 2001. 'Optimal Marginality: Innovation and Orthodoxy in Fromm's Revision of Psychoanalysis', *The Sociological Quarterly*, 42(2), 271–88.

Meadows, D. 1999. *Leverage Points: Places to Intervene in a System*. Hartland, VT: The Sustainability Institute.

Meadows, D. H., Meadows, D. L., Randers, J., and Behrens, W. I. 1972. *The Limits to Growth*. New York: Signet.

Melosi, M. V. 2008. *The Sanitary City: Environmental Services in Urban America from Colonial Times to the Present*. Pittsburgh, PA: University of Pittsburgh Press.

Melucci, A. 1985. 'The Symbolic Challenge of Contemporary Movements', *Social Research*, 52, 780–816.

Mertig, A. G. and Dunlap, R. E. 2001. 'Environmentalism, New Social Movements, and the New Class: A Cross-National Investigation', *Rural Sociology*, 66, 113–36.

Meyer, J. M. 2015. *Engaging the Everyday: Environmental Social Criticism and the Resonance Dilemma*. Cambridge, MA: MIT Press.

Micheletti, M. 2003. *Political Virtue and Shopping: Individuals, Consumerism, and Collective Action*. New York: Palgrave Macmillan.

Micheletti, M. and Stolle, D. 2012. 'Sustainable Citizenship and the New Politics of Consumption', *The Annals of the American Academy of Political and Social Science*, 644, 88–120.

Middlemiss, L. 2018. *Sustainable Consumption: Key Issues*. London and New York: Routledge.

Mol, A. 1999. 'Ontological Politics. A Word and Some Questions', *Sociological Review*, 47, 74–89.

Mol, A. 2013. 'Mind your Plate! The Ontonorms of Dutch Dieting', *Social Studies of Science*, 43, 379–96.

Newell, P. 2008. 'CSR and the Limits of Capital', *Development and Change*, 39, 1063–78.

Nixon, R. 2011. *Slow Violence*. Cambridge, MA: Harvard University Press.

Nussbaum, M. C. 2000. *Women and Human Development: The Capabilities Approach*. Cambridge: Cambridge University Press.

Nussbaum, M. C. 2006. *Frontiers of Justice: Disability, Nationality, Species Membership*. Cambridge, MA: Harvard University Press.

Nussbaum, M. C. 2011. *Creating Capabilities: The Human Development Approach*. Cambridge, MA: Harvard University Press.

Office for National Statistics. 2011. Population Statistics for the UK. https://www.ons.gov. uk/census/2011census/2011censusdata/2011censusdatacatalogue/populationstatisticsfor theuk (accessed 28 September 2018).

Ornetzeder, M. and Rohracher, H. 2013. 'Of Solar Collectors, Wind Power, and Car Sharing: Comparing and Understanding Successful Cases of Grassroots Innovations', *Global Environmental Change*, 23, 856–67.

Ostrom, E. 2009. 'A General Framework for Analyzing Sustainability of Social-Ecological Systems', *Science*, 325, 419–22.

Ottinger, G. 2013. 'Changing Knowledge, Local Knowledge, and Knowledge Gaps: STS Insights into Procedural Justice', *Science, Technology & Human Values*, 38, 250–70.

Papadopoulos, D. 2018. *Experimental Practice: Technoscience, Alterontologies, and More-Than-Social Movements*. Durham, NC: Duke University Press.

Payne, K. 2011. *The Hip Girl's Guide to Homemaking*. New York: Harper Design.

Peck, J. and Tickell, A. 2002. 'Neoliberalizing space', *Antipode*, 34(3), 380–404.

Pellow, D. N. 2004. *Garbage Wars: The Struggle for Environmental Justice in Chicago*. Boston, MA: MIT Press.

Pellow, D. N. 2007. *Resisting Global Toxics*. Boston, MA: MIT Press.

Pellow, D. N. 2017. *What is Critical Environmental Justice?* Cambridge: Polity Press.

Peña, D. G. (ed.) 1998. *Chicano Culture, Ecology, Politics: Subversive Kin*. Tucson, AZ: University of Arizona Press.

Petrini, C. 2010. *Terra Madre: Forging a New Global Network of Sustainable Food Communities*. White River Junction, VT: Chelsea Green.

Phillips, M. 2017. 'Embodied Care and Planet Earth: Ecofeminism, Maternalism and Postmaternalism', *Australian Feminist Studies*, 31, 468–85.

Piso, Z., Werkheiser, I., Noll, S., and Leshko, C. 2016. 'Sustainability of What? Recognising the Diverse Values that Sustainable Agriculture Works to Sustain', *Environmental Values*, 25, 195–214.

Plumwood, V. 2002. *Environmental Culture: The Ecological Crisis of Reason*. London: Routledge.

Pollan, M. 2007. *The Omnivore's Dilemma*. New York: Penguin.

Puig de la Bellacasa, M. 2017. *Matters of Care. Speculative Ethics in more than Human Worlds*. Minneapolis, MN: University of Minnesota Press.

Pulido, L. 2015. 'Geographies of Race and Ethnicity 1: White Supremacy vs. White Privilege in Environmental Racism Research', *Progress in Human Geography*, 39, 809–17.

Pynchon, T. 2006. *The Crying of Lot 49*. New York: Harper Perennial.

Rancière, J. 2004. *The Politics of Aesthetics: The Distribution of the Sensible*. New York: Continuum International.

Reel, M. 2014. 'Saving Detroit, One Tree at a Time', *Bloomberg Businessweek*, 2 September.

Robeyns, I. 2017. *Wellbeing, Freedom and Social Justice: The Capability Approach Re-Examined*. Cambridge: Open Book Publishers.

Rockström, J., Steffen, W., Noone, K., Persson, Å., Chapin III, F. S., Lambin, E., Lenton, T. M., Scheffer, M., Folke, C., and Schellnhuber, H. J. 2009. 'Planetary Boundaries: Exploring the Safe Operating Space for Humanity', *Ecology and Society*, 14, 1–33.

Romero-Lankao, P., Bulkeley, H., Pelling, M., Burch, S., Gordon, D., Gupta, J., Johnson, C., Kurian, P., Lecavalier, E., Simon, D., Tozer, L., Ziervogel, G., and Munshi, D. 2018. 'Urban Transformative Potential in a Changing Climate', *Nature Climate Change*, 8 (9), 754–6.

Roth, L. and Russell, B. 2018. 'Translocal Solidarity and the New Municipalism', *Roar*. https://roarmag.org/magazine/municipalist-movement-internationalism-solidarity/.

Ruger, J. 2010. *Health and Social Justice*. New York: Oxford University Press.

Salatin, J. 2011. *Folks, This Ain't Normal.* New York: Center Street.

Salleh, A. 1995. 'Nature, Woman, Labor, Capital: Living the Deepest Contradiction', *Capitalism Nature Socialism,* 6, 21–39.

Sandilands, C. 1997. 'Mother Earth, the Cyborg, and the Queer: Ecofeminism and (More) Questions of Identity', *National Women's Studies Association Journal* 9, 18–40.

Sbicca, J. 2014. 'The Need to Feed: Urban Metabolic Struggles of Actually Existing Radical Projects', *Critical Sociology,* 40(6), 817–34.

Sbicca, J. 2018. *Food Justice Now! Deepening the Roots of Social Struggle.* Minneapolis, MN: University of Minnesota Press.

Schattschneider, E. E. 1960. *The Semisovereign People: A Realist's View of Democracy in America.* New York: Holt, Rhinehart and Winston.

Schatzki, T. 2010. 'Materiality and Social Life', *Nature and Culture,* 5, 123–49.

Schelly, C. 2017. *Dwelling in Resistance.* New Brunswick, NJ: Rutgers University Press.

Schlosberg, D. 1995. 'Communicative Action in Practice: Intersubjectivity and New Social Movements', *Political Studies,* 43, 291–311.

Schlosberg, D. 1999a. 'Networks and Mobile Arrangements: Organizational Innovation in the U.S. Environmental Justice Movement', *Environmental Politics,* 8, 122–48.

Schlosberg, D. 1999b. *Environmental Justice and the New Pluralism.* New York: Oxford University Press.

Schlosberg, D. 2007. *Defining Environmental Justice: Theories, Movements, and Nature.* Oxford: Oxford University Press.

Schlosberg, D. 2013. 'Theorizing Environmental Justice: The Expanding Sphere of Discourse', *Environmental Politics,* 22, 37–55.

Schlosberg, D. and Carruthers, D. 2010. 'Indigenous Struggles, Environmental Justice, and Community Capabilities', *Global Environmental Politics,* 10, 12–35.

Schlosberg, D. and Coles, R. 2016. 'The New Environmentalism of Everyday Life: Sustainability, Material Flows and Movements', *Contemporary Political Theory,* 15, 160–81.

Schlosberg, D. and Collins, L. B. 2014. 'From Environmental to Climate Justice: Climate Change and the Discourse of Environmental Justice', *WIREs Climate Change,* 5, 359–74.

Schlosberg, D., Rickards, L., and Byrne, J. 2017. 'Environmental Justice and Attachment to Place: Australian Cases', in Holifield, R., Chakraborty, J., and Walker, G. (eds.) *The Routledge Handbook of Environmental Justice.* London and New York: Routledge.

Schrader-Frechette, K. 2005. *Environmental Justice: Creating Equality, Reclaiming Democracy.* Oxford: Oxford University Press.

Schram, S. 2015. *The Return of Ordinary Capitalism: Neoliberalism, Precarity, Occupy.* New York: Oxford University Press.

Seddon, J. 2008. *Systems Thinking in the Public Sector.* Axminster: Triarchy Press.

Sen, A. 1985. *Commodities and Capabilities.* Oxford: Elsevier Science Publishers.

Sen, A. 1993. 'Capability and Well-being', in Nussbaum, M. C. and Sen, A. (eds.) *The Quality of Life.* Oxford: Clarendon Press.

Sen, A. 1999. *Development as Freedom.* New York: Oxford University Press.

Senge, P. 1992. *The Fifth Discipline: The Art and Practice of the Learning Organisation.* New York: Doubleday.

Seyfang, G. and Haxeltine, A. 2012. 'Growing Grassroots Innovations: Exploring the Role of Community-Based Initiatives in Governing Sustainable Energy Transition', *Environment and Planning C,* 30, 381–400.

Shiva, V. 2007. *Manifestos on the Future of Food and Seed.* Boston, MA: South End Press.

Shiva, V. 2008. *Soil Not Oil.* Boston, MA: South End Press.

Simms, A. and Potts, R. 2012. *The New Materialism: How our Relationship with the Material World can Change for the Better*. London: The Real Press.

Smith, A. 2006. 'Green Niches in Sustainable Development: The Case of Organic Food in the United Kingdom', *Environment and Planning C: Government and Policy*, 24, 439–58.

Solnit, D. 2003. 'The New Radicalism: Uprooting the System and Building a Better World', in Solnit, D. (ed.) *Globalize Liberation: How to Uproot the System and Build a Better World*. San Francisco, CA: City Lights Publishers.

Stanton, A. (dir.) 2008. 'Wall-E', Los Angeles, CA: Walt Disney Studios Motion Pictures.

Steffen, W., Richardson, K., Rockström, J., Cornell, S. E., Fetzer, I., Bennett, E. M., Biggs, R., Carpenter, S. R., De Vries, W., and De Wit, C. A. 2015. 'Planetary Boundaries: Guiding Human Development on a Changing Planet', *Science*, 347 (6223), 1259855.

Sterman, J. D. 1994. 'Learning in and about Complex Systems', *System Dynamics Review* 10(2–3), 291–330.

Stewart, F. 2005. 'Groups and Capabilities', *Journal of Human Development*, 6, 185–204.

Stolle, D. and Micheletti, M. 2013. *Political Consumerism: Global Responsibility in Action*. Cambridge: Cambridge University Press.

Stolle, D., Hooghe, M., and Micheletti, M. 2005. 'Politics in the Supermarket: Political Consumerism as a Form of Political Participation', *International Political Science Review*, 26, 245–69.

Strom, S. 2012. 'Has Organic Been Oversized?' *New York Times*, 7 July.

Sturgeon, N. 1995. 'Theorizing Movements: Direct Action and Direct Theory', in Epstein, B., Darnovsky, M., and Flacks, R. (eds.) *Cultural Politics and Social Movements*. Philadelphia, PA: Temple University Press.

Swyngedouw, E. 2009. 'The Antinomies of the Postpolitical City: In Search of a Democratic Politics of Environmental Production', *International Journal of Urban and Regional Research*, 33, 601–20.

Swyngedouw, E. 2010. 'Apocalypse Forever? Post-Political Populism and the Spectre of Climate Change', *Theory, Culture & Society*, 27, 213–32.

Sze, J. 2006. *Noxious New York: The Racial Politics of Urban Health and Environmental Justice*. Cambridge, MA: MIT Press.

Sze, J. and London, J. K. 2008. 'Environmental Justice at the Crossroads', *Sociological Compass*, 2, 1331–54.

Taleb, N. N. 2012. *Antifragile: How to Live in a World We Don't Understand*. London: Allen Lane London.

Tarrow, S. G. 1994. *Power in Movement: Social Movements and Contentious Politics*. Cambridge: Cambridge University Press.

Tormey, S. 2015. *The End of Representative Politics*. Cambridge: Wiley.

Tronto, J. C. 1993. *Moral Boundaries: A Political Argument for an Ethic of Care*. New York: Psychology Press.

Tsing, A. L. 2015. *The Mushroom at the End of the World: On the Possibility of Life in Capitalist Ruins*. Princeton, NJ and Oxford: Princeton University Press.

United States Census Bureau. 2017. Quick Facts: People. https://www.census.gov/quickfacts/fact/table/US/PST045217 (accessed 28 September 2018).

van Deth, J. W. 2014. 'A Conceptual Map of Political Participation', *Acta Politica*, 49, 349–67.

Venkatapuram, S. 2013. *Health Justice: An Argument from the Capabilities Approach*. Hoboken, NJ: Wiley.

Venn, L., Kneafsey, M., Holloway, L., Cox, R., Dowler, E., and Toumainen, H. 2006. 'Researching European "Alternative" Food Networks: Some Methodological Considerations', *Area*, 38, 248–58.

Wahlen, S. and Laamanen, M. 2015. 'Consumption, Lifestyle and Social Movements', *International Journal of Consumer Studies*, 39, 397–403.

Walker, G. 2009. 'Beyond Distribution and Proximity: Exploring the Multiple Spatialities of Environmental Justice', *Antipode*, 41, 614–36.

Walker, G. 2011. 'The Role for "Community" in Carbon Governance', *WIREs Climate Change*, 2, 777–82.

Walker, G. 2012. *Environmental Justice: Concepts, Evidence and Politics*. London: Routledge.

Walker, G. and Day, R. 2012. 'Fuel Poverty as Injustice: Integrating Distribution, Recognition and Procedure in the Struggle for Affordable Warmth', *Energy Policy*, 49, 69–75.

Walker, G., Devine-Wright, P., Hunter, S., High, H., and Evans, B. 2010. 'Trust and Community: Exploring the Meanings, Contexts and Dynamics of Community Renewable Energy', *Energy Policy*, 38, 2655–63.

Washick, B., Wingrove, E., Ferguson, K. E., and Bennett, J. 2015. 'Politics that Matter: Thinking about Power and Justice with the New Materialists', *Contemporary Political Theory*, 14, 63–89.

Weick, K. E. 1984. '*Small Wins: Redefining the Scale of Social Problems*', American Psychologist, 39(1), 40–9.

Welch, D. and Yates, L. 2018. 'The Practices of Collective Action: Practice Theory, Sustainability Transitions and Social Change', *Journal for the Theory of Social Behaviour*, 48, 288–305.

Whiteside, K. H. 2013. 'A Representative Politics of Nature? Bruno Latour on Collectives and Constitutions', *Contemporary Political Theory*, 12, 185–205.

Whyte, K. P. 2011. 'The Recognition Definitions of Environmental Justice in Indian Country', *Environmental Justice*, 4, 199–205.

Williams, R. 1976. *Keywords: A Vocabulary of Culture and Society*. London: Collins.

Winne, M. 2011. *Food Rebels, Guerrilla Gardeners, and Smart-Cookin' Mamas: Fighting Back in an Age of Industrial Agriculture*. Boston, MA: Beacon Press.

Wolff, J. and De-Shalit, A. 2007. *Disadvantage*. Oxford: Oxford University Press.

Wright, E. O. 2010. *Envisioning Real Utopias*. New York: Verso.

Yates, L. 2015. 'Rethinking Prefiguration: Alternatives, Micropolitics and Goals in Social Movements', *Social Movement Studies*, 14, 1–21.

Young, I. M. 1990. *Justice and the Politics of Difference*. Princeton, NJ: Princeton University Press.

Young, I. M. 2004. 'Responsibility and Global Labor Justice', *Journal of Political Philosophy*, 12, 365–88.

Young, I. M. 2006. 'Responsibility and Global Justice: A Social Connection Model', *Social Philosophy and Policy*, 23, 102–30.

# Index

Printed and bound by CPI Group (UK) Ltd, Croydon, CR0 4YY